THANK YOUR LUCKY STARS!

In the 2012 Astrological Guide, you'll find:

- All 12 signs individually represented—for a personalized look at *each month* in the year to come
- The days that will be most memorable for you
- Answers to many questions
- An essay by a leading astrologer
- And much more!

"Astrology told me about my life even before I wrote it as an autobiography." —Bette Davis

"Whether or not I would have succeeded without astrology, I don't know." —Sylvester Stallone

SYDNEY OMARR'S®
ASTROLOGICAL GUIDE FOR YOU IN
2012

by Trish MacGregor
with Rob MacGregor

A SIGNET BOOK

SIGNET
Published by New American Library, a division of
Penguin Group (USA) Inc., 375 Hudson Street,
New York, New York 10014, USA
Penguin Group (Canada), 90 Eglinton Avenue East, Suite 700, Toronto,
Ontario M4P 2Y3, Canada (a division of Pearson Penguin Canada Inc.)
Penguin Books Ltd., 80 Strand, London WC2R 0RL, England
Penguin Ireland, 25 St. Stephen's Green, Dublin 2,
Ireland (a division of Penguin Books Ltd.)
Penguin Group (Australia), 250 Camberwell Road, Camberwell, Victoria 3124,
Australia (a division of Pearson Australia Group Pty. Ltd.)
Penguin Books India Pvt. Ltd., 11 Community Centre, Panchsheel Park,
New Delhi - 110 017, India
Penguin Group (NZ), 67 Apollo Drive, Rosedale, Auckland 0632,
New Zealand (a division of Pearson New Zealand Ltd.)
Penguin Books (South Africa) (Pty.) Ltd., 24 Sturdee Avenue,
Rosebank, Johannesburg 2196, South Africa

Penguin Books Ltd., Registered Offices:
80 Strand, London WC2R 0RL, England

First published by Signet, an imprint of New American Library,
a division of Penguin Group (USA) Inc.

First Printing, July 2011
10 9 8 7 6 5 4 3 2 1

Copyright © The Estate of Sydney Omarr, 2011
All rights reserved

Sydney Omarr's is a registered trademark of Writers House, LLC.

Sydney Omarr® is syndicated worldwide by Los Angeles Times Syndicate.

REGISTERED TRADEMARK—MARCA REGISTRADA

Printed in the United States of America

Without limiting the rights under copyright reserved above, no part of this publication may be reproduced, stored in or introduced into a retrieval system, or transmitted, in any form, or by any means (electronic, mechanical, photocopying, recording, or otherwise), without the prior written permission of both the copyright owner and the above publisher of this book.

PUBLISHER'S NOTE
While the author has made every effort to provide accurate telephone numbers and Internet addresses at the time of publication, neither the publisher nor the author assumes any responsibility for errors, or for changes that occur after publication. Further, publisher does not have any control over and does not assume any responsibility for author or third-party Web sites or their content.

If you purchased this book without a cover you should be aware that this book is stolen property. It was reported as "unsold and destroyed" to the publisher and neither the author nor the publisher has received any payment for this "stripped book."

The scanning, uploading and distribution of this book via the Internet or via any other means without the permission of the publisher is illegal and punishable by law. Please purchase only authorized electronic editions, and do not participate in or encourage electronic piracy of copyrighted materials. Your support of the author's rights is appreciated.

CONTENTS

PART ONE

1. The Basics	3
2. Aries	15
3. Taurus	39
4. Gemini	65
5. Cancer	90
6. Leo	114
7. Virgo	138
8. Libra	161
9. Scorpio	184
10. Sagittarius	208
11. Capricorn	231
12. Aquarius	254
13. Pisces	277

PART TWO: Another Viewpoint

14. Navigating the Waves of Change *by Nancy McMoneagle*	303

PART THREE: The Emergence of a Thirteenth Zodiac Sign

	317

PART ONE

1
The Basics

On the day you were born, what was the weather like? If you were born at night, had the moon already risen? Was it full or the shape of a Cheshire cat's grin? Was the delivery ward quiet or bustling with activity? Unless your mom or dad has a very good memory, you'll probably never know the full details. But there's one thing you can know for sure: on the day you were born, the sun was located in a particular zone of the zodiac, an imaginary 360-degree belt that circles the earth. The belt is divided into twelve 30-degree portions called signs.

If you were born between July 23 and August 22, then the sun was passing through the sign of Leo, so we say that your sun sign is Leo. Each of the twelve signs has distinct attributes and characteristics. Leos, for instance, love being the center of attention. They're warm, compassionate people with a flair for the dramatic. Virgos, born between August 23 and September 22, are perfectionists with discriminating intellects and a genius for details. Capricorns, born between December 22 and January 19, are the worker bees of the zodiac, serious minded, ambitious, industrious.

How Signs Are Classified

The twelve signs are categorized according to element and quality or modality. The first category, element, reads like a basic science lesson—fire, earth, air, and water—and describes the general physical characteristics of the signs.

Fire signs—Aries, Leo, Sagittarius—are warm, dynamic individuals who are always passionate about what they do.

Earth signs—Taurus, Virgo, Capricorn—are the builders of the zodiac, practical and efficient, grounded in everything they do.

Air signs—Gemini, Libra, Aquarius—are people who live mostly in the world of ideas. They are terrific communicators.

Water signs—Cancer, Scorpio, Pisces—live through their emotions, imaginations, and intuitions.

The second category describes how each sign operates in the physical world, how adaptable it is to circumstances:

Cardinal signs—Aries, Cancer, Libra, Capricorn—are initiators. These people are active, impatient, restless. They're great at starting things, but unless a project or a relationship holds their attention, they lose interest and may not finish what they start.

Fixed signs—Taurus, Leo, Scorpio, Aquarius—are deliberate, controlled, resolute. These individuals tend to move more slowly than cardinal signs, are often stubborn, and resist change. They seek roots and stability and are always in the game for the long haul. They aren't quitters.

Mutable signs—Gemini, Virgo, Sagittarius, Pisces—are adaptable. These people are flexible, changeable, communicative. They don't get locked into rigid patterns or belief systems.

Sun Signs

Sign	Date	Element	Quality
Aries ♈	March 21–April 19	Fire	Cardinal
Taurus ♉	April 20–May 20	Earth	Fixed
Gemini ♊	May 21–June 21	Air	Mutable
Cancer ♋	June 22–July 22	Water	Cardinal
Leo ♌	July 23–August 22	Fire	Fixed
Virgo ♍	August 23–September 22	Earth	Mutable
Libra ♎	September 23–October 22	Air	Cardinal
Scorpio ♏	October 23–November 21	Water	Fixed

Sign	Date	Element	Quality
Sagittarius ♐	November 22–December 21	Fire	Mutable
Capricorn ♑	December 22–January 19	Earth	Cardinal
Aquarius ♒	January 20–February 18	Air	Fixed
Pisces ♓	February 19–March 20	Water	Mutable

The Planets

The planets in astrology are the players who make things happen. They're the characters in the story of your life. This story always begins with the sun, the giver of life.

Your sun sign describes your self-expression, your primal energy, the essence of who you are. It's the archetypal pattern of your Self. When you know another person's sun sign, you already have a great deal of information about that person. Let's say you're a Taurus who has just started dating a Gemini. How compatible are you?

On the surface, it wouldn't seem that you have much in common. Taurus is a fixed earth sign; Gemini is a mutable air sign. Taurus is persistent, stubborn, practical, a cultivator as opposed to an initiator. Gemini is a chameleon, a communicator, social, with a mind as quick as lightning. Taurus is ruled by Venus, which governs the arts, money, beauty, love, and romance, and Gemini is ruled by Mercury, which governs communication and travel. There doesn't seem to be much common ground. But before we write off this combination, let's look a little deeper.

Suppose the Taurus has Mercury in Gemini and suppose the Gemini has Venus in Taurus? This would mean that the Taurus and Gemini each have their rulers in the other person's sign. They probably communicate well and enjoy travel and books (Mercury) and would see eye to eye on romance, art, and music (Venus). They might get along so well, in fact, that they collaborate on creative projects.

Each of us is also influenced by the other nine planets (the sun and moon are treated like planets in astrology) and the signs they were transiting when you were born. Suppose our Taurus and Gemini have the same moon sign? The moon rules our inner needs, emotions, and intuition, and all that makes us feel secure within ourselves. Quite often, compatible moon signs can overcome even the most glaring difference in sun signs because the two people share similar emotions.

In the sections on monthly predictions, your sun sign always takes center stage, and every prediction is based on the movement of the transiting planets in relation to your sun sign. Let's say you're a Sagittarius. Between January 7 and February 4 this year, Venus will be transiting your sign. What does this mean for you? Well, since Venus rules—among other things—romance, you can expect your love life to pick up significantly during these weeks. Other people will find you attractive and be more open to your ideas, and you'll radiate a certain charisma. Your creative endeavors will move full steam ahead.

Table 2 provides an overview of the planets and the signs that they rule. Keep in mind that the moon is the swiftest-moving planet, changing signs about every two and a half days, and that Pluto is the snail of the zodiac, taking as long as thirty years to transit a single sign. Although the faster-moving planets—the moon, Mercury, Venus, and Mars—have an impact on our lives, it's the slow pokes—Uranus, Neptune, and Pluto—that bring about the most profound influence and change. Jupiter and Saturn fall between the others in terms of speed. This year, Jupiter spends the first six months in Taurus, then enters Gemini on June 11 and doesn't leave that sign until late June 2013.

In the section on predictions, the most frequent references are to the transits of Mercury, Venus, and Mars. In the daily predictions for each sign, the predictions are based primarily on the transiting moon.

Now glance through Table 2. When a sign is in parentheses, it means the planet corules that sign. This assignation dates back to when we thought there were only seven planets in the solar system. But since there were still twelve signs, some of the planets had to do double duty!

The Planets

Planet	Rules	Attributes of Planet
Sun ☉	Leo	Self-expression, primal energy, creative ability, ego, individuality
Moon ☽	Cancer	Emotions, intuition, mother or wife, security
Mercury ☿	Gemini, Virgo	Intellect, mental acuity, communication, logic, reasoning, travel, contracts
Venus ♀	Taurus, Libra	Love, romance, beauty, artistic instincts, the arts, music, material and financial resources
Mars ♂	Aries (Scorpio)	Physical and sexual energy, aggression, drive
Jupiter ♃	Sagittarius (Pisces)	Luck, expansion, success, prosperity, growth, creativity, spiritual interests, higher education, law
Saturn ♄	Capricorn (Aquarius)	Laws of physical universe, discipline, responsibility, structure, karma, authority
Uranus ♅	Aquarius	Individuality, genius, eccentricity, originality, science, revolution
Neptune ♆	Pisces	Visionary self, illusions, what's hidden, psychic ability, dissolution of ego boundaries, spiritual insights, dreams
Pluto ♇	Scorpio	The darker side, death, sex, regeneration, rebirth, profound and permanent change, transformation

Houses and Rising Signs

In the instant you drew your first breath, one of the signs of the zodiac was just passing over the eastern horizon. Astrologers refer to this as the rising sign or ascendant. It's what makes your horoscope unique. Think of your ascendant as the front door of your horoscope, the place where you enter into this life and begin your journey.

Your ascendant is based on the exact moment of your birth, and the other signs follow counterclockwise. If you have Taurus rising, for example, that is the cusp of your first house. The cusp of the second would be Gemini, of the third Cancer, and so on around the horoscope circle in a counterclockwise direction. Each house governs a particular area of life, which is outlined below.

The best way to find out your rising sign is to have your horoscope drawn up by an astrologer. For those of you with access to the internet, though, there are a couple of sites that provide free birth horoscopes: www.astro.com and www.cafeastrology.com.

In a horoscope, the ascendant (cusp of the first house), IC (cusp of the fourth house), descendant (cusp of the seventh house), and MC (cusp of the tenth house) are considered to be the most critical angles. Any planets that fall close to these angles are extremely important in the overall astrological picture of who you are. By the same token, planets that fall in the first, fourth, seventh, and tenth houses are also considered to be important.

Now here's a rundown on what the houses mean.

ASCENDANT OR RISING: THE FIRST OF FOUR IMPORTANT CRITICAL ANGLES IN A HOROSCOPE
- How other people see you
- How you present yourself to the world
- Your physical appearance

FIRST HOUSE, PERSONALITY
- Early childhood
- Your ego
- Your body type and how you feel about your body
- General physical health
- Defense mechanisms
- Your creative thrust

SECOND HOUSE, PERSONAL VALUES
- How you earn and spend your money
- Your personal values
- Your material resources and assets
- Your attitudes and beliefs toward money

- Your possessions and your attitude toward those possessions
- Your self-worth
- Your attitudes about creativity

THIRD HOUSE, COMMUNICATION AND LEARNING
- Personal expression
- Intellect and mental attitudes and perceptions
- Siblings, neighbors, and relatives
- How you learn
- School until college
- Reading, writing, teaching
- Short trips (the grocery store versus Europe in seven days)
- Earth-bound transportation
- Creativity as a communication device

IC OR FOURTH HOUSE CUSP: THE SECOND CRITICAL ANGLE IN A HOROSCOPE
- Sign on IC describes the qualities and traits of your home during early childhood
- Describes roots of your creative abilities and talents

FOURTH HOUSE, YOUR ROOTS
- Personal environment
- Your home
- Your attitudes toward family
- Early childhood conditioning
- Real estate
- Your nurturing parent

Some astrologers say this house belongs to Mom or her equivalent in your life, others say it belongs to Dad or his equivalent. It makes sense to me that it's Mom because the fourth house is ruled by the moon, which rules mothers. But in this day and age, when parental roles are in flux, the only hard and fast rule is that the fourth belongs to the parent who nurtures you most of the time.

- The conditions at the end of your life
- Early childhood support of your creativity and interests

FIFTH HOUSE, CHILDREN AND CREATIVITY
- Kids, your first-born in particular
- Love affairs, romance
- What you enjoy
- Creative ability
- Gambling and speculation
- Pets

Traditionally, pets belong in the sixth house. But that definition stems from the days when "pets" were chattel. These days, we don't even refer to them as pets. They are animal companions who bring us pleasure.

SIXTH HOUSE, WORK AND RESPONSIBILITY
- Day-to-day working conditions and environment
- Competence and skills
- Your experience of employees and employers
- Duty—to work, to employees
- Health and the daily maintenance of your health

DESCENDANT/SEVENTH HOUSE CUSP: THE THIRD CRITICAL ANGLE IN A HOROSCOPE
- The sign on the house cusp describes the qualities sought in intimate or business relationships
- Describes qualities of creative partnerships

SEVENTH HOUSE, PARTNERSHIPS AND MARRIAGE
- Marriage
- Marriage partner
- Significant others
- Business partnerships
- Close friends
- Open enemies
- Contracts

EIGHTH HOUSE: TRANSFORMATION
- Sexuality as transformation
- Secrets
- Death, taxes, inheritances, insurance, mortgages, and loans
- Resources shared with others
- Your partner's finances
- The occult (read: astrology, reincarnation, UFOs, everything weird and strange)
- Your hidden talents
- Psychology
- Life-threatening illnesses
- Your creative depths

NINTH HOUSE, WORLDVIEW
- Philosophy and religion
- The law, courts, judicial system
- Publishing
- Foreign travel and cultures
- College, graduate school
- Spiritual beliefs
- Travel abroad

MC OR CUSP OF TENTH HOUSE: THE FOURTH CRITICAL ANGLE IN A HOROSCOPE
- Sign on cusp of MC describes qualities you seek in a profession
- Your public image
- Your creative and professional achievements

TENTH HOUSE, PROFESSION AND CAREER
- Public image as opposed to a job that merely pays the bills (sixth house)
- Your status and position in the world
- The authoritarian parent and authority in general
- People who hold power over you
- Your public life
- Your career/profession

ELEVENTH HOUSE, IDEALS AND DREAMS
- Peer groups
- Social circles (your writers' group, your mother's bridge club)
- Your dreams and aspirations
- How you can realize your dreams

TWELFTH HOUSE, PERSONAL UNCONSCIOUS
- Power you have disowned that must be claimed again
- Institutions—hospitals, prisons, nursing homes, what is hidden
- What you must confront this time around, your karma, issues brought in from other lives
- Psychic gifts and abilities
- Healing talents
- What you give unconditionally

In the section on predictions, you'll find references to transiting planets moving into certain houses. These houses are actually solar houses that are created by putting your sun sign on the ascendant. This technique is how most predictions are made for the general public rather than for specific individuals.

Lunations

Every year there are twelve new moons and twelve full moons, with some years having thirteen full moons. The extra full moon is called the Blue Moon. New moons are typically when we should begin new projects, set new goals, seek new opportunities. They're times for beginnings. They usher in new opportunities according to house and sign.

Two weeks after each new moon, there's a full moon. This is the time of harvest, fruition, when we reap what we've sown.

Whenever a new moon falls in your sign, take time to

brainstorm what you would like to achieve during weeks and months until the full moon falls in your sign. These goals can be in any area of your life. Or you can simply take the time on each new moon to set up goals and strategies for what you would like to achieve or manifest during the next two weeks—until the full moon—or until the next new moon.

Here's a list of all the new moons and full moons during 2012. The asterisk beside any new-moon entry indicates a solar eclipse; the asterisk next to a full-moon entry indicates a lunar eclipse.

New Moons	**Full Moons**
January 23—Aquarius	January 9—Cancer
February 21—Pisces	February 7—Leo
March 22—Aries	March 8—Virgo
April 21—Taurus	April 6—Libra
*May 20—Gemini	May 5—Scorpio
June 19—Gemini	*June 4—Sagittarius
July 19—Cancer	July 3—Capricorn
August 17—Leo	August 1—Aquarius
September 15—Virgo	August 31—Pisces
October 15—Libra	September 29—Aries
*November 13— Scorpio	October 29—Taurus
December 13—Sagittarius	*November 28—Gemini
	December 28—Cancer

Every year there are two lunar and two solar eclipses, separated from each other by about two weeks. Lunar eclipses tend to deal with emotional issues and our internal world and often bring an emotional issue to the surface related to the sign and house in which the eclipse falls. Solar eclipses deal with events and often enable us to see something that has eluded us. They also symbolize beginnings and endings.

Read more about eclipses in the big picture for your sign for 2012. I also recommend Celeste Teal's excellent book *Eclipses*.

Mercury Retrograde

Every year Mercury—the planet that symbolizes communication and travel—turns retrograde three times. During these periods our travel plans often go awry, communication breaks down, computers go berserk, cars or appliances develop problems. You get the idea. Things in our daily lives don't work as smoothly as we would like.

Here are some guidelines to follow for Mercury retrogrades:

Try not to travel. But if you have to, be flexible and think of it as an adventure. If you're stuck overnight in an airport in Houston or Atlanta, though, the adventure part of this could be a stretch.

Don't sign contracts—unless you don't mind revisiting them when Mercury is direct again.

Communicate as succinctly and clearly as possible.

Back up all computer files. Use an external hard drive and/or a flash drive. If you've had a computer crash, you already know how frustrating it can be to reconstruct your files.

Don't buy expensive electronics. Expensive anything.

Don't submit manuscripts or screenplays, pitch ideas, or launch new projects.

Revise, rewrite, rethink, review.

In the overview for each sign, check out the dates for this year's Mercury retrogrades and how these retrogrades are likely to impact you. Do the same for eclipses.

2

Aries

The Big Picture for 2012

Welcome to 2012, Aries. This year highlights your work, creativity, originality, personal unconscious, and many sudden, unexpected events. Let's take a closer look.

Mars, your ruler, begins the year in Virgo, in your solar sixth house of daily work, where it will be until July 3, thanks to a long retrograde. While it's moving direct, your daily work life should be hectic, but you'll have the physical energy to get things done. You may have to schedule your time more efficiently, however, so that everything on your agenda receives the attention it deserves.

Pluto, the snail of the zodiac, starts off the year in Capricorn, where it has consistently been since November 2008. You're accustomed to its energy now. Its transit, which lasts until 2024, is bringing profound and permanent change, evident in the economic challenges that now face the U.S. Most institutions are in the throes of great change—the health-care industry, the petroleum and insurance industries, mortgages/lending, housing, aviation, even the Internet. You name it, and Pluto's fingerprint can be found.

On a personal level, this planet's transit through the career sector of your chart until 2024 probably started bringing about professional change in 2008. That trend will continue.

Neptune entered Pisces and your solar twelfth house on April 4, 2011. But by early August 2011, it had slipped back into Aquarius. On February 3, 2012, it enters Pisces again and won't move on until January 2026. For hints about what this may mean for you, look back to that period in 2011 when Neptune was in Pisces.

Neptune symbolizes our higher ideals, escapism, fiction, spirituality, and our blind spots. It seeks to dissolve boundaries between us and others. One possible repercussion of this transit is prolonged religious wars, which proliferated during Uranus's transit in Pisces from early 2003. On a personal level, though, Neptune's transit through your twelfth house is likely to increase your intuitive ability. It will be easier for you to recognize other people's motives and hidden agendas—and your own. You may be scrutinizing your spiritual beliefs more deeply, perhaps delving into your own past lives and taking workshops or seminars to develop your intuitive ability.

That brings us to Uranus, which entered your sign in March 2011. Undoubtedly you've already found this transit to be a wild, unpredictable ride. Uranus's job is to shake up the status quo, to move us out of our ruts and routines, to wake us up so that we recognize where we have become rigid and inflexible. For an Aries, this will be an exciting time that will last until March 2019. Few elements in your life will be predictable during this transit. Relationships will begin and end suddenly. What was certain yesterday will be uncertain by tomorrow. You'll attract idiosyncratic individuals into your life. These people are apt to be highly creative, unusually bright, or even geniuses at what they do. During the seven years of this transit, you'll experience many changes—moves, changes in your job and career, personal life, and living situation.

Saturn begins the year in Libra, your opposite sign. It has been there since the summer of 2010 and will be there until October 2012. This transit brings structure to business and personal partnerships, can cause delays and restrictions, and prompts you to strive for cooperation and balance in your relationships. During this opposition to your sun, you may feel discouraged at times because it seems that nothing is moving in your direction. You could encounter problems with bosses and other authority figures, and if you resist what's going on, could suffer from health problems. That said, this transit teaches you to "go with the flow," whatever that flow may be, and to continue to reach for your dreams, to move forward even when you're discouraged, and to simply put one foot in front of the other and believe in yourself.

Once Saturn enters Scorpio in October, your spouse or partner's income may be restricted in some way. There could be delays or difficulties in obtaining mortgages or loans. However, with metaphysical work you find the right structures for studying and pursuing intuitive development.

Expansive Jupiter begins the year in Taurus, your solar second house. This transit, which lasts until June 11, should plump up your bank account and expand your money-making options. You may have opportunities to travel internationally, perhaps as a result of new business deals. Then on June 11 Jupiter enters compatible air sign Gemini and your solar third house. This transit, which lasts until late June 2013, should be fabulous for you. Your communication abilities expand, you may move to a neighborhood that suits you better, and depending on your age, may see the addition of a brother or sister in your family.

They say that timing is everything, so with that in mind let's look at some specific areas in your life.

ROMANCE/CREATIVITY

The most romantic and creative time for you all year falls between September 6 and October 3, when Venus transits Leo and the romance/creativity area of your chart. If you're not involved before this transit begins, you probably will be before the transit ends. If you're not, it won't matter because you're having too much fun. Or you're deeply immersed in a creative project that consumes a lot of your time and energy. Great backup dates: February 8 to March 5, when Venus transits your sign. Things really seem to flow your way then in many areas, but particularly with romance and creative ventures.

The best time for serious involvement and deepening commitment in an existing relationship occurs when Venus transits Libra and your seventh house from October 28 to November 21. You and your partner may decide to move in together, get engaged, or get married. Just be sure that you don't do any of this under a Mercury retrograde period. Take a look under the appropriate section below to find out when Mercury will be retrograde this year.

Other good backup dates: July 3 to August 23, when Mars transits Libra and your solar seventh house. This stirs up a lot of activity with a partner.

CAREER

Usually Venus and Jupiter transits to your career area are the times to look for, but those transits don't happen this year. However, between November 16 and December 25, your ruler, Mars, will be in Capricorn, moving through your career area. This is the time to push your professional agenda forward, make new professional contacts, and keep your nose to the grindstone, completing projects and brainstorming with coworkers for new ideas. Also, between January 1 and June 11, when Jupiter is transiting Taurus, it forms a harmonious angle to your career area, so your professional life should run smoothly, with expanding options and greater pay.

When Venus is in Capricorn and your tenth house between February 4 and March 1, don't hesitate to pitch ideas, submit manuscripts and screenplays, and ask for a raise. It's also an excellent time to launch a Web site, start your own business, or to make new professional contacts. Other people will be receptive to your ideas. A great backup period falls between April 2 and May 11, when Mars transits your sign.

BEST TIMES FOR

Buying or selling a home: August 7 to September 6, when Venus is in Cancer and your fourth house; June 7 to 25, when Mercury transits Cancer.

Family reunions: Any of the dates above.

Financial matters: The period from January 1 to June 11, when Jupiter transits your house of money. Also, March 5 to April 3, when Venus moves through the same area.

Signing contracts: When Mercury is moving direct!

Overseas travel, publishing, and higher-education endeavors: December 15 to January 9, 2013, while Venus transits your solar ninth house and fellow fire sign Sagittarius.

MERCURY RETROGRADES

Every year Mercury—the planet of communication and travel—turns retrograde three times. During this period it's wise not to sign contracts (unless you don't mind negotiating when Mercury is moving direct), to check and recheck travel plans, and to communicate as succinctly as possible. Refrain from buying any large-ticket items or electronics during this time too. Often computers and appliances go on the fritz, cars act up, data is lost . . . you get the idea. Be sure to back up all files before the dates below:

March 12–April 4: Mercury retrograde in your sign. Ouch!

July 14–August 8: Mercury retrograde in Leo, your solar fifth house of romance and creativity.

November 6–26: Mercury retrograde in Sagittarius, your solar ninth house. This one impacts publishing, higher education, and foreign travel.

ECLIPSES

Solar eclipses tend to trigger external events that bring about change according to the sign and house in which they fall. Lunar eclipses trigger inner, emotional events according to the sign and house in which they fall. Any eclipse marks both beginnings and endings. The solar and lunar eclipse in a pair falls in opposite signs. If you're interested in detailed information on eclipses, take a look at Celeste Teal's excellent and definitive book, *Eclipses: Predicting World Events & Personal Transformation.*

If you were born under or around the time of an eclipse, it's to your advantage to take a look at your birth chart to find out exactly where the eclipses will impact you.

Most years feature four eclipses—two solar, two lunar, with the set separated by about two weeks. In November and December 2011, there were solar and lunar eclipses, so this year the first eclipses fall during May and June.

May 20: Solar eclipse at 0 degrees Gemini, in your third house. This one brings new opportunities in communication, travel, your neighborhood, and with your siblings.

June 4: Lunar eclipse in Sagittarius, your ninth house. This should be a positive eclipse for you and brings news from abroad.

November 13: Solar eclipse in Scorpio, your solar eighth house. New opportunities in shared resources. Your partner or spouse could see a raise on or around the time of this eclipse. Deep emotions surface.

November 28: Lunar eclipse, Gemini. Jupiter forms a five-degree conjunction to the eclipse degree, suggesting that whatever news comes your way, it's positive, and you're in an upbeat, expansive mood.

LUCKIEST DAY OF THE YEAR
Every year there's one day when Jupiter and the sun meet up, and luck, serendipity, and expansion are the hallmarks. This year that day falls on May 13, with a conjunction in Taurus, your money house!

January—Aries

LUNAR HIGHLIGHTS
The year gets off to a running start for you, Aries, with the full moon in Cancer on January 9. This one occurs in your solar fourth house—your domestic environment. News and insights generally accompany full moons, and with one in Cancer there may be news connected to the past—about relative or friends you haven't seen in eons. The moon also represents mom or her equivalent or a nurturing individual, so there may be news about this individual too.

The new moon in compatible air sign Aquarius on January 23 should usher in new opportunities to connect with like-minded people. You may join new groups whose interests are in line with yours.

FINANCES, OTHER STUFF
Between January 1 and June 11, expansive Jupiter is in Taurus and your solar second house of finances. Lucky you! This transit continues from June of 2011 and should be lining your pockets with gold and silver coins, Aries. Because Jupiter expands, however, it can also mean you spend beyond your means. Practice paying for everything in cash. It will make you more aware of what you spend on what.

CAREER
Strongest communication in terms of your career occurs between January 8 and 27, when Mercury moves through Capricorn and the professional area of your chart. Lay down your goals, figure out how to attain them, push your own agenda forward. Do NOT be shy. Pluto is transiting your career area, which gives you a major edge. Power plays are likely.

ROMANCE
Single or involved, the first two weeks of the month favor romance and love. Venus is in compatible air sign Aquarius then, and it's possible you meet a special someone through friends or through a group to which you belong. If you're committed, then you and your partner enjoy the company of friends between January 1 and 14.

From January 14 to February 8, Venus is in Pisces, your solar twelfth house. Your intuitive connection to your partner is strong, perhaps almost telepathic.

BEST DAYS, CHALLENGING DAYS
January 1 to 7: Excellent communication with a partner or loved one. Favors travel abroad.

January 24: Mars (your physical and sexual energy) turns retrograde in Virgo, in the daily work area of your chart.

February—Aries

LUNAR HIGHLIGHTS
You'll love the full moon in fellow fire sign Leo on February 7. It should bring news about a romance, creative project, or a child. Or there's news about something you find enjoyable. Mercury is opposed to this full moon, suggesting a lot of activity and chaos generally. It's the sort of chaos that suits you, Aries.

The new moon in Pisces on February 21 occurs in your solar twelfth house and ushers in new opportunities to delve into your own psyche. You might enter therapy or take a workshop on dreams or intuitive development, or you could decide a past-life regression is your ticket to understanding who you are. Neptune is closely conjunct this new moon, indicating that you're acting from a place within yourself of higher inspiration and idealism.

FINANCES, OTHER STUFF
With Jupiter in Taurus and the money area of your chart, you're in good shape. This month Jupiter has some help too. Between February 13 and March 2, Mercury transits Pisces, so you're more intuitive about financial decisions you make. Then, between February 8 and March 5, Venus moves through your sign. Your self-confidence soars, and whenever you feel good about yourself and your love life, the rest of your life tends to run more smoothly.

CAREER
With Uranus in your sign until March 2019, you can expect the unexpected, and nothing will be easy to predict or anticipate. You've got Pluto moving through your career area until 2024, so whenever a new moon or a planet forms a beneficial angle to Pluto, you're in a powerful position. The new moon in Pisces is one of those dates (February 21), and so is the time frame between February 13 and March 2, when Mercury is in Pisces.

Also, on February 3, Neptune enters Pisces for a run of

about fourteen years. This transit suggests that idealism, inspiration, and creativity are more prominent in your professional life.

ROMANCE
The period from February 8 to March 5 is one of the most romantic and creative for you all year. Venus is in your sign, Aries, and life certainly looks very nice indeed. Since Venus is traveling with Uranus, unexpected and surprising twists and turns are the norm in romance.

BEST DAYS, CHALLENGING DAYS
Saturn in Libra is retrograde between February 6 and June 25, so your personal and business partnerships may not be quite up to par. Delays or restrictions could occur. February 16 looks beautiful for communication and news about finances.

March—Aries

LUNAR HIGHLIGHTS
March 8: Full moon in Virgo, in your solar sixth house. News about your daily work routine or health. Mars forms a wide conjunction to this full moon, suggesting heightened activity and a need for precision.

March 22: The new moon is in your sign, with close conjunctions from both Uranus and Mercury. This is a date to circle. Expect unexpected new personal opportunities. Communication, travel, siblings, and other relatives are highlighted. This new moon happens just once a year and sets the tone for the next six months. Visualize what you want and reach for it.

FINANCES, OTHER STUFF
Mercury enters your sign on March 2, turns retrograde on the twelfth, turns direct again in Pisces on April fourth, and enters your sign again on April 16. Before it turns retro-

grade, be sure to solidify travel plans, back up computer files, and tie up loose ends on every front.

Venus joins Jupiter in Taurus between March 5 and April 3, so your finances should be really humming this month. A raise? A royalty check? Insurance settlement?

CAREER
While Venus and Jupiter travel together between March 5 and April 3, they form a beneficial angle to Pluto and your career area. For the first week of this transit, Mercury is direct, so pitch your ideas, submit your manuscript, move your own projects forward. You're in the driver's seat. Once Mercury turns retrograde, it's time to rethink, revise, review.

ROMANCE
With Venus in Taurus from March 5 to April 3, you're in a sensuous mood, and your partner responds to it. Sensuality isn't just sex, though. You're after the romance part of the relationship too, whether it's moonlit walks on a beach, a delicious meal by candlelight, or sweet nothings whispered through text messages, emails, or in person!

BEST DAYS, CHALLENGING DAYS
March 12, the day that Mercury turns retrograde in your sign, is likely to be challenging. Appliances may go on the fritz, travel plans could change without notice, your computer may shut down forever. Sometimes these snafus occur right before the retrograde begins. Before a Mercury retrograde in December 2009, for instance, we had to buy a new printer, a new washing machine, and a new hot water heater! During the retrograde, the major mishap was a dishwasher that stopped draining, but a dose of vinegar and Drano did the trick.

March 11 to 14 should be terrific days. Venus and Jupiter are traveling together in Taurus, in your financial area.

April—Aries

LUNAR HIGHLIGHTS
The full moon in Libra on April 6 should bring news about partnerships—personal or professional. There could be an element of surprise to this news, which will somehow expand your pocketbook and creative venues. Strive to balance the various elements of your life around this time, but don't bend over backward to please others.

On April 21, the new moon in Taurus should usher in new financial opportunities. You're still enjoying Jupiter's bounties in your money area, which makes this new moon one to anticipate. There can be a tendency to overspend when Jupiter is in your financial area, which makes it smart to pay cash as often as possible. That will make you more aware of what you're spending.

FINANCES, OTHER STUFF
Mercury turns direct in Pisces, your solar twelfth house, on April 4. So it's now safe to pack your bags and head out for some exotic global spot. You may want to do that with a friend or even a romantic interest, because on April 3, Venus enters compatible air sign Gemini. The trip certainly won't be boring, and the friend or romantic partner with whom you travel is sure to keep things lively.

CAREER
Mars has been in Virgo since the beginning of the year and will be there until July 3. It forms a beneficial angle to your career area and Pluto, which is transiting that area. Think of Mars as a booster rocket that gets professional stuff moving by working daily to make sure you tend to details and connect all the dots, i.e., that you do the detail work. Even if details aren't your thing, Aries, it's best to do what Mars—your sign's ruler—requires!

ROMANCE

This area is very active in April. Venus enters Gemini on April 4 and until May 15, when it turns retrograde, triggers all sorts of interesting experiences in the romance department. Your new romantic interest may be someone who lives closer than you think—perhaps in your neighborhood. You could meet this individual through a book group to which you belong, a sibling or other relative, or a neighbor.

In an existing relationship—or a new one—the level of communication should be excellent. You and your partner may be traveling together during this period or spending more time than usual with friends.

Venus is retrograde between May 15 and June 27, then moves forward again in Gemini until August 7. So you're treated to two delightful periods when your love life unfolds smoothly, with just the right amount of excitement and fun.

BEST DAYS, CHALLENGING DAYS

Circle April 9. Venus and Uranus form a beneficial angle to each other and your sun. Expect the unexpected in love and creativity, with plenty of fun and excitement tossed in for good measure. On April 10, Pluto turns retrograde in Capricorn and remains that way until September 17. Career stuff slows down!

May—Aries

LUNAR HIGHLIGHTS

May 5: The full moon in Scorpio should bring news about a mortgage, loan, insurance, or even about taxes. It occurs in your solar eighth house, which also rules the weird, strange, hidden, mysterious, and psychic. You may have unusual psychic experiences around the time of this moon—precognitive dreams or instances of telepathy, clairvoyance, clairaudience, even remote seeing. It would be a great time to take a workshop in intuitive development.

May 20: The first solar eclipse of the year, in Gemini, your third house. This eclipse should bring new opportunities to express yourself. If you're a writer, for example, then you may have an opportunity to write something completely different from what you've been doing. You may start a blog, build a Web site, start a newsletter. Whatever it is, it's new.

FINANCES, OTHER STUFF

Until June 11, Jupiter remains in Taurus and your solar second house, so your finances look good. If you've been creating a solid financial base for yourself, then you'll enjoy Jupiter's transit through Gemini, an air sign more compatible with your fire-sign sun. More on that under the June entry.

Interestingly enough, between May 9 and 24, Jupiter gets a nice boost from Mercury as it travels through Taurus. This suggests discussions and communication about money. Perhaps you're asking for a raise, Aries?

CAREER

Neptune in Pisces forms a harmonious angle to your career area and Pluto, which is moving through Capricorn. This transit will continue for some time because both of these planets move like snails. But the bottom line for this year—and the next fourteen years—is that your ideals play a larger part in your professional decisions and options. Also, with Uranus in your sign for the next seven years, you're thinking way outside the box and may be discovering ideals you didn't even realize you had.

ROMANCE

Venus turns retrograde in Gemini on May 15, so best to bite your tongue between then and June 27. Don't blurt out everything you think and feel to and about your partner. Strive for introspection first; revise and review an existing relationship. If you're single, it's possible that old flames resurface in your life. You'll have a chance to move ahead again between June 27 and August 7.

BEST DAYS, CHALLENGING DAYS
May 28 could be quite an interesting day in terms of intellect, ideas, communication. Mercury and Uranus form a beneficial angle to each other, so you're conscious thought process is cutting edge. Jot down all your ideas. You'll be able to use them soon.

Challenging days? Not really, not unless you choose to make a day that way!

June—Aries

LUNAR HIGHLIGHTS
The lunar eclipse in Sagittarius on June 4 should bring exciting news for you, Aries, and it looks like you may be happy enough to celebrate with loved ones. You might land an overseas position, win admission to the college or graduate school of your choice, or have an opportunity to travel overseas. Uranus forms a beneficial angle to the eclipse degree, suggesting that the news is sudden and unexpected. Maybe a shift in your beliefs has brought it about.

The second new moon in Gemini occurs on June 19. This one should bring new opportunities in your daily life to communicate more widely and frequently. You may have opportunities to spend time with siblings, other relatives, and neighbors. If you've been hoping to move, this would be a good time to look for a new neighborhood. Put out feelers with friends about what you're searching for. On the day of this new moon, Uranus forms a beneficial angle to Venus, so there could be sudden and unexpected surprises in your love life.

FINANCES, OTHER STUFF
Jupiter enters Gemini on June 11, when it leaves your financial area and enters your solar third house. This

transit—which lasts until June 25, 2013—forms a harmonious angle to your sun, so various areas of your life will feel as if they are particularly lucky. It's to your advantage to take a look at your natal chart to find out where Gemini appears. Whatever that house represents will experience the most expansion during the next year.

Between June 7 and 25, Mercury transits Cancer, your solar fourth house, and forms a beneficial angle to Neptune in Pisces and Mars in Virgo. The combination of transits brings a strong intuitive flavor to your conscious mind. It may prompt you to take a workshop in intuitive development or to remove that unfinished manuscript from your desk and get to work on it!

CAREER
Mars in Virgo, where it remains until July 3, continues to form a beneficial angle to your career area and Pluto in Capricorn. Think of this angle as a professional booster rocket that makes it possible for you to get things done. You forge ahead on your projects, explore new ideas and methods, and basically barrel through any obstacles you encounter.

ROMANCE
Venus is retrograde in Gemini until June 27, creating bumps and bruises and misunderstandings in your partnerships. But more than likely, Venus retrograde can bring about physical discomforts and inconveniences that create tension between you and a partner. Your air conditioning could go on the fritz, for instance, or your car breaks down.

Once Venus turns direct again, it will be in Gemini until August 7, lighting up your love life close to home.

BEST DAYS, CHALLENGING DAYS
June 30 looks like a really good day, Aries. Mercury and Jupiter form a beneficial angle to each other and your sun. This expands your opportunities in education, foreign travel, romance, and sheer enjoyment. A confusing day falls on June 4, when Neptune turns retrograde in Pisces.

July—Aries

LUNAR HIGHLIGHTS
The month gets off to a running start with a full moon in Capricorn on July 3. Pluto is closely conjunct to this moon, suggesting power plays in your career or with an authority figure. There could also be professional news that impacts you emotionally. Earth isn't an element that mixes well with your fire-sign sun, but it does serve to ground you, Aries.

July 19 features a new moon in Cancer, your solar fourth house. This one should bring new opportunities related to your home life, family, and personal environment. Thanks to a challenging angle from Saturn to this new moon, you have to fulfill your obligations and responsibilities to others before you gain full advantage of the opportunity.

FINANCES, OTHER STUFF
Mercury turns retrograde in fellow fire sign Leo on July 14 and remains that way until August 8. The first rule for these periods is simple to remember: revise, rethink, review. Don't sign contracts, do recheck travel plans and itinerary, and be sure to communicate clearly. The possibility of misunderstandings is strong.

Jupiter is now in compatible air sign Gemini, your solar third house, which enhances your general luck in communication, education, and daily life.

CAREER
As of July 3, Mars joins Saturn in Libra, your opposite sign, and forms a challenging angle to your career sector and Pluto in Capricorn. You're strongly motivated now to move ahead and make professional strides, but may encounter challenges or obstacles. Nothing is insurmountable for you, however. Just put on your entrepreneur hat, and take the competition by storm.

ROMANCE
Since Venus went direct on June 27, in Gemini, where it will be until August 7, you're a much happier camper. Your

love life, if you're involved, hums along at a pleasurable pace. You and partner agree on the fundamentals. If you're uninvolved right now, that could change, and a romantic interest could be right around the corner, as close as your own neighborhood.

With Uranus in your sign, Aries, romantic interludes occur suddenly and unexpectedly.

BEST DAYS, CHALLENGING DAYS
July 1 looks like a green light day. Venus, Mercury, Uranus, and Jupiter are all forming beneficial angles to each other and your sun sign. Bottom line? Love, creativity, heightened communication abilities are all part of the day's parcel.

July 13 could be troublesome. Uranus turns retrograde in your sign and doesn't turn direct again until December 13. Once you get accustomed to the energy, you'll do fine. But lie low on the thirteenth.

August—Aries

LUNAR HIGHLIGHTS
There are three lunar events this month, and it all begins on August 1, with a full moon in Aquarius in your solar eleventh house. Uranus forms a close, beneficial angle to this full moon, so news that you hear is unexpected, may come through friends, and certainly looks good. Jupiter also forms an exact, harmonious angle to this moon, suggesting the news is lucky and expansive. A date to circle!

The new moon in Leo on August 17 occurs in your solar fifth house and should be ideal for you, Aries. New opportunities in love and romance and new opportunities to show off your creativity. You have a chance to shine now. Don't waste it!

August 31 features a full moon in Pisces, your solar twelfth house. It's easier to access your own psyche during this full moon, to figure out your own motives, to recall your dreams.

Insights come through imagination and intuition. News could concern something going on behind the scenes.

FINANCES, OTHER STUFF
On August 7, Venus enters Cancer and your solar fourth house, where it will be until September 6. This transit suggests that your financial decisions during the next several weeks will be colored by your emotions and guided by your intuition. Adjustments may have to be made at home or in your domestic environment, i.e., you may spend money refurbishing your home or redecorating. Just be sure you've got the money in the bank—so that you can pay off the credit card when the bill comes due.

CAREER
Venus in Cancer between August 7 and September 6 has repercussions for your professional life. You may have to be more careful now about balancing obligations at home and in your career. You could feel torn between one and the other. Meanwhile, Saturn in Libra, your opposite sign, requests that you fulfill your responsibilities in all areas of your life. So you could be feeling a bit overwhelmed, Aries. Just put one foot in front of the other and move ahead.

ROMANCE
On August 8, Mercury turns direct in Leo, the romance area of your chart. Good news, indeed! You and your partner can now talk about whatever is on your respective minds—topics you may have avoided during the retrograde period. This change in Mercury also favors all your creative projects.

BEST DAYS, CHALLENGING DAYS
August 8, of course, is a day to circle. Mercury turning direct is always something to celebrate, but especially when it happens in a fellow fire sign. August 22 and 23 are green light days too. Mercury and Jupiter form strong angles to each other, strengthening your communication ability and your luck!

Red light days? August 23 could be touchy. Your ruler, Mars, enters Scorpio, your solar eighth house. Energy shifts, but the good news is that your sexuality is heightened.

September—Aries

LUNAR HIGHLIGHTS
The new moon in Virgo on September 15 falls in your solar sixth house—daily work and the daily maintenance of your health. New communication opportunities surface—a chance to build a Web site or start a blog or newsletter. You might join a gym, start a new exercise regimen, or start working out of your home. Mars forms a wide, beneficial angle to this new moon, which suggests a lot of activity and forward thrust around this time.

The full moon in your sign on September 29 promises unexpected and exciting news that somehow expands your life. Your personal life is illuminated in some way and even though you might feel a bit nuts around the time of this moon, it's the kind of nuts that suits you. There could be news, too, concerning a romantic relationship or creative project.

FINANCES, OTHER STUFF
Venus transits fellow fire sign Leo between September 6 and October 3. This transit has ramifications for your love life, which we'll talk about under Romance, but it also has financial ramifications. You may find that you spend more on jewelry, art, and other beautiful but high-ticket items. Just be sure you've got the money in the bank to pay for the bills when they come due.

You could receive a payment for something you create or may be spending money on pleasurable pursuits.

CAREER
On September 17, Pluto turns direct in Capricorn and your career area. Anything that has been stalled in your profession can now move forward. You're on top of your goals

and desires again and can easily make things happen and manifest your desires. The new moon in Virgo on September 15 helps you connect the dots in your daily work, and that in turn helps you professionally.

ROMANCE
Okay, about that Venus transit through Leo. This transit is one of the most romantic and creative for you all year. Others find you attractive, appealing, perhaps even seductive. You're the magnet in any crowd, and yes, admit it, Aries—you love the attention. If you're involved already, your partner is extraattentive. If you're not involved, you may be before the transit is over.

Creatively, you're on a roll during this transit. Others also like your ideas and projects, and it shouldn't be too difficult to get the attention you deserve.

BEST DAYS, CHALLENGING DAYS
September 20 and 21 look like stellar days for romance, creativity, and just plain luck. Maybe it's time to buy a lottery ticket, Aries! With both Venus and Jupiter forming beneficial angles to each other and to your sun sign, how can you lose?

October—Aries

LUNAR HIGHLIGHTS
The new moon in Libra on October 15 falls in your partnership area. This is good news, Aries! It suggests that a new, serious romance may be on its way into your life, or you and your existing partner deepen your commitment to each other. In business ventures, you find the right partner at the right time. Jupiter forms a beneficial angle to this new moon—and your sun sign—suggesting that the new opportunities expand your horizons.

The full moon in Taurus on October 29 occurs in your financial area and should bring news about money. Pluto forms a beneficial angle to this new moon, suggesting there may be a promotion and a raise for you around this time. If there's any confusion, just ride the tide and let things work out on their own.

FINANCES, OTHER STUFF

Between October 5 and 29, Mercury transits Scorpio and your solar eighth house. Your mind is like a psychic sponge during this transit, and decisions will be made from a deeply intuitive level. You may be dealing with things like taxes, insurance, wills, financial resources you share with a partner or someone else. It's smart to keep plans to yourself or to share them only with people you trust implicitly.

CAREER

On October 5, Saturn enters Scorpio and your solar eighth house, where it will travel several weeks with Mercury. Both Mercury and Saturn are making beneficial angles to your career area and Pluto in Capricorn. You're focused on professional matters and relationships. You're able to grasp the deeper, often hidden truths behind people's actions and motives. Saturn's transit through Scorpio should strengthen your career options and work. Just don't take shortcuts!

ROMANCE

Between October 28 and November 21, Venus transits Libra, your opposite sign. This transit favors romantic partnerships and may take yours to the next level. You and your partner could move in together, get engaged or married, or start a family. It's even possible that you go into business together, combining business with love. Not a bad proposition, right, Aries?

Between October 6 and November 16, your ruler, Mars, transits fellow fire sign Sagittarius. This transit probably fires up your libido, so why not get out of town for a few days? Or a few weeks?

BEST DAYS, CHALLENGING DAYS
October 30 and 31 look great for open, honest communication with your partner. Toss in some travel, and you'll be as happy as a clam.

October 7 to 13, Saturn in Scorpio and Neptune in Pisces form beneficial angles to each other—but not to your sun. This period could be challenging.

November—Aries

LUNAR HIGHLIGHTS
The two eclipses this month stimulate a number of events and emotions for you, Aries. On November 13, a solar eclipse in Scorpio brings new opportunities for research and investigation, to explore your sexuality, to hone your intuition. In addition, opportunities in terms of taxes, insurance, mortgages, and loans come your way too. The bottom line in any area you take on is revealed.

The lunar eclipse in Gemini on November 28 should bring positive news connected to communication, travel, siblings, your neighborhood and community. Jupiter is conjunct this moon by five degrees, close enough so that the good news you receive expands your world in some way. You might, for instance, hear that your scholarship for college or grad school has been approved. Or that your novel has been bought.

FINANCES, OTHER STUFF
The solar eclipse in Scorpio on November 13 highlights that area of your chart concerned with shared resources—usually those shared with a partner. So it's likely that your partner's income could spike upward. Don't sign any financial contracts (or any contracts, for that matter!) between November 6 and 26, while Mercury is retrograde in Sagittarius. Mars will be traveling with Mercury between November 6 and 16, so you may feel mentally restless, eager to get out on the road and travel, and spend money you may not have!

Between November 21 and December 15, Venus transits

Scorpio and the shared resources area of your chart. This should greatly enhance the promises mentioned earlier of the new moon.

CAREER
The big career news this month is the transit of Mars through Capricorn, your solar tenth house. It occurs between November 16 and December 25. This transit brings great forward thrust with professional matters, particularly when Mercury is moving direct, after November 26. Be sure to get out and about and make contacts that may be useful to you in your career. You're better able to set goals and figure out how to achieve them.

ROMANCE
The lunar eclipse in Gemini on November 28 could have you feeling very good about a romantic relationship. Perhaps you and your partner get out of town together for a few days. Or maybe you decide to work on a creative project together, move in together, or even get married. Your feel-good mood attracts much more that makes you happy.

BEST DAYS, CHALLENGING DAYS
November 9 looks very nice overall, but especially for romance and travel. Tread carefully during the Mercury retrograde period between November 6 and 26.

December—Aries

LUNAR HIGHLIGHTS
You'll love the new moon in fellow fire sign Sagittarius on December 13. This one ushers in new opportunities for foreign travel and sales and expanding your business into overseas markets. This new moon occurs with Mercury in Sadge and also happens on the same day that Uranus turns direct in your sign. Nice combination of energies. Get out and enjoy yourself.

The full moon in Cancer on December 28 occurs in your solar fourth house. News related to your domestic situation, your personal environment, or one of your parents. Saturn forms a close, beneficial angle with this moon, suggesting that the news is solid, a done deal.

FINANCES, OTHER STUFF
You may be getting your financial house in order for the end of the year. Lots of calls and emails are exchanged—with your bank, a mortgage company, your insurance company. Most of this is likely to occur while Mercury transits Scorpio until December 10.

Mercury transits fellow fire sign Sagittarius between December 10 and 31, so you may be thinking about traveling or could be traveling for the holidays.

CAREER
You'll be set up nicely for the new year when Mercury transits Capricorn and your career area between December 31 and January 19. That will be the time to pitch ideas, push your agenda forward, submit manuscripts and résumés. For the rest of the month, stick to the program, don't make waves.

ROMANCE
On the fifteenth, Venus enters fellow fire sign Sagittarius, your solar ninth house. You're ready to hit the road, Aries, with just your backpack and an ATM card. Travel with your partner, or if you're not involved, be prepared to meet someone while you're traveling. Jupiter is still in compatible air sign Gemini, so you've got plenty of luck in your court.

BEST DAYS, CHALLENGING DAYS
From December 16 to the end of the month, Mercury and Venus travel together in Sadge. You're in the mood for love and romance, and the feeling is reflected in your creative endeavors.

Happy New Year!

3

Taurus

The Big Picture in 2012

Welcome to 2012, Taurus! This year highlights partnerships, cooperation, spirituality. Let's take a closer look.

Your ruler, Venus, starts off the year in Aquarius, your solar tenth house, your career area, where it will be until the fourteenth. This beautiful transit favors all your professional endeavors and generally enables you to move your ambitions forward without much effort. On the fourteenth, Venus enters compatible water sign Pisces, which we'll scrutinize more closely under the Romance section.

Pluto, the snail of the zodiac, starts off the year in fellow earth sign Capricorn, where it has consistently been since November 2008. You're accustomed to its energy now. Its transit, which lasts until 2024, is bringing profound and permanent change, evident in the economic challenges that now face the U.S. Most institutions are in the throes of great change—the health-care industry, the petroleum and insurance industries, mortgages/lending, housing, aviation, even the Internet. You name it, and Pluto's fingerprint can be found.

On a personal level, this planet's transit through your solar ninth house has been changing your worldview since 2008. Your spiritual beliefs and educational and publishing goals are in flux. Your beliefs about foreigners and foreign cultures are changing, and so are your traveling habits. More frequent overseas travel is possible. The Pluto transit doesn't end until 2024.

Neptune entered Pisces and your solar eleventh house on April 4, 2011. But by early August 2011, it had slipped back into Aquarius. On February 3, 2012, it enters Pisces again and won't move on until January 2026. For hints about what this may mean for you, look back to that period in 2011 when Neptune was in Pisces.

Neptune symbolizes our higher ideals, escapism, fiction, spirituality, and our blind spots. It seeks to dissolve boundaries between us and others. One possible repercussion of this transit is prolonged religious wars, which proliferated during Uranus's transit in Pisces from early 2003. On a personal level, though, Neptune's transit through your eleventh house suggests that you may join spiritual or metaphysical groups or seek out friends with spiritual or metaphysical interests. You also may join charitable groups that support your ideals. Your intuitive ability should deepen. Among groups, you may meet up with people you have known in past lives.

Uranus entered Aries and your solar twelfth house in March 2011. This transit has undoubtedly stirred up plenty of stuff in your unconscious already and will do so again this year and for the next seven, right up until March 2019. But that's its job. Uranus shakes up the status quo so that we're forced to move beyond our ruts and routines. It wakes us up so that we recognize where we have become rigid and inflexible.

The trick in navigating this transit successfully, Taurus, is to delve into your own unconscious for a deeper understanding of your motives and needs. If you don't meditate already, now is a good time to start. Also, your dream recall should be quite good during this transit, with lucid dreams and out-of-body experiences much easier to achieve. Few elements in your life will be predictable during this transit, but your inner world will be the least predictable area, so it behooves you to pay attention to what's going on within.

Saturn begins the year in Libra, your solar sixth house. It has been there since the summer of 2010 and will be there until October 2012. This transit brings structure to your daily work—perhaps due to increased responsibilities, a new job, a change in your domestic routine that requires you to use your time more efficiently. Saturn can cause delays and restrictions, so if you encounter challenges in your daily work, don't push against them. Just try to go with the flow. If challenges with a coworker surface, be as diplomatic as possible and walk in the other person's shoes. Do they really have an issue or are they simply complainers?

Once Saturn enters Scorpio in October, there may be delays or restrictions in business and romantic partnerships. Or you find the ideal structure for a relationship. There will be an emphasis on cooperation, teamwork. You'll want greater balance in your partnerships, and one way or another, you'll find it.

Expansive Jupiter begins the year in your sign! You've been experiencing this transit since June 2011, so by the beginning of this year you should know how Jupiter's expansiveness and luck are unfolding in your life. It lasts until June 11, so take advantage of all opportunities for growth that present themselves. With Jupiter in your sign, you may head overseas more frequently, could publish a book, go to college or graduate school, even launch your own business.

Once Jupiter enters Gemini and your solar second house on June 11—until June 25, 2013—you're in for a treat! This transit should increase your earnings and open up new financial venues. Even if it seems you're initially spending more than usual, don't worry about it. Your income should increase significantly.

They say that timing is everything, so with that in mind let's look at some specific areas in your life.

ROMANCE/CREATIVITY

The most romantic and creative time for you all year falls between October 3 and 28, when Venus transits Virgo and your solar fifth house. If you're not involved before this transit begins, you probably will be before the transit ends. If you're not, it won't matter because you're having too much fun. Or you're deeply immersed in a creative project that consumes a lot of your time and energy. Great backup dates: March 5 to April 3, when Venus transits your sign. Things really seem to flow your way then in many areas, but particularly with romance and creative ventures.

The best time for serious involvement and deepening commitment in an existing relationship occurs when Venus transits Scorpio and your seventh house from November 21 to December 15. You and your partner may decide to move in together, get engaged, or get married. Just be sure that you don't do any of this under a Mercury retrograde period. Take a look under the appropriate section below to find out when Mercury will be retrograde this year.

Other good backup dates: August 23 to October 6, when Mars transits Scorpio and your solar seventh house. This stirs up a lot of activity with a partner.

CAREER

Usually Venus and Jupiter transits to your career area are the times to look for. But those transits don't happen this year. However, between December 25 and February 2, 2013, Mars will be transiting Aquarius and your career area. This is the time to push your professional agenda forward, make new professional contacts, and keep your nose to the grindstone, completing projects and brainstorming with coworkers for new ideas. Even though it begins during the holidays, don't let that hold you back! Also, from June 11, 2012, to June 25, 2013, when Jupiter is transiting Gemini, it forms a harmonious angle to your career area, so your professional life should run smoothly during this period, with expanding options and greater pay.

Since your career area misses the boat on Venus this year, look to April 3 to May 15, when Venus is moving direct in Gemini and forming a beneficial angle to your career area. This occurs again (because of a retrograde) between June 27 and August 7. Don't hesitate to pitch ideas, submit manuscripts and screenplays, and ask for a raise. It's also an excellent time to launch a Web site, start your own business, or make new professional contacts. Other people will be receptive to your ideas.

BEST TIMES FOR
Buying or selling a home: September 6 to October 3, when Venus is in Leo and your fourth house; June 25 to July 14 and August 8 to 31, when Mercury is moving direct in Leo.

Family reunions: Any of the dates above.

Financial matters: The period from June 11, 2012, to June 25, 2013, when Jupiter transits your house of money. Also, April 3 to May 15 and June 27 to August 7, when Venus is moving direct through the same area.

Signing contracts: When Mercury is moving direct!

Overseas travel, publishing, and higher-education endeavors: December 15 to January 9, 2013, while Venus transits your solar eighth house and fire sign Sagittarius.

MERCURY RETROGRADES
Every year Mercury—the planet of communication and travel—turns retrograde three times. During this period it's wise not to sign contracts (unless you don't mind renegotiating when Mercury is moving direct), to check and recheck travel plans, and to communicate as succinctly as possible. Refrain from buying any large-ticket items or electronics during this time too. Often computers and appliances go on the fritz, cars act up, data is lost ... you get the idea. Be sure to back up all files before the dates below:

March 12–April 4: Mercury retrograde in Aries, your twelfth house. Revisiting old issues, Taurus. Old friends may surface too.

July 14–August 8: Mercury retrograde in Leo, your solar fourth house of family and home.

November 6–26: Mercury retrograde in Sagittarius, your solar eighth house. This one impacts shared resources, particularly those shared with a partner.

ECLIPSES
Solar eclipses tend to trigger external events that bring about change according to the sign and house in which they

fall. Lunar eclipses trigger inner, emotional events according to the sign and house in which they fall. Any eclipse marks both beginnings and endings. The solar and lunar eclipse in a pair falls in opposite signs. If you're interested in detailed information on eclipses, take a look at Celeste Teal's excellent and definitive book, *Eclipses: Predicting World Events & Personal Transformation*.

If you were born under or around the time of an eclipse, it's to your advantage to take a look at your birth chart to find out exactly where the eclipses will impact you.

Most years feature four eclipses—two solar, two lunar, with the set separated by about two weeks. In November and December 2011, there were solar and lunar eclipses, so this year the first eclipses fall during May and June.

May 20: Solar eclipse at 0 degrees Gemini, your second house. This one brings new financial opportunities.

June 4: Lunar eclipse in Sagittarius, your eighth house. This should be a positive eclipse for you and your partner. You land a loan or a mortgage that you wanted, have a terrific psychic reading, get a break on taxes or insurance.

November 13: Solar eclipse in Scorpio, your solar seventh house. New opportunities surface for you and your romantic or business partner.

November 28: Lunar eclipse, Gemini. Jupiter forms a five-degree conjunction to the eclipse degree, suggesting that financial news coming your way is positive, and you're in an upbeat, expansive mood.

LUCKIEST DAY OF THE YEAR
Every year there's one day when Jupiter and the sun meet up, and luck, serendipity, and expansion are the hallmarks. This year that day falls on May 13, with a conjunction in Taurus. The fact that it's in your sign makes it a very lucky day indeed.

January—Taurus

LUNAR HIGHLIGHTS
The full moon in Cancer on January 9 is compatible with your earth-sign sun, so it should be quite a good day for you. You may receive news about a writing project, siblings, someone or something in your community. Thanks to a beneficial angle from Mars, January 9 and a few days on either side of it are apt to be chaotic, filled with movement, people, and activities.

The new moon in Aquarius on January 23 falls in your career area, a fantastic harbinger for the new year. This moon should bring new career opportunities and new ways of tackling your professional life. Aquarius is usually visionary, and whatever hunches and gut certainties you have at this time should be heeded.

FINANCES, OTHER STUFF
Venus transits compatible water sign Pisces between January 14 and February 8. This period favors all activities with friends and groups. You may be dealing more with groups, perhaps to sell or promote a product or service, and doing more public speaking.

With Mercury in fellow earth sign Capricorn between January 8 and 27, Mars in fellow earth sign Virgo until July 3, and Jupiter in your sign until June 11, you're pretty well set financially. You also have the will and determination to budget and save your money.

CAREER
From January 27 to February 13, Mercury transits Aquarius and your career area. This period favors professional communication, pitching ideas, submitting manuscripts, and garnering support of coworkers when needed. Whenever you feel you're up against an obstacle or challenge, use Jupiter's energies to move through it. Jupiter in Taurus bolsters the qualities for which you're admired—resoluteness, carrying things through to completion, and grounding your goals.

ROMANCE
Venus and Uranus travel together in Pisces between January 14 and February 8. This duo promises unexpected experiences with friends and groups, which could lead to a sudden romance. The excitement builds for you during this period, and there will be a deep intuitive flow between you and a potential love interest.

BEST DAYS, CHALLENGING DAYS
January 15 to 16 looks very nice. Expansive Jupiter and Venus form beneficial angles to each other, making it likely that any romantic relationship will expand and flourish during this period.

With Uranus in Aries for the next seven years, your inner world—your psyche, your unconscious—may be rocking and rolling, Taurus. The best use of this energy is to delve within. Meditate, take up yoga, keep track of your dreams, hone your intuitive ability.

February—Taurus

LUNAR HIGHLIGHTS
The full moon in Leo on February 7 occurs in your solar fourth house. It should bring insights and news about your domestic environment. This moon and Mercury are directly opposed to each other, suggesting that your conscious mind is active, sifting through ideas, new ways to communicate. Visitors could arrive unexpectedly, disturbing your routines, but you manage to take it in stride.

The new moon in Pisces on February 21 fits nicely with your earth-sign sun. Expect new opportunities for working with groups, new opportunities to meet people and make friends. Keep your social calendar open, Taurus. No telling who may be at that party you attend, that concert you get tickets to. Neptune is closely conjunct this new moon, suggesting that the new opportunities could have a spiritual component to them. Your idealism and ideals are also part of this new-moon equation.

FINANCES, OTHER STUFF

With Jupiter still in your sign, many areas of your life continue to expand, and your finances could certainly be one of those areas. It depends on your intent and beliefs. Do you believe you should be earning more for your skills and talent? Do you actively work to remain upbeat and positive, to see everything as an opportunity, even what other people might call a setback?

With Mercury in intuitive Pisces from February 13 to March 2, any hunches you get about investments or ways to make more money should be explored. Mars is still in fellow earth sign Virgo, your solar fifth house, suggesting that your quotient for enjoyment is high and that you actively pursue what you enjoy.

CAREER

On February 7, Saturn turns retrograde in Libra, your solar sixth house, suggesting that things in your daily work life could hit a few bumps. Just try to relax into your work routine and let events unfold. Practice nonresistance. Once Saturn turns direct again on June 25, you'll be able to use the structures you've built in a more positive way.

Neptune enters Pisces on February 3. Since Pisces is a water sign compatible with your sun, your professional ambitions may begin to integrate your spiritual beliefs and ideals more readily into your work. Also, you've got Pluto in Capricorn on your side until 2024, which brings self-empowerment, ambition, and a deeper sense of purpose.

ROMANCE

Between February 8 and March 5, Venus transits Aries, your solar twelfth house. You may be spending more time alone with a new romantic interest. It could be that you simply enjoy each other's company too much right now to share your time with others. Or perhaps there's a reason your relationship is secretive. If that's the case, the relationship won't be secretive after March 5, when Venus moves into your sign, Taurus!

BEST DAYS, CHALLENGING DAYS
February 16 and 17 look like very nice days for you. Mercury in Pisces and Jupiter in your sign beam friendly vibes at each other. Your intuition should be strong, your feelings expansive. Make the most of it!

March—Taurus

LUNAR HIGHLIGHTS
You're in tip-top shape this month, Taurus. The full moon in Virgo on March 8 is very much to your liking. Virgo is a fellow earth sign, and this full moon falls in your solar fifth house of romance and creativity. Read about that facet in more depth in the Romance section. Romance aside for the moment, one possible ramification of this full moon is a tremendous amount of creative activity and stuff going on with your kids, if you have children. You have Mars to thank for this. It forms a wide conjunction to this moon.

The new moon in Aries on March 22 ushers in new opportunities to trailblaze. If you've thought about striking out on your own, starting your own company, creating a new product, writing a novel or screenplay, this new moon can help to make things happen. Both Mercury and Uranus form close conjunctions to this new moon, indicating that the opportunities may occur suddenly, out of the blue, so you need to be on your toes. Mercury's proximity suggests a flood of ideas.

FINANCES, OTHER STUFF
Between March 2 and May 9, Mercury transits Aries, your solar twelfth house. The reason the transit lasts so long is that Mercury is retrograde for part of that time—March 12 to April 4. While it's moving direct, though, it should be easy for you to spot new financial opportunities or ways you can increase your income. You'll be doing more work behind the scenes—perhaps touching

base with clients through email, your blog or Web site. Your big financial boom will occur between June 11, 2012, and June 25, 2013, while Jupiter transits Gemini and your financial area.

CAREER
You're at the cutting edge this month, Taurus. Get your new ideas and projects out there between March 2 and 12, while Mercury is traveling in direct motion with edgy Uranus. Then after the twelfth, backtrack, revise, review, and rethink what you're doing until Mercury turns direct again on April 4. Then move forward.

If you're hunting for a job, be sure to send out résumés while Mercury is direct. In fact, reread the Mercury retrograde section in the Big Picture for your sign.

ROMANCE
Now for the really good stuff. Venus enters your sign on March 5, marking the start of one of the best periods for you all year—in romance, creative ventures, in any area where you place your intent and focus. Venus remains in your sign until April 3, traveling with lucky and expansive Jupiter. Possibilities? A wonderful relationship develops that expands your life and worldview; an existing relationship is taken to a deeper level of commitment; you enjoy multiple relationships and commit to none of them because you're having so much fun.

This transit also indicates that your muse will be at your beck and call 24/7. So put up that DO NOT DISTURB sign on your door and brainstorm.

BEST DAYS, CHALLENGING DAYS
The most challenging time is likely to be the Mercury retrograde in Aries, between March 12 and April 4.

April—Taurus

LUNAR HIGHLIGHTS
The full moon in Libra on April 6 should be terrific for you. It brings news and insights about your daily work routine, relationships, art and beauty generally. This moon is also quite social, so be sure to have free time that day and night to enjoy the company of a lover, spouse, and friends.

Then there's the new moon in your sign on April 21. Mark that date. This new moon rolls around just once a year and sets the tone for the next twelve months. Before it arrives, be sure to make a wish list. Post it where you'll see it frequently. Then back these desires with strong emotion. Focus on them, make them real, imagine them in detail. Mars forms a close, beneficial angle to the degree of this moon, so you'll have plenty of energy at your disposal to manifest these desires.

FINANCES, OTHER STUFF
From April 3 to August 7, Venus will be in Gemini, your financial sector. This transit is a harbinger of good things for your earnings, beliefs and attitudes toward money, and communicating about money. In other words, this could be an excellent time to make your pitch for a raise, to sell a novel, start a blog, or build a Web site. Between May 15 and June 27, however, Venus will be retrograde, so be sure to have your ducks lined up before this period begins or after it ends.

Fortunately, Mercury turns direct on April 4, which mitigates communication snafus. You can travel again without having to worry about mix-ups.

CAREER
Venus's transit in Gemini forms a strong, beneficial angle for the same dates listed above. Make your moves while the planet is in direct motion—pitch your ideas, submit manuscripts, résumés, and portfolios, sign contracts, push your agenda forward. You'll be in a sociable mood, too, so it would be to your advantage to attend all professional

social functions and to generally make it known that you're on top of things. Nothing is slipping past your radar.

ROMANCE
A bit more, now, about Venus in Gemini. This transit makes for an interesting relationship—conversation is avid, constant, lively. Ideas are exchanged; you and your partner may get involved in some sort of creative project together.

Venus in Jupiter also forms a beneficial angle to Saturn in Libra, so it's possible that your partner or new love interest is older than you are. Or has an air of seriousness. If you're not in a relationship at this time, then Venus in Gemini may prompt you to spend more time with friends or people with whom you work.

BEST DAYS, CHALLENGING DAYS
Circle April 9. Venus in Gemini and Uranus in Aries form a beneficial angle to each other, suggesting a visceral, unexpected romantic attraction. Or some cutting edge creative ideas. Or both!

May—Taurus

LUNAR HIGHLIGHTS
The full moon in Scorpio, your opposite sign, on May 5 brings news about a business or romantic partner or spouse. Scorpio is an emotionally intense and deeply intuitive sign, so it's possible that you have an inkling about this news before you officially hear it. With Pluto forming a wide but beneficial angle to this full moon, there's a sense of empowerment that accompanies it.

On May 20, there's a solar eclipse in Gemini. This eclipse should bring new financial opportunities. Thanks to a wide and beneficial angle from Uranus to the eclipse degree, the opportunities are likely to happen suddenly, so you'll have to be vigilant, Taurus. You want to be sure that you seize the opportunities the instant you recognize them! This eclipse is at zero degrees Gemini, which means there will be another new moon in Gemini at a larger degree—in about a month.

FINANCES, OTHER STUFF

The big financial news for the month is, of course, the solar eclipse in your financial area. With Venus turning retrograde in that same sign and house on May 15, the opportunities the eclipse promises may be somewhat delayed in arriving. If so, things will straighten out after June 27, when Venus turns direct again. Hold off on any big-ticket purchases till then.

That said, it's sometimes possible to get good deals when Venus is retrograde, but there could be unforeseen glitches. We once bought a used car during a Venus retrograde, got a good price on it, but later discovered it had been in an accident. Since the owner hadn't taken it to the dealer for repairs, the warranty was null and void. We went back to the dealer, who paid for the repairs. A year later, we sold the car for nearly what we'd paid for it.

CAREER

On May 9, Mercury enters your sign, joining Jupiter there, so you should be in rare form indeed! Communication suddenly becomes so easy that you may feel inspired to start a blog, build a Web site, write a newsletter for your company's clients or for your own services/company. Your mind is expansive. During this same period, Mars is also in fellow earth sign Virgo, so you've got plenty of physical energy to do whatever needs to be done. You're focused, goal oriented.

ROMANCE

Mars remains in Virgo and your solar fifth house until July 3, so your pursuit of pleasure, fun, and romance continues unabated until then. Since Mars symbolizes, among other things, your sexuality, your sex life is certainly highlighted. Virgo tends to be picky, though, and that could mean you're discriminating about your partners. You're not interested in sex just for sex. There has to be some deeper emotion.

BEST DAYS, CHALLENGING DAYS
May 15, when your ruler, Venus, turns retrograde, could be problematic. You're sensitive to what this planet does. Try not to get into arguments with your partner! May 9 looks very nice. Mercury joins expansive Jupiter in your sign! The sky is, suddenly, the limit.

June—Taurus

LUNAR HIGHLIGHTS
Two weeks after the solar eclipse in Gemini comes a lunar eclipse in the opposite sign, Sagittarius. Circle June 4. This one occurs in your solar eighth house and should be quite good for you, Taurus. There's news about resources you share with others (like a partner, parents, child), publishing, overseas travel, higher education. Uranus forms a wide, beneficial angle to the degree of this eclipse, suggesting the news takes you by surprise or that it has some sort of unexpected twist.

On June 19, there's a second new moon in Gemini, so it looks as if your new financial opportunities are coming around twice in a single month. Saturn forms a wide, beneficial angle to this new moon, indicating that the opportunities are grounded, solid, serious.

FINANCES, OTHER STUFF
We've talked about the financial issues related to the new moon. What else is going on? Well, the best portent for your finances begins on June 11 and lasts until June 25, 2013, when Jupiter transits Gemini and your money area. Look back twelve years, the last time this transit occurred, for clues about how this transit could unfold for you. Here are some possibilities: you earn more, but may also spend more; you land a significant raise, sell a novel or screenplay, or start your own business; you earn money through public speaking or public relations.

It's to your advantage to check your natal chart to see

where Gemini actually falls. That house will feel the most expansion from this transit.

CAREER
Jupiter in Gemini forms a beneficial angle to your career area between the dates listed above. Use this period to push your professional agenda forward. Go back to school for additional training. Write your novel or nonfiction book. If you're dissatisfied with your work, this transit may help you find a more meaningful career. In short, this transit enables you to make significant professional strides.

ROMANCE
Mercury entered Gemini last month, on the twenty-fourth, and joined Venus retrograde in Gemini. Granted the retrograde can be annoying, but with these two planets traveling together until June 7, you and your sweetie should be communicating deeply and well. From June 11 to August 7, Venus and Jupiter travel together, and after June 27, Venus will be moving direct. Your love life during that period should be expanding like crazy—you get engaged, move in with the one you love, perhaps even get married.

This period should also be one of great creative drive and accomplishment.

BEST DAYS, CHALLENGING DAYS
Not only is June 19 the day of the new moon, but Uranus and Venus form an exact and beneficial angle to each other. This combination could spark an unusual and edgy romantic attraction or creative endeavor.

July—Taurus

LUNAR HIGHLIGHTS
July 3 features a full moon in fellow earth sign Capricorn, your solar ninth house. This full moon brings news concerning higher education, foreign travel, foreign countries and

investments, your career, your worldview. Pluto is closely conjunct this moon, so the news you hear is powerful and potentially transformative.

The new moon in compatible water sign Cancer on July 19 should usher in new communication opportunities. You may have a chance to nurture a writing project, attend a different school, travel. Your daily routine may change somewhat, providing more opportunities for doing the things you really enjoy.

FINANCES, OTHER STUFF
We've talked about the effects of Jupiter in Gemini on your finances, i.e., expansion, luck! In addition, Venus in Gemini turned direct on June 27, which means these two planets are now traveling together in your financial sector. You could be making money from the arts; women who work in artistic professions could prove helpful. You could be spending more money, too, particularly on things you find aesthetically pleasing—jewelry, for instance, art, gourmet foods.

CAREER
Mercury enters Leo on June 25, moves retrograde between July 14 and August 8, and enters Virgo on August 31. While it's moving direct in Leo, your communication abilities really shine. So push your agenda forward, make your pitches, update your blog and Web site. If you're self-employed, now is the time to gain publicity for your company and/or product. In addition, Saturn in Libra forms a favorable angle to your career, so the structures you put into place are strong, lasting.

ROMANCE
Now that Venus is in direct motion, any bumps and glitches in your love life should be history. However, once Mercury turns retrograde on July 14, you may have to be extra careful about saying what you mean so that your actions aren't misinterpreted. Once Mercury enters fellow earth sign Virgo on August 31, you'll be feeling

very much in your element and your communications will reflect this.

BEST DAYS, CHALLENGING DAYS
Exert extra care during Mercury's retrograde in Leo from July 14 to August 8. It occurs in your solar fourth house—home and domestic environment. Read more about this retrograde in the Big Picture section for your sign.

Uranus turns retrograde on July 13 and stays that way until December 13. This movement could stir up stuff in your unconscious. So if you overreact to a situation, look within first for the reason.

August—Taurus

LUNAR HIGHLIGHTS
Buckle up, Taurus! August features three moons, and it all starts on August 1 with a full moon in Aquarius, your career area. There will be more on that under the Career section, but one thing's for sure with this full moon. Life could get chaotic quickly. Mars forms a wide, beneficial angle to this full moon, and Uranus forms a tighter, beneficial angle, suggesting that any news you hear is an unexpected and positive surprise!

On August 17, the new moon in Leo occurs in your solar fourth house. This should bring new opportunities related to your domestic environment, one of your parents, and your home life generally. Perhaps you buy a new home or someone moves into your place. There could be a birth or a positive change in the lives of your parents. Saturn forms an exact and beneficial angle to this new moon, suggesting that the opportunities that surface are serious, grounded, and deserve your consideration.

The full moon in Pisces on August 31 should ramp up your social life, Taurus. Leave your calendar open for a few days on either side of the thirty-first, so that you can be part of the festivities. Both Mars and Pluto form beneficial angles to this full moon and your sun sign. The combination of energies suggests intensity, heightened sexuality, and power—your power!

FINANCES, OTHER STUFF
Circle August 8. Mercury turns direct in Leo and now moves toward its appointment with Virgo, a transit that will be more pleasing to you. It's safe to pack your bags now and head out on that adventure!

Mars is in Libra until August 23, then enters Scorpio, your opposite sign, where it will be until October 6. This transit places a focus on your business and personal partnerships. Emotions may be intense and powerful.

CAREER
The full moon in Aquarius on August 1 brings news about a professional matter. You might land your dream job, be promoted, secure a major account, sell a book ... you get the idea. Since full moons also bring important insights, you may realize that your career is perfect—or not what you want. Either way, the insight benefits you.

Until June 25, 2013, you've got Jupiter forming a beneficial angle to your career area, helping to expand your professional options and venues.

ROMANCE
Venus enters compatible water sign Cancer on August 7. You're in for a treat! This transit lasts until September 6, and during this period a new relationship could be as close as your back yard. You may meet someone new through siblings, a neighbor, even another relative. For an existing relationship, this transit brings a certain softness and intuitive flow to your feelings for each other.

BEST DAYS, CHALLENGING DAYS
Circle August 31. Mercury enters Virgo and your solar fifth house. This transit, which lasts until September 16, promises vibrant communication with the one you love. Your muse will be in attendance 24/7, so be sure to carve out time for your creative projects.

September—Taurus

LUNAR HIGHLIGHTS
The new moon in Virgo on September 15 should be a good one for you, Taurus. Look for new opportunities related to romance, pleasure and enjoyment, and creativity. Mercury forms a close conjunction to this new moon, indicating that part of the creativity picture here could involve communication, travel, and education. If you're not involved with anyone now, this new moon could bring the right person at the right time!

The full moon in Aries on September 29 occurs in your solar twelfth house. This moon should bring insights into the workings of your own psyche and into your motives and those of others. Uranus falls within a degree of this full moon, suggesting that any news you hear is likely to catch you by surprise. In fact, for several days on either side of the twenty-ninth, expect the unexpected.

FINANCES, OTHER STUFF
By now you should be experiencing some of Jupiter's largesse in your finances. You get an additional boost this month when Venus enters Leo on September 6, a transit that lasts until October 3 and forms a beneficial angle to Jupiter in Gemini. In addition, Mercury enters fellow earth sign Virgo on August 31, and between then and October 5 your capacity for enjoyment and talking about your enjoyment increases. The more fun you have, Taurus, the better you feel. The better you feel, the greater the likelihood that your life generally will improve. If your life improves, so will your finances!

CAREER
Jupiter continues to form a harmonious angle to your career area—true until late June 2013. So now it's up to you to make things happen through your intentions, desires, visualizations. If you don't meditate already, then start doing it daily for five or ten minutes. If you don't have an exer-

cise regimen, start one. In other words, tend to each area of your life with equal attention and care.

ROMANCE
Venus enters Leo on September 6, firing up your domestic environment. You and your partner should enjoy plenty of stimulating conversation, cozy togetherness, and some drama. The drama could revolve around your need to be recognized by your partner, to be openly appreciated. Best not to obsess about it. State your case and move on.

BEST DAYS, CHALLENGING DAYS
Circle September 5–6. Mercury, Mars, and Pluto form close angles to each other. This trio of energies brings great passion, a penchant for details, and self-empowerment.

October—Taurus

LUNAR HIGHLIGHTS
The new moon in Libra on October 15 occurs in your solar sixth house and should bring new work opportunities. Jupiter is sending friendly beams to this new moon, suggesting that any opportunities that surface will be expansive and lucky and will benefit your work routine, social contacts, and relationships.

On October 29, the full moon in Taurus brings news about a personal issue, and the news looks good. This full moon receives a friendly beam from Pluto and Neptune, suggesting that your ideals may be involved in the events that unfold. If power issues surface, you're in control.

FINANCES, OTHER STUFF
Mars transits Sagittarius from October 6 to November 16, highlighting your partner's income and any resources you share with others. Your partner, for instance, could be working longer hours to make ends meet, doing more business travel, and could get a raise. The eighth house, where

this transit occurs, governs resources you share with others, so these possibilities could also apply to a parent, child, or anyone else with whom you share resources.

On October 29, Mercury joins Mars in your solar eighth house, so there could be discussions about obtaining a mortgage or loan, your credit rating, or insurance and taxes.

CAREER
Your business partnerships are highlighted once Saturn enters Scorpio, your opposite sign, on October 5. This transit lasts two and a half years. During this period, there could be delays in your business partnerships. Perhaps you and your partners don't see eye to eye on everything. Your partners could be older than you or have worked in the business longer than you have and bring great expertise.

ROMANCE
The period from October 3 to 28 looks like it's made for romance. If you're uncommitted, Venus in fellow earth sign Virgo is sure to attract potential partners made to order for your needs and desires. You may be pickier than usual, more discriminating about what you're really looking for, but even so, by the end of this transit a relationship could be brewing. If not, your creativity is flowing, and you're having so much fun that you decide to just play the field.

If you're in a committed relationship, this transit should enable the relationship to hum along at a pace that's pleasing to both you and your partner. You may get away together for a long weekend.

BEST DAYS, CHALLENGING DAYS
The entire Venus transit through Virgo is something to anticipate, Taurus! Also the full moon in your sign on October 15 looks positive.

November—Taurus

LUNAR HIGHLIGHTS
The big lunar news this month revolves around two eclipses. The first, a solar eclipse on November 13, falls in Scorpio, your opposite sign. This eclipse brings new opportunities related to partnerships—both business and personal—and in psychic development, research and investigation, all the areas that Scorpio rules. This eclipse should be positive for you, Taurus.

The second eclipse, a lunar eclipse, falls on November 28 in Gemini, your second house. With Jupiter close to the eclipse degree, you can expect positive news about your finances, education, and communication/writing projects. The news expands your worldview in some way and your financial options.

FINANCES, OTHER STUFF
We've discussed the financial aspects of the lunar eclipse, so let's take a closer look at what else is occurring this month. Mercury turns retrograde for the last time this year on November 6, in Sagittarius, and doesn't turn direct again until November 26. This retrograde affects your partner's income, resources you share with others, and areas like mortgages and insurance. Some possible repercussions include: delays with any mortgage or loan applications that you've submitted, revisiting insurance and tax issues. Read over the Mercury retrograde section in the Big Picture section for your sign.

CAREER
On November 16, Mars enters fellow earth sign Capricorn and your solar ninth house, where it will be until December 25. This transit should prove illuminating for you. Your ambitions are stronger and your goals more clearly defined. You've got plenty of physical energy to get things done. This transit strengthens all your innate qualities and bolsters your resoluteness and determination.

Between October 28 and November 21, Venus transits Libra and your solar sixth house. This transit facilitates your daily work schedule, which in turn helps to attract the people and experiences and opportunities that benefit you professionally.

ROMANCE
An office flirtation may be in the offing, particularly between October 3 and November 21, while Venus transits Virgo and then Libra. If you're involved already, this transit may unfold as creative brainstorming with employees and coworkers. You'll be a much happier camper once Mercury turns direct again on November 26!

Venus enters Scorpio on November 21. Between then and December 15, your sexuality is heightened, and an existing relationship may be taken to a whole new level. You and your partner could move in together, get engaged, or even tie the knot.

BEST DAYS, CHALLENGING DAYS
November 26 is a day to circle. Mercury turns direct, and now you can pack your bags and head out for parts unknown, sign contracts, and rest assured that communication snafus are history—at least until the next Mercury retrograde!

December—Taurus

So here we are, at the final month of 2012. Depending on who is talking, the world may end on December 21, right? Uh—uh. But there will undoubtedly be a lot of media hype about it, so just ignore it. You also might want to read the conclusion of the book, about why the world won't end on December 21.

LUNAR HIGHLIGHTS
The new moon on December 13 falls in Sagittarius, your solar eighth house. This one should usher in new opportu-

nities for your partner's income, resources you share with others, foreign travel and business dealings, in insurance, taxes, inheritances, publishing, and higher education. Those are the areas ruled by the eighth house and Sagittarius. But the eighth house also has that metaphysical component, so it's possible that the new opportunities could involve psychic development and heightened sensitivity to ghosts and things that go bump in the night.

The full moon in Cancer on December 28 feels comfortable to you. It occurs in your solar third house, so there should be news about a communication project. A novel, perhaps? Screenplay? There could also be news about a sibling. Neptune forms a beneficial angle to this full moon, suggesting higher inspiration and idealism.

FINANCES, OTHER STUFF
Your ruler, Venus, enters Sagittarius on December 15, so between then and early January 2013, your joint resources should be running smoothly. Your partner could land a raise, you may get a break in taxes or insurance, or you could be paid a plump bonus. Mercury will also be in Sadge from December 10 to 31, suggesting a lot of talk and activity in the area of shared resources. You could get a contract for something you've written or sign up a new client for your business. It's also possible that you're in negotiations for expanding your product or services to overseas markets.

CAREER
Between December 25 and February 1, 2013, your professional life will pick up its pace considerably. Mars will be transiting Aquarius and your career sector, and you'll be able to make things happen. Be sure to mark this period on your calendar, and have your agenda lined up by the time the new year begins!

ROMANCE
In each area of your life, romance included, it's a good idea to list goals and wishes that you have for the new year. If

you're single, what kind of person would you like to meet in the new year? If you're in a committed relationship, where would you like things to go? What are your expectations? What are your true feelings for this other person? By December 13, all the planets are moving in direct motion—functioning as they should—so that might be a good time to make your lists.

BEST DAYS, CHALLENGING DAYS
The entire month looks promising. But even if you run into a glitch here and there, remember that you can turn a challenging day around just through a change in your attitude!

Happy New Year!

4

Gemini

The Big Picture in 2012

Welcome to 2012, Gemini. This year highlights your finances as well as finances that you share with a partner. It's a year of communication and investigation, of research and exploration.

Your ruler, Mercury, starts the year in Sagittarius, your opposite sign, then on the eighth enters Capricorn and your solar eighth house. So the year gets off to an interesting start, with your conscious focus on partnerships and your career ambitions.

Venus starts the year in fellow air sign Aquarius, your solar ninth house, a beautiful transit that could send you overseas. Or you may meet someone special from another country or while you're traveling abroad. Your solar ninth house governs publishing, higher education, and your worldview and spiritual beliefs, so with Venus here, all those areas should run smoothly. For more details on romance in 2012, look below under the Romance section.

Pluto, the snail of the zodiac, starts off the year in Capricorn, where it has consistently been since November 2008. You're accustomed to its energy now. Its transit, which lasts until 2024, is bringing profound and permanent change globally, evident in the economic challenges that now face the U.S. Most institutions are in the throes of great change—the health-care industry, the petroleum and insurance industries, mortgages/lending, housing, aviation, even the Internet. You name it, and Pluto's fingerprint can be found.

On a personal level, this planet's transit through your solar eighth house has been altering resources you share with others since 2008. You may be delving more deeply into metaphysics—divination systems, past lives, communication with the dead, all the cosmic biggies.

Neptune entered Pisces and your solar tenth house on April 4, 2011. But by early August 2011, it had slipped back into Aquarius. On February 3, 2012, it enters Pisces again and won't move on until January 2026. For hints about what this may mean for you, look back to that period in 2011 when Neptune was in Pisces.

Neptune symbolizes our higher ideals, escapism, fiction, spirituality, and our blind spots. It seeks to dissolve boundaries between us and others. One possible repercussion of this transit is prolonged religious wars, which proliferated during Uranus's transit in Pisces from early 2003. On a personal level, though, Neptune's transit through your career area suggests that you may try to integrate spirituality more readily into your career. You may start volunteering for a charitable organization or for your local animal shelter. One way or another, your ideals become more prevalent in your professional life. It's also possible that through your career you meet people you have known in past lives.

Uranus entered Aries and your solar eleventh house in March 2011. This transit probably has already attracted new and unusual people into your life and will continue to do so. Friendships begin and end suddenly, your social life spikes to exciting new highs, and your dreams and goals change without warning. But Uranus shakes up the status quo so that we're forced to move beyond our ruts and routines. It wakes us up so that we recognize where we have become rigid and inflexible.

Until March 2019, Uranus in Aries forms a beneficial angle to your sun, so your ideas are cutting edge, and you benefit from the unusual people you meet.

Saturn begins the year in Libra, your solar fifth house. It has been there since the summer of 2010 and will be there until October 2012. This transit brings structure to your creativity. Instead of just having an idea for a novel or book, you actually start writing it. Or if you've thought about launching your own business, this is when you do it. Even romance and things you do for enjoyment now have a definite structure. Instead of just taking a vacation, your travel has a purpose. You might travel for educational reasons or for some sort of vision quest. Saturn forms a beneficial angle to your sun while it's in Libra, so make good use of it!

Once Saturn enters Scorpio in October, there may be delays or restrictions in your daily work. You may have more responsibility, which means you could be working longer hours. As long as you enjoy your work, this shouldn't be a big deal. But if you don't like what you do, then you may consider finding a new job. The sixth house also governs your daily health, so it's smart to have some sort of regular exercise routine during this transit.

Expansive Jupiter begins the year in Taurus, your solar twelfth house. You should be acquainted by now with the energies associated with this transit; it's been going on since June 2011 and lasts until June 11, 2012. Jupiter here expands your inner world and your access to your own unconscious and should make it easier for you to recall and work with your dreams.

Once it enters your sign on June 11, you're in for a treat! Jupiter will expand everything you do, Gemini. For hints about what may be involved, look back twelve years to when this transit last occurred—2000. Possibilities? You move, land the dream job, get married, get a raise. You get the idea, right? Let the good times roll!

They say that timing is everything, so with that in mind let's look at some specific areas in your life.

ROMANCE/CREATIVITY

The most romantic and creative time for you all year falls between October 28 and November 21, when Venus transits Libra and your solar fifth house. If you're not involved before this transit begins, you probably will be before the transit ends. If you're not, it won't matter because you're having too much fun. Or you're deeply immersed in a creative project that consumes a lot of your time and energy. Great backup dates: April 3 to May 15 and June 27 to August 7, when Venus is moving direct in your sign. Things really seem to flow your way then in many areas, but particularly with romance and creative ventures.

The best time for serious involvement and deepening commitment in an existing relationship occurs when Venus transits Sagittarius and your seventh house of partnerships. That occurs from December 15, 2011, to January 10, 2013. You and your partner may decide to move in together, get engaged, or get married. Just be sure that you don't do any of this under a Mercury retrograde period. Take a look under the appropriate section below to find out when Mercury will be retrograde this year.

Other good backup dates: October 6 to November 16, when Mars transits Sagittarius and your solar seventh house. This stirs up a lot of activity with a partner.

CAREER

Usually Venus and Jupiter transits to your career area are the times to look for. There's no transit of Jupiter in Pisces in 2012, but Venus transits this area from January 14 to February 8, so this should be an excellent time to push your professional agenda forward, pitch new ideas, and socialize with bosses and peers. When Jupiter is in Taurus between January and June 11, it forms a beneficial angle to your career area. Expect expansion, luck, and perhaps more foreign travel in the professional arena. A salary hike and promotion are possible, too.

Mars transits Scorpio between August 23 and October 6 and forms a beneficial angle to your career area. This is the time to make new professional contacts and keep your nose to the grindstone, completing projects and brainstorming with coworkers for new ideas.

With Neptune in your career area from February 3 onward for the next fourteen years, there can be some confusion about professional matters. But if you integrate your ideals more completely into your career, you can mitigate some of the confusion associated with this transit.

BEST TIMES FOR
Buying or selling a home: October 3 to 28, when Venus is in Virgo and your fourth house; August 31 to September 16, when Mercury is moving direct in Virgo.

Family reunions: Any of the dates above.

Financial matters: The period from August 7 to September 6, when Venus transits Cancer and your financial sector.

Signing contracts: When Mercury is moving direct!

MERCURY RETROGRADES
Every year Mercury—the planet of communication and travel—turns retrograde three times. During this period it's wise not to sign contracts (unless you don't mind renegotiating when Mercury is moving direct), to check and recheck travel plans, and to communicate as succinctly as possible. Refrain from buying any large-ticket items or electronics during this time too. Often computers and appliances go on the fritz, cars act up, data is lost . . . you get the idea. Be sure to back up all files before the dates below:

March 12–April 4: Mercury retrograde in Aries, your eleventh house. This one affects friendships, groups to which you belong.

July 14–August 8: Mercury retrograde in Leo, your solar third house of communication.

November 6–26: Mercury retrograde in Sagittarius, your solar seventh house, partnerships.

ECLIPSES
Solar eclipses tend to trigger external events that bring about change according to the sign and house in which they fall. Lunar eclipses trigger inner, emotional events according to the sign and house in which they fall. Any eclipse marks both beginnings and endings. The solar and lunar eclipse in a pair falls in opposite signs. If you're interested in detailed information on eclipses, take a look at Celeste

Teal's excellent and definitive book, *Eclipses: Predicting World Events & Personal Transformation.*

If you were born under or around the time of an eclipse, it's to your advantage to take a look at your birth chart to find out exactly where the eclipses will impact you.

Most years feature four eclipses—two solar, two lunar, with the set separated by about two weeks. In November and December 2011, there were solar and lunar eclipses, so this year the first eclipses fall during May and June.

May 20: Solar eclipse at 0 degrees Gemini. This one should bring in new opportunities in many different areas of your life.

June 4: Lunar eclipse in Sagittarius, your seventh house. This should be a positive eclipse for you and your partner.

November 13: Solar eclipse in Scorpio, your solar sixth house. New opportunities surface in your daily work.

November 28: Lunar eclipse, Gemini. Jupiter forms a five-degree conjunction to the eclipse degree, suggesting that news you receive around this time will be cause for celebration!

LUCKIEST DAY OF THE YEAR
Every year there's one day when Jupiter and the sun meet up, and luck, serendipity, and expansion are the hallmarks. This year that day falls on May 13, with a conjunction in Taurus.

January—Gemini

LUNAR HIGHLIGHTS
So it's a new year, Gemini, and it gets off to a running start with a full moon in Cancer on January 9. On or around this date, you may hear news about your finances. Possibilities? A raise, bonus, commission or royalty check. This water-sign moon probably isn't your favorite unless you have a natal moon or rising in a water sign, but it does serve to heighten certain memories and perhaps create nostalgia for the bygone days.

The new moon in fellow air sign Aquarius on January 23 is much more to your liking. It should usher in new opportunities for foreign travel and business, higher education, publishing, and coming up with innovative ideas. Uranus forms a beneficial angle to this new moon, so these opportunities are likely to surface quickly and unexpectedly.

FINANCES, OTHER STUFF

On January 8, your ruler, Mercury, enters Capricorn and your solar eighth house. This transit, which lasts until January 27, spurs discussions about mortgages, loans, taxes, insurance. You may make a contribution to your IRA or Keogh, which can save you on taxes.

Jupiter is in Taurus as the year begins, in your solar twelfth house. This transit expands your inner life, your personal unconscious. It's easier for you to understand your dreams, which may contain important insights and information about any concerns you have. Jupiter forms a beneficial angle to Mercury while it's in Capricorn, which suggests that your conscious mind is expansive, curious, seeking.

CAREER

Jupiter in Taurus also has an impact on your career. It forms a beneficial angle to your career area and brings luck and serendipity related to professional matters. You're in the right place at the right time, and with your natural gift of gab, Gemini, you can make things happen. In addition to help from Jupiter, your professional life is aided by Venus's transit in Pisces and your career area from January 14 to February 8. So push your agenda forward, pitch your ideas, gather support among peers and coworkers. If you're job hunting, the Venus transit should help you out considerably.

ROMANCE

For most of the year—until October 5—Saturn is in fellow air sign Libra, your fifth house of romance. It forms a beneficial angle to your sun. This transit has been going on for some time, so you should have a clear idea by now about its impact on your love life, creativity, and what you do for fun and enjoyment. Some possible repercussions for the rest of the year? You get involved with someone older than you or someone who brings greater structure to your life. If you're already involved, the relationship may take on more serious undertones, a deeper level of commitments.

BEST DAYS, CHALLENGING DAYS
Circle January 14, when Venus enters Pisces and your career area. This transit is very positive.

February—Gemini

LUNAR HIGHLIGHTS
It's likely that you'll enjoy the full moon in compatible fire sign Leo on February 7. Not only will there be news about a writing/communication project or an upcoming trip, but you'll have a chance to strut your stuff, Gemini. For you, that usually means exhibiting your knowledge, your communication skills, or your ability to talk to anyone about anything. Another possibility is that the Leo full moon could bring news about siblings or other relatives or about your neighbors and neighborhood. With most full moons, there's a lot of general activity, hustle and bustle, and a tad of craziness.

The new moon in Pisces on February 21 occurs in your career area. Expect new opportunities to surface concerning your profession. Perhaps you get a job offer you simply can't refuse. Or you might get a promotion or a raise, land a new project that thrills you, or have an opportunity to study intuitive development or use your imagination in a new way.

FINANCES, OTHER STUFF
Right now expansive Jupiter is in Taurus, your solar twelfth house, and expands your access to your personal uncon-

scious. You benefit from working behind the scenes, finishing what you start, and staying in the game long after the competition has dropped away. In one way or another, this benefits you professionally and financially. Self-knowledge, after all, is empowerment.

With Mars retrograde in Virgo until April 4 and in this sign until July 3, your home life is a whirl of activity. However, because Mars is in Virgo, the activity may have a distinctive finesse, with some unexpected twists and turns.

CAREER

On February 13, Mercury enters Pisces and your career area, where it will be until March 2. This transit is favorable for pitches about new ideas, projects, and possibilities. It favors sitting down with your boss and explaining things from your point of view. Whether you work for someone else or are self-employed, this transit suggests an intuitive approach to your work. Go with your hunches.

Neptune enters Pisces and your career area on February 3, a transit that lasts for fourteen years. There can be confusion with Neptune transits, but idealism and creative inspiration are also hallmarks of this planet. You may experience both.

ROMANCE

Between February 8 and March 5, Venus transits compatible fire sign Aries and your solar eleventh house. This transit sure favors romance between friends, Gemini. You know the drill: you and a friend have an honest discussion about life, love, and everything else and suddenly realize that your feelings for each other have gone well beyond friendship. Now the question becomes: do you act on these feelings? Suppose the relationship goes south? Will your friendship remain intact?

BEST DAYS, CHALLENGING DAYS

On February 7, Saturn in Libra turns retrograde, where it stays until June 25. During this period you don't have the benefit of strength and structures in your love life or in creative ventures, at least not as you've enjoyed in recent months. Take heart, though. You've got some other good stuff going on this year. Read on.

March—Gemini

LUNAR HIGHLIGHTS
The full moon in Virgo on March 8 brings news about a domestic issue. Perhaps you've been considering a move, but your house hasn't sold. So now you could get an offer that suits you and things start to move. Mars forms a wide conjunction to this full moon, indicative of a lot of activity and energy. Pluto forms a wide, beneficial angle to this moon that suggests power issues may surface.

The new moon in Aries on March 22 should be right up your alley. Both Mercury, your ruler, and Uranus are closely conjunct this new moon. New opportunities surface with writing/communication projects and social networks, friendships, and groups. Keep your social calendar wide open around the time of this new moon and accept any invitations that come your way. Due to the unexpected nature of these opportunities, you've got to be on your toes, ready to seize the opportunity as it appears!

FINANCES, OTHER STUFF
Your financial expansion is likely to occur between June 11, 2012, and June 25, 2013, when Jupiter transits your sign. So be sure that as you approach the beginning of this transit, you plant seeds carefully, with forethought. Make investments based on a combination of facts and intuition. Don't spend recklessly. Try to stash away a percentage of what you earn so that you always have backup funds.

Mercury turns retrograde in Aries on March 12 and turns direct again on April 4. During this period don't sign contracts, make your travel arrangements on either side of these dates, and make backups of your computer data before it begins. It's always best to revise, rethink, and re-evaluate during a Mercury retrograde.

CAREER
You're still enjoying the influence of that Pisces new moon at the end of February. New professional opportunities may continue to surface until around March 8. Between March 5 and April 3, lovely Venus transits Taurus and forms a beneficial angle to your career area. Some possibilities? A project or idea you have pitched is picked up or approved; you pursue something with a dogged determination that pays off; women are helpful professionally. Whenever Venus is involved, there's a possibility of making money through the arts.

ROMANCE
With Venus in Taurus and your solar twelfth house between March 5 and April 3, a flirtation or romance may be kept under wraps for some reason. You usually don't run your life in a secretive manner, Gemini, and probably aren't very adept at keeping secrets. If that's the case with a relationship, rest assured that once Venus enters your sign on April 3, you'll be spilling the beans to the world!

BEST DAYS, CHALLENGING DAYS
Whenever your ruler, Mercury, turns retrograde, you feel the effect more than most signs. So circle March 12 through April 4, when Mercury is retrograde in Aries.

April—Gemini

LUNAR HIGHLIGHTS
The full moon in fellow air sign Libra on April 6 occurs in your solar fifth house. You can expect news about a romantic relationship or a creative project. Or, if you have children, news about them. This full moon can also light up your social calendar and whatever you do for pleasure

and enjoyment. It forms a beneficial angle to your sun sign, Gemini, suggesting that you're in an upbeat, fun-loving mood.

The new moon in Taurus on April 21 falls in your solar twelfth house. New opportunities to work behind the scenes in some capacity should surface. These opportunities will expand your creative venue in some way. There are two new moons in your sign coming up, so whatever seeds you sow now could begin to flourish in late May and June.

FINANCES, OTHER STUFF

Venus enters your sign this month, so you may be in the mood to spend, spend, spend. But you could be earning more too. Between May 15 and June 27, Venus moves retrograde in your sign, so try to buy any large-ticket items on either side of those dates. More on this in the May section.

Mercury turns direct on April 4, welcome news for everyone, but especially for you and Virgo, also ruled by Mercury. So pack your bags and get out of town, sign your contracts, move your life into high gear again.

CAREER

With Uranus in compatible fire sign Aries until May 2018, you have an opportunity to really think and create outside the box. Your social contacts will be very important during this long transit, so don't hesitate to work a crowd of strangers, hand your business cards whenever possible, and schmooze.

With Neptune in your career area now, you may be feeling some of the ramifications mentioned earlier—confusion, perhaps, about your professional path or you may feel incredibly inspired to dive into your creative projects.

ROMANCE

Right now you're in one of the most romantic periods this year. Your self-confidence is soaring, you're an attractor. Whether you're involved or not, people are aware of you. They find you seductive, intriguing. Law of attraction, Gemini. If you're uncommitted and wish otherwise, then now is the time to visualize what you want in a partner, to make a list of qualities you would like in a partner, and to back these desires with powerful emotion. So read Esther and Jerry Hicks's book *The Law of Attraction* and Jane Robert's book, *The Nature of Personal Reality*.

BEST DAYS, CHALLENGING DAYS
On April 10, Pluto turns retrograde in Capricorn, your solar eighth house, and remains that way until September 17. During this period Pluto goes into a kind of dormant state.

May—Gemini

LUNAR HIGHLIGHTS
On May 5, the full moon in Scorpio should bring news about your daily work routine or health, or you may find yourself deep in some sort of research or investigative work. Pluto forms a wide, beneficial angle to this full moon, indicative of power issues, transformative change. With a wide angle from Mars tossed into the equation, you can expect quite a bit of activity. Perhaps you'll be putting in longer hours at work—to meet a deadline, for the love of it, no telling.

The new moon in your sign on May 20 is also a solar eclipse, so think of this as double the new opportunities. These opportunities will surface suddenly and unexpectedly, so you'll have to be ready to seize them as they occur. Some possibilities? You have a chance to do whatever you feel passionate about. Focus your attention on your desires a few days before this new moon, back the desires with emotion, and then get out of the way so the universe can do its work and manifest the desires.

FINANCES, OTHER STUFF
On May 9, Mercury enters Taurus, where it will be until the twenty-fourth. This transit brings a rock-solid resoluteness to your conscious mind, enabling you to outlast the com-

petition in just about any area you choose. You'll be more aware of what you spend and what you buy, what you earn and what you wish you earned. Your personal unconscious will be more accessible to you, and if there are issues that aren't resolved, you may opt for therapy. Or perhaps you'll simply turn your unconscious inside out and blog about your self-discoveries.

CAREER

Mars continues to transit Virgo, your solar fourth house, and it's moving in opposition to your career area. You may experience a conflict between your personal and professional responsibilities and could feel that you're carrying more than your share of the load at work. Best not to fret about it and just go with the flow, Gemini. If you obsess about what you dislike, you'll just get more of it!

Venus turns retrograde in your sign on May 15 and remains there until June 27. This retrograde could impact your career—a few bumps in the road with a coworker, a flirtation distraction, or even something that goes awry in the physical environment at work. Again, take it in stride.

ROMANCE

The main impact of Venus retrograde is on your love life. If you're involved you and your partner could find yourselves embroiled in arguments over small things—an idea on which you differ, for example, or differing opinions about a book or movie. Silly stuff, in other words. If you're not involved, then you probably don't want to get involved during the retrograde. But if you do, enjoy it but don't let your expectations carry you away.

BEST DAYS, CHALLENGING DAYS

May 24. Circle it. Mercury enters your sign and will be there until June 7.

June—Gemini

LUNAR HIGHLIGHTS
Busy month, Gemini! On the fourth, the lunar eclipse in Sagittarius, your opposite sign, brings news about a partnership—business or romantic. Since Sagittarius rules publishing, higher education, foreign travel and countries, there could be news, too, in any of those areas. You might, for instance, sell a novel or book, hear about a college or graduate school that interests you, or your business could expand to overseas markets.

The new moon in your sign on the nineteenth is the second one in a month! Look for new opportunities that thrill you personally. Some possibilities? Communication and writing opportunities, a chance to travel somewhere you've never been before, new opportunities in romance, career... well, you get the idea. Wherever you place your focus and desires, opportunities are likely to surface. Saturn forms a beneficial angle to this new moon, too, an additional bonus that brings form to your desires.

FINANCES, OTHER STUFF
The big news: Jupiter enters your sign on June 11 and will remain there until June 25, 2013. This transit should expand any number of areas in your life—including your finances. Your mood is more buoyant and optimistic, you feel good generally about life and where you are. You may decide to obtain further educational training or take workshops in topics that interest you, or your spiritual beliefs may expand. Or all of the above. The only risk with this transit is excess. Try not to spread yourself too thinly.

Your ruler, Mercury, transits Cancer and your financial sector from June 7 to 25, so there will be plenty of discussions about money.

CAREER
With Jupiter now in your sign, forming a square to your midheaven, you may try to take on too much. It's the "ex-

cess" part of the Jupiter equation. You'll have plenty of opportunities to strut your stuff, but pick and choose wisely.

Saturn turns direct in Libra on June 25, which should help to stabilize things in your career and personal life. When your personal life is humming along with contentment, the rest of your life tends to function more smoothly as well.

ROMANCE
The best news is that Venus in your sign turns direct on June 27. This movement should help straighten out anything in your love life that has been bumpy or not quite to your liking. You can now enjoy a delightful period of renewed self-confidence that lasts until Venus enters Cancer on August 7.

BEST DAYS, CHALLENGING DAYS
Next month, on July 3, energetic Mars enters fellow air sign Libra and leaves your solar fourth house. This transit will be much more fitting for you. Right now, Mars may be creating some chaos and uncertainty at home. Circle June 27, when Venus turns direct, finally, in your sign!

July—Gemini

LUNAR HIGHLIGHTS
The full moon in Capricorn on July 3 falls in your solar eighth house of shared resources. Your business or romantic partner may hear news about his or her income. A raise, perhaps? There could also be news for you related to taxes, insurance, or wills. With the moon in ambitious Capricorn, your professional ambitions could be highlighted in some way too. Pluto forms a close conjunction to this moon, suggesting that the news you hear is powerful and transformative.

Your bank account benefits with the new moon in Cancer on July 19. It occurs in your financial sector, so new opportunities to earn more money should surface on or around the date of this moon. The Cancer moon is intuitive and nurturing, and you may have opportunities to deepen your intuitive ability and nurture a dream that you hold.

FINANCES AND OTHER STUFF
Mercury went into compatible fire sign Leo on June 25 and remains there until August 31. It will be retrograde between July 14 and August 8. On either side of the retrograde, this transit brings fire and passion to your ideas and to the way you communicate. Be sure that before the retrograde starts, you follow the drill: firm up travel plans, back up all computers, sign contracts, pitch ideas, make deals, apply for mortgages, loans.

CAREER
On February 3, Neptune entered Pisces and your career area. It will be there for fourteen years, and with these lengthy transits the most challenging times are often at the beginning. Possibilities? Your career goals may feel muddled, vague, confusing. You may feel dissatisfied with your professional life. On the other hand, you could feel more inspired, your ideals will have a greater power and force in your life, and you may consider integrating your spiritual beliefs more readily into your career. You could also become involved with a charity or humanitarian organization.

ROMANCE
Venus turned direct on June 27 in your sign, so now you should be enjoying all the benefit of this transit. The bonus is that Venus now travels with Jupiter in your sign. It hardly gets better than this, Gemini. You enjoy increased self-confidence, you and your partner may decide to deepen your commitment to each other, or you're playing the field because you have so many options! In addition to having both Venus and Jupiter in your sign, Mars enters fellow air sign Libra on July 3, in the romance sector of your chart. This transit suggests a lot of your physical energy is poured into romance, enjoyment, and creativity.

BEST DAYS, CHALLENGING DAYS
Challenging day? Circle July 14, when Mercury in Leo turns retrograde.

August—Gemini

LUNAR HIGHLIGHTS
Buckle up, Gemini. It's going to be a wild month. There are three lunations in August—two full moons and a new moon. The first, on August 1, is a full moon in fellow air sign Aquarius. Jupiter forms an exact trine to this full moon, indicative of positive news that somehow broadens options for you in any number of areas. This one should bring news that you'll love. You're in the right place, at the right time.

The new moon in Leo on August 17 should usher in new opportunities for your talents and abilities to shine, to be recognized. Something new surfaces in your daily life too. You may have an opportunity to study an area that intrigues you, to return to school or take workshops. Or perhaps you're teaching the workshops! Geminis usually have multiple talents and interests, so the sky may be the limit here.

The full moon in Pisces on August 31 occurs in your career area. Neptune forms a wide conjunction with this full moon, suggesting there could be an element of confusion surrounding news. If a decision is required of you, don't make it until after Mercury turns direct on August 8.

FINANCES, OTHER STUFF
Reread the section on Mercury retrogrades in the Big Picture for your sign. After August 8, when Mercury turns direct, you're home free—at least for another three months, until Mercury acts up again. In terms of your finances, the most important thing to remember is to not apply for mortgages or loans during the retrograde period or to sign any contracts related to them.

On August 7, Venus enters Cancer and your financial area. This transit lasts until September 6 and should ramp up your earnings. You may be spending more too, particularly on luxury items. Resist that urge unless you've got the money in the bank to cover the bill. Your earnings could increase because of a raise, an unexpected royalty check, or even the repayment of a loan.

On August 31, Mercury enters Virgo and your solar fourth house, where it will be until September 16. During this transit, your conscious mind is meticulous and detailed, and the gift of gab is certainly yours!

CAREER

Now that Saturn is moving direct in Libra, you are better able to use its energy to solidify your career goals. In addition, you've got Uranus in compatible fire sign Aries on your side, pushing you to think outside the box, to move beyond your comfort zone.

On August 23, Mars enters water sign Scorpio, where it will be until October 6. It forms a beneficial angle to your career area and acts as a booster rocket, moving you forward professionally. Scorpio is a secretive, intuitive sign, however, so to benefit fully from this transit, it's important that you listen to and follow your hunches.

ROMANCE

With Venus's transit through Cancer from August 7 to September 6, you may meet someone whose values match your own. Also, Jupiter is still in your sign, Gemini, seeking to expand and broaden your venues. So if you're looking for romance, it can work its magic in that department too. In addition, once Mars enters Scorpio, it forms a beneficial angle to Venus in Cancer, bringing a nice intuitive flow to all romantic encounters.

BEST DAYS, CHALLENGING DAYS

Circle August 17, that new moon in Leo. It should be a humdinger for you!

September—Gemini

LUNAR HIGHLIGHTS
On September 15, the new moon in Virgo brings new opportunities in communication/writing, on the domestic front, and in your personal environment. Mercury forms a close conjunction with this new moon, suggesting a lot of activity and discussion about these new opportunities that surface. If you've been hoping to move, this new moon could make it happen or, at the least, get the process started.

September 29 features a full moon in compatible fire sign Aries, your solar eleventh house. This moon should stir up your social life, so be sure to keep your options open and to accept invitations that come your way. Uranus is closely conjunct to this moon, suggesting news that catches you by surprise.

FINANCES, OTHER STUFF
Mars continues its trek through Scorpio until October 6 and certainly lights up your daily work routine, which in turn affects your finances. What's the connection? You may be putting in a lot of overtime or working a second job to earn more money. On the sixteenth, Mercury enters Libra, forming a beneficial angle to your sun, and your gift of gab may translate to a creative project—a book? a speaking gig?—that brings in more money.

CAREER
Mercury transits sociable Libra from September 16 to October 5, joining Saturn in that sign. This duo brings order and structure to your conscious mind, your writing, your communication abilities. You're able to make a powerful case for your ideas, agenda, and pitches and find the support you need. Get out and socialize with coworkers and bosses whenever you can. Network.

ROMANCE
Venus enters Leo on September 6 and remains there until October 3. This transit suggests that romance may be as close as your own neighborhood. Or you could meet a new

romantic interest through a neighbor, sibling, or other relative or even during the course of your normal day. This transit brings passion to your romantic relationships and perhaps a bit of jealousy, too, particularly if you feel your partner isn't paying enough attention to you!

BEST DAYS, CHALLENGING DAYS
September 23 looks good for you, Gemini. The sun enters fellow air sign Libra and your solar fifth house, lighting up your love life and revving your creative adrenaline.

October—Gemini

LUNAR HIGHLIGHTS
The new moon in Libra on October 15 is one to anticipate. It occurs in your solar fifth house and should usher in positive energy and new opportunities in romance and creativity, with your children, and in everything you do for fun and enjoyment. It occurs at 22 degrees Libra, so those Geminis born in the later part of the Gemini cycle will benefit the most. However, every Gemini will enjoy this one, particularly with lucky Jupiter forming a beneficial angle to it. Possibilities? A new relationship, a pregnancy or the birth of a child, you sell a novel or book, get a chance to exhibit your photos. You get the idea. Embrace whatever comes your way.

The full moon in Taurus on October 29 occurs in your solar twelfth house. Insights and news revolve around issues you may have buried. You're able to see these issues in a brighter light now and deal with and resolve them. Pluto forms a close and beneficial angle to this full moon, suggesting a transformative quality to insights you have.

FINANCES, OTHER STUFF
On October 5, both Mercury and Saturn enter Scorpio. The Saturn transit is discussed under the career area. The Mercury transit, which lasts until the twenty-ninth, brings a

deep, intuitive bent to your conscious mind. You're able to dig for answers and won't be satisfied until you find what you're looking for. This transit forms a beneficial angle to your financial area, so it's important for you to follow your hunches about investments.

CAREER
Saturns enters Scorpio and your solar sixth house on October 5 and will remain there for the next two and a half years. This transit forms a beneficial angle to your career area and Neptune in Pisces. In many ways, it can counterbalance the confusion of the Neptune transit and provides strength and deep resolve to do things your own way. Your intuition should be much stronger, and you may find that you're after the absolute bottom line in whatever you tackle.

ROMANCE
Venus transits Virgo from October 3 to 28, when it then enters Libra. Let's look at the Virgo transit first. This one should allow your domestic life to unfold more smoothly. It's excellent for your love life too and suggests that you and partner may be sticking close to home for the next few weeks. One or both of you could be feeling a bit picky or critical. Best to remember the famous words of Dale Carnegie (*How to Win Friends and Influence People*): Don't criticize, condemn, or complain.

Once Venus enters Libra on the twenty-eighth, you'll be in for a real treat. This transit, which lasts until November 21, marks one of the most romantic and creative times for you all year.

BEST DAYS, CHALLENGING DAYS
October 28 is a day to anticipate. So is the new moon in Libra on October 15.

November—Gemini

LUNAR HIGHLIGHTS
The new moon in Scorpio on November 13 is also a solar eclipse. This one should bring multiple opportunities related to your daily work life, the maintenance of your health, and intuitive development. Today would be a terrific time to send out résumés, if you're looking for a job, or to advertise your services on craigslist. Or, equally likely, perhaps you land the job you've wanted. Today is also favorable for joining a gym, signing up for yoga classes, or starting an exercise program that you know you can stick to. A new diet or nutritional program may be in the offing, too.

The full moon on November 28 is a lunar eclipse in your sign! Expect news that excites and delights you. With Jupiter closely conjunct to this full moon, the news somehow expands your world and options, and you feel mighty lucky indeed!

FINANCES, OTHER STUFF
By now you should be seeing Jupiter's magic lighting up various areas of your life. The best news is that it's going to remain in your sign for another seven months! Where is the greatest expansion occurring for you, Gemini?

On November 16, Mars enters earth sign Capricorn, your solar eighth house. This transit, lasting until December 25, stirs up a lot of activity in resources you share with others. Your partner may be working longer hours, but the payoff could be significant. Your professional ambitions increase during this transit. You may be more focused and directed, certain of your goals, and this self-confidence translates into a financial gain.

CAREER
Neptune turned direct on June 4, so now you should be back on track professionally. Yes, some of the confusion may persevere, but your adaptability and versatility enable you to use it to your advantage somehow. Also, with both

Pluto and Mars in Capricorn now, you are a power to be reckoned with in your career.

ROMANCE
Between October 28 and November 21, romance and creativity flow your way. Single or committed, there's much to enjoy during this transit. Your creative drive is as strong as your drive to enjoy yourself, to take pleasure in even the smallest details. You and your partner should be getting along well, on the same page regarding most things. If you're not in a relationship when this transit begins, you probably will meet someone before it ends, and if not, it doesn't matter. You're having too much fun!

BEST DAYS, CHALLENGING DAYS
The entire Venus transit. Challenging: Mercury's retrograde in Sagittarius between November 6 and 26.

December—Gemini

LUNAR HIGHLIGHTS
The new moon in Sagittarius on December 13 occurs in your opposite sign, your partnership area. This one should usher in new opportunities related to business and personal partnerships, publishing, foreign travel, and higher education. It should be a good one for you, Gemini, especially if you're in the mood for a party. Around the holidays, who isn't?

The full moon on December 28, the last of 2012, falls in nurturing Cancer, your financial area. Pluto is within two degrees of an exact opposition, so there could be some tension around this time concerning finances. Maybe you're worrying about everything you spent for holiday gifts!

FINANCES, OTHER STUFF
Pay for your holiday gifts in cash this holiday season so you don't have to suffer through the angst of credit card

bills coming due in January. With Mercury in Sadge, Venus entering that sign on the fifteenth, Uranus in fire sign Aries, you've got plenty of fire in your belly and an eagerness to hit the open road. You're the intrepid explorer this month.

CAREER
Professional activities and endeavors should be a big challenge this month. Everyone is in a festive spirit as the holidays approach. There could be some distractions, however, with what will undoubtedly be media hype about December 21, 2012. Ignore it. There's enough turmoil in the world without adding your energy to it!

ROMANCE
Venus enters Sagittarius on December 15, assuring fun-filled times for the holidays and a love life that should hum along much to your liking. It travels with Mercury until New Year's Eve, suggesting that you and your honey enjoy lively conversations and some quick trips as well.

BEST DAYS, CHALLENGING DAYS
Christmas Day brings Mars into fellow air sign Aquarius, making it possible that one of your trips could be to a far-flung locale.

Happy New Year!

5

Cancer

The Big Picture in 2012

Welcome to 2012, Cancer. This year is one of beginnings and endings for you, of sweeping change and excitement.

Mercury, the planet of communication, begins the year in Sagittarius, in your solar sixth house of work. This transit sets the stage for discussions and dealings with employees and coworkers. In the wake of the Christmas and New Year holidays, it will feel good to get things back on track. On the eighth, Mercury enters Capricorn, your opposite sign, and your attention shifts to partnerships—business and romantic.

Venus starts the year in Aquarius, easing the way for obtaining mortgages and loans and studying metaphysics. On the fourteenth, it enters fellow water sign Pisces, so between then and February 8, it's a good time to travel overseas, submit a manuscript to publishers, and work on deepening your intuition. Romance while traveling is a good possibility, but we explore romance more under the Romance/Creativity section below.

Mars begins the year in compatible earth sign Virgo, your solar third house, triggering more activities and movement in your daily life until July 3.

From January 1 to June 11, Jupiter transits compatible earth sign Taurus, a wonderful aspect that expands your circle of friends and wishes and dreams and opens doors to new opportunities in many different areas of your life.

You should be acquainted with Jupiter's energies by now. It's been in Taurus since June of 2011, and should continue to bring luck and expansion into your life.

Between June 11, 2012, and June 25, 2013, it transits Gemini and your solar twelfth house. Here it expands your inner world and your access to your own unconscious and should make it easier for you to recall and work with your dreams.

Pluto, the snail of the zodiac, starts off the year in Capricorn, your solar seventh house, where it has consistently been since November 2008. You're accustomed to its energy now. Its transit, which lasts until 2024, is bringing profound and permanent change globally, evident in the economic challenges that now face the U.S. Most institutions are in the throes of great change—the health-care industry, the petroleum and insurance industries, mortgages/lending, housing, aviation, even the Internet. You name it, and Pluto's fingerprint can be found.

On a personal level, this planet's transit through your partnership area has been altering your closest partnerships and bringing profound inner change. Your own psyche is more accessible to you now, particularly as it relates to your attitudes and beliefs concerning relationships. During this transit, it's possible that you delve more deeply into psychology and perhaps even metaphysics.

Neptune entered Pisces and your solar ninth house on April 4, 2011. But by early August 2011, it had slipped back into Aquarius. On February 3, 2012, it enters Pisces again and won't move on until January 2026. This transit forms a beneficial angle to your sun, so its impact should be positive. For hints about what this may mean for you, look back to that period in 2011 when Neptune was in Pisces.

Neptune symbolizes our higher ideals, escapism, fiction, spirituality, and our blind spots. It seeks to dissolve boundaries between us and others. One possible repercussion of this transit is prolonged religious wars, which proliferated during Uranus's transit in Pisces from early 2003. On a personal level, though, Neptune's transit through your solar ninth house suggests that you may try to integrate your spiritual beliefs more readily into other areas of your life. You may start volunteering for a charitable organization or for your local animal shelter. You could embark on some sort of spiritual quest that takes you to sacred sites overseas. You may meet people you have known in past lives.

Uranus entered Aries and your solar tenth house in March 2011. This transit probably has already attracted new and unusual people into your life and will continue to do so. It may be altering the landscape of your career in new, unprecedented ways. If you lose your job under this transit, another comes along quickly and is more in alignment with your passions and interests. Events occur suddenly and without warning, but that's Uranus's job, to shake up the status quo so that we're forced to move beyond our ruts and routines. It wakes us up so that we recognize where we have become rigid and inflexible.

Until March 2019, Uranus in Aries forms a challenging angle to your sun, urging you to reach for the new, the different, the innovative.

Saturn begins the year in Libra, your solar fourth house. It has been there since the summer of 2010 and will be there until October 2012. This transit brings greater structure and a need for compromise to your home life. You may have to deal with greater responsibility, or there could be delays or restrictions concerning your home—selling it, moving to a different home.

Once Saturn enters fellow water sign Scorpio on October 5, you'll feel more in your element. Saturn will then be forming a beneficial angle to your sun. This transit should bring greater structure to your romantic relationships, creative projects, and everything you do for fun and enjoyment. Instead of just taking a vacation, for instance, you may travel for creative inspiration or on a spiritual quest.

They say that timing is everything, so with that in mind let's look at some specific areas in your life.

ROMANCE/CREATIVITY

The most romantic and creative time for you all year falls between November 21 and December 15, when Venus transits Scorpio and your solar fifth house. If you're not involved before this transit begins, you probably will be before the transit ends. If you're not, it won't matter because you're having too much fun. Your creativity soars during this transit, too, with your muse up close and personal.

Another good period: August 7 to September 6, when Venus is moving direct in your sign. Things really seem to flow your way then in many areas, but particularly with romance and creative ventures. The best time for serious involvement and deepening commitment in an existing relationship occurs when Venus transits Capricorn and your seventh house of partnerships. That doesn't happen this year. So Venus's transit of your sign is the period to look for. You and your partner may decide to move in together, get engaged, or get married. Just be sure that you don't do any of this under a Mercury retrograde period. Take a look under the appropriate section below to find out when Mercury will be retrograde this year.

Other good backup dates: November 16 to December 25, when Mars transits Capricorn and your solar seventh house. This stirs up a lot of activity with a partner.

CAREER

Usually Venus and Jupiter transits to your career area are the times to look for. There's no transit of Jupiter in Aries—your tenth house and career area—in 2012, but Venus transits this area from February 8 to March 5, so this should be an excellent time to push your professional agenda forward, pitch new ideas, and socialize with bosses and peers. When Jupiter is in Gemini from June 11, 2012, to June 25, 2013, it forms a beneficial angle to your career area. Expect expansion, luck, and perhaps more foreign travel in the professional arena. A salary hike and promotion are possible too.

Mars transits Sagittarius between October 6 and November 16 and forms a beneficial angle to your career area. This is the time to make new professional contacts and to keep your nose to the grindstone, completing projects and brainstorming with coworkers for new ideas.

BEST TIMES FOR
Buying or selling a home: October 28 to November 21, when Venus is in Virgo and your fourth house; September 16 to October 5, when Mercury is moving direct in Libra.

Family reunions: Any of the dates above.

Financial matters: The period from September 6 to October 3, when Venus transits Leo and your financial sector.

Signing contracts: When Mercury is moving direct!

MERCURY RETROGRADES
Every year Mercury—the planet of communication and travel—turns retrograde three times. During this period it's wise not to sign contracts (unless you don't mind renegotiating when Mercury is moving direct), to check and recheck travel plans, and to communicate as succinctly as possible. Refrain from buying any large-ticket items or electronics during this time too. Often computers and appliances go on the fritz, cars act up, data is lost . . . you get the idea. Be sure to back up all files before the dates below:

March 12–April 4: Mercury retrograde in Aries, your tenth house, career area.

July 14–August 8: Mercury retrograde in Leo, your solar second house of finances.

November 6–26: Mercury retrograde in Sagittarius, your solar sixth house, daily work and health.

ECLIPSES
Solar eclipses tend to trigger external events that bring about change according to the sign and house in which they fall. Lunar eclipses trigger inner, emotional events according to the sign and house in which they fall. Any eclipse marks both beginnings and endings. The solar and lunar eclipse in a pair falls in opposite signs. If you're interested in detailed information on eclipses, take a look at Celeste Teal's excellent and definitive book, *Eclipses: Predicting World Events & Personal Transformation.*

If you were born under or around the time of an eclipse, it's to your advantage to take a look at your birth chart to find out exactly where the eclipses will impact you.

Most years feature four eclipses—two solar, two lunar, with the set separated by about two weeks. In November and December 2011, there were solar and lunar eclipses, so this year the first eclipses fall during May and June.

May 20: Solar eclipse at 0 degrees Gemini. This one should bring in new opportunities to delve into your own unconscious—through therapy, meditation, a past-life regression, communication.

June 4: Lunar eclipse in Sagittarius, your solar sixth house. This should be a positive eclipse for your daily work and health.

November 13: Solar eclipse in Scorpio, in your solar fifth house. New opportunities surface in romance and creativity.

November 28: Lunar eclipse, Gemini. Jupiter forms a five-degree conjunction to the eclipse degree, suggesting that news you receive around this time will be cause for celebration!

LUCKIEST DAY OF THE YEAR
Every year there's one day when Jupiter and the sun meet up, and luck, serendipity, and expansion are the hallmarks. This year that day falls on May 13, with a conjunction in Taurus.

January—Cancer

LUNAR HIGHLIGHTS
What a beautiful way to start the year, with a full moon in your sign on January 9. Expect news of a personal nature, plenty of activity, maybe even a tad of chaos. Perhaps the holiday visitors haven't gone home yet, and you're chafing at the bit for privacy and solitude. If that's the case, it may be time to put your foot down and usher the visitors on their way!

The new moon on January 23 falls in Aquarius, your financial area. Expect new money opportunities, Cancer. A raise? Repayment of a loan? Whatever it is, your coffers benefit.

FINANCES, OTHER STUFF
The new moon mentioned above is a day to anticipate financially. Also, Mars in Virgo forms a favorable angle to your sun and becomes your impetus to get up and move, to make things happen. Your attention to details benefits your checkbook. Perhaps you catch an error in your favor? On the twenty-fourth, Mars turns retrograde, however, and will be that way until April 14.

CAREER
Your career is probably filled with unexpected changes right now. You have Uranus in Aries to thank for that. Some of these changes will seem too abrupt to suit you, but all will prove to be beneficial in the long run. Uranus is simply shaking up your professional status quo. Read more about it in the Big Picture section for your sign. Between now and March 2019 when this transit ends, your career journey is filled with surprises.

ROMANCE
From January 14 to February 8, Venus transits fellow water sign Pisces. This period should be quite pleasant for you, with just the right amount of romantic excitement and quietude. It's possible that any relationship that begins during this transit could be with someone born in another country. Or perhaps you meet this person while traveling abroad. Thanks to Mercury's transit of Capricorn, your opposite sign, from January 8 to 27, you may at times feel conflicted about this new relationship. Don't obsess about it, though. Go with the flow.

BEST DAYS, CHALLENGING DAYS
It's a new year. Cause to celebrate!

February—Cancer

LUNAR HIGHLIGHTS
The full moon in Leo on February 7 should bring financial news. This could be anything from a raise in your salary to the arrival of an unexpected bonus or royalty check. You also may have an opportunity to strut your stuff, Cancer, and exhibit your talents. Others applaud and appreciate your work and creative skills.

On February 21, the new moon in Pisces should be very much to your liking. Pisces is a fellow water sign, so there's a nice intuitive flow to your day. This new moon should bring new opportunities for intuitive development and stretching your imagination and in higher education, publishing, and overseas travel. It's possible that your business expands to foreign markets or that you have an opportunity to study abroad.

FINANCES, OTHER STUFF
In addition to the new moon mentioned above, Venus enters Aries and your career area on February 8. This transit, which lasts until March 5, forms a beneficial angle to your financial sector and helps set you up for the new opportunities that are ushered in by the new moon. There are professional ramifications with this transit too, which we'll talk about under the Career section. Uranus is also in Aries (reread the Big Picture for your sign for the details), which brings insight into unusual ways to make money.

CAREER
Between February 8 and March 5, Venus travels with Uranus in Pisces, through your career area. This duo should bring a remarkable energy and an element of luck to everything you undertake professionally. You come up with exactly the right ideas at the right time and present them to the right people.

Mercury transits Pisces from February 13 to March 2. This transit enables you to talk about what exists in your imagination—ideas, images, hopes, and dreams. It also deepens your intuitive ability. You may be discussing college or graduate school plans with family and friends. You could be entertaining the possibility of studying abroad for six months or a year.

ROMANCE
Back to Venus in Aries. An office flirtation or romance heats up. Just be careful that you don't break any hearts, Cancer. If you see this individual daily, it could get uncomfortable if the relationship goes south. Mars in Virgo turned retrograde on January 24, which means it won't be functioning normally, and your energy may feel a bit down. Increase your vitamin intake!

BEST DAYS, CHALLENGING DAYS
Jupiter continues its transit of compatible earth sign Taurus, which lasts until June 11, so this entire period should be quite pleasant for you. Your network of acquaintances and friends expands tremendously.

March—Cancer

LUNAR HIGHLIGHTS
The full moon in Virgo on March 8 should be to your liking. Virgo is an earth sign compatible with your water-sign sun. This full moon occurs in the communication area of your chart, so you can expect news regarding a speaking engagement, something you've written, or a project you're working on now. Mars is also in Virgo and even though it's retrograde, it infuses your communication with lots of energy.

The new moon in Aries on March 22 occurs in your career sector and should usher in new professional opportunities. If you've been looking for a new career or job, this new moon could help you find it. Other possibilities: a significant promotion, an opportunity to strike out on your own, perhaps by launching your own business, or you may come up with a cutting edge idea. Both Mercury and Uranus form close conjunctions to this new moon, suggesting that opportunities surface unexpectedly, out of the blue.

FINANCES, OTHER STUFF
With expansive Jupiter in compatible earth sign Taurus until June 11, your social contacts should be expanding like crazy. The larger your network, the more likely it is that financial and professional opportunities come your way.

On February 3, Neptune entered Pisces and your solar ninth house. Read more about this under the Big Picture section for your sign. But in a nutshell, this fourteen-year transit infuses your belief system with idealism and a higher consciousness so that you are acutely aware of doing no harm. You may reach out to others more compassionately, could work for a charitable organization, or travel abroad on some sort of spiritual quest.

CAREER
The new moon in Aries on March 22 is a definite professional boost. In addition, however, Uranus in Aries will be in your career arena for the next seven years, bringing elements of uncertainty and surprise. You may change jobs or professions. You may end up at the top of your game—or at the bottom. There's just no predicting specifics when Uranus is involved in the equation. Much of what you experience depends on your belief system.

ROMANCE
With Venus in Taurus from March 5 to April 3, it looks as if romance could be headed your way with someone you meet through friends or a social contact. If you're involved already, then this transit promises that your love life will hum along at a steady pace and in a way that pleases you.

BEST DAYS, CHALLENGING DAYS
Circle March 5. Venus enters compatible earth sign Taurus that day, lighting up your social life until April 3. On March 12, Mercury turns retrograde in Aries, in your ca-

reer area. It turns direct again on April 4. Reread the Mercury retrograde section in the Big Picture for your sign and refresh your memory about the DOs and DON'Ts of this period.

April—Cancer

LUNAR HIGHLIGHTS
April 6. The full moon in Libra falls in your solar fourth house, so you can expect a lot of socializing at your place. Either you're entertaining more than usual or, if you have kids, they're inviting their friends home. Life around the time of this full moon could be hectic, so be sure to watch your nutrition and exercise regularly.

April 21 features a new moon in compatible earth sign Taurus. In addition to new opportunities surfacing to achieve your wishes and dreams, you can look forward to new friends, group associations, and plenty of action and activity. Nothing boring at this time, Cancer! Mars in compatible earth sign Virgo forms a close and beneficial angle to this new moon, and Neptune in fellow water sign Pisces also forms a beneficial angle. The result? You're perfectly attuned to your imagination and have the skills to make the intangible tangible.

FINANCES, OTHER STUFF
With Jupiter still in Taurus, your finances are one area that could be expanding big time. You're thinking in larger terms these days and are more aware of how you feel about yourself and the various areas of your life. The clearer your beliefs about money, the more likely it is that you can manifest what you need, when you need it, or even that you can manifest more than you need.

CAREER
You'll be relieved when Mercury turns direct again on April 4. Anything that has been stalled professionally should

now move forward. Your communication skills should be more enhanced once it turns direct, so you won't have to try as hard to make yourself understood. On April 3, Venus enters Gemini and forms a beneficial angle to your career area, enabling you to garner support for your ideas. Other people find merit in your ideas, skills, and projects.

ROMANCE
Venus transits your solar twelfth house from April 4 to August 7. It's a long transit due to a retrograde between May 15 and June 27. While it's moving direct, you could be involved in a relationship that is secretive or so private that the two of you don't spend much time with others. It's also possible that you're involved in a creative project that requires a lot of solitude. Or both!

Any romantic relationship during this time will require a lot of honest communication!

BEST DAYS, CHALLENGING DAYS
April 4: Mercury turns direct. That's good in any language!

May—Cancer

LUNAR HIGHLIGHTS
The full moon in fellow water sign Scorpio on May 5 should bring news about a romantic relationship, a creative project, or your children. There could also be news about anything you do for pleasure and enjoyment. Emotions may be high pitched around the time of this full moon, and you could have some intense psychic experiences.

The new moon in Gemini on May 20 is also a solar eclipse. Think of it as a double new moon, bringing twice the number of new opportunities to express yourself. You might sell a novel or book, for example, or have a chance to build a Web site, start a blog, a newsletter. The solar eclipse occurs at 0 degrees and 21 minutes of Gemini, which means there will be another new moon in this sign in June, in a later degree.

FINANCES, OTHER STUFF
From May 9 to 24, Mercury transits Taurus and your solar eleventh house. Your conscious mind is resolute, firm, grounded. It's an ideal time to take care of any financial business you have put off. Mercury is traveling with Jupiter, which expands your thinking and communication abilities.

With Saturn continuing its trek through Libra and your fourth house until October 5, you may be experiencing some setbacks or delays in your domestic situation. Don't get discouraged. Once Saturn enters fellow water sign Scorpio, your situation improves, and the structures in your life are strengthened.

CAREER
Just stay focused this month, that's the primary challenge professionally. You may experience some distractions between May 15 and June 27, when Venus in Gemini is retrograde. But listen to your intuition and follow hunches to mitigate whatever challenges you confront. After May 24, things should ease up somewhat, what with Mercury entering Gemini and your solar twelfth house. You'll have a firmer grasp on any issues that surface and will know how to resolve them.

ROMANCE
Venus retrograde. Generally, it's not as noticeable as a Mercury retrograde. But it can bring about bumps in a romantic relationship, so when you encounter one, just take a few deep breaths and remind yourself that this too shall pass. Mars is now moving direct in compatible earth sign Virgo, suggesting that your physical energy is strong and resilient enough to get you through virtually anything.

BEST DAYS, CHALLENGING DAYS
The full moon in fellow water sign Scorpio should be good, but a tad chaotic.

June—Cancer

LUNAR HIGHLIGHTS
The month gets off to a running start on June 4, with a lunar eclipse in Sagittarius. Expect news concerning a work situation, a relationship with a coworker or employee, or with your daily work routine generally. The news looks good and has a positive impact on your career. Since the eclipse is in Sagittarius, there could also be news in any of the areas that Sagittarius rules—overseas travel, foreigners, higher education, publishing.

The new moon in Gemini on June 19—the second one in Gemini—looks very nice for new communication venues and new opportunities to work behind the scenes in some capacity. With both Venus and now Jupiter in Gemini as well, your personal unconscious will be much more readily accessible to you.

FINANCES, OTHER STUFF
On June 11, Jupiter enters Gemini and your solar twelfth house. This transit lasts until June 25, 2013, and should expand your personal unconscious. You may find, for instance, that your dreams are easier to recall and that they hold insights and valuable information. Make a habit of keeping a dream journal for the next year. You may find that some of your dreams are precognitive.

Mars continues its transit through Virgo and your solar third house, increasing your communication skills. Until July 3, you should be able to talk circles around anyone!

CAREER
Jupiter's transit through Gemini should give your career a major boost, Cancer. It forms a beneficial angle to your career area, so some of the planet's luck and expansive qualities will be putting you in the right place at the right time. If you're looking to change jobs or careers, this transit could help bring it about.

During this transit, you might even have more than one job—your day job and something else that you do for fun and because you're passionate about it. If you'd like to make your passion your job, then Jupiter helps in this regard too. It would be beneficial, though, it you practice visualization techniques that clearly define what you desire.

ROMANCE
Mercury enters your sign on June 7, and this impacts every area of your life. Your conscious mind is much more intuitive now, and you're better able to communicate with your partner or new romantic interest. Venus turns direct on June 27, a bonus for any relationship, and begins to move toward its appointment with Cancer on August 7. If you're not involved with anyone right now, then use the period from June 27 to August 7 to define what you're looking for in a relationship. Make lists of qualities you would like in a partner.

BEST DAYS, CHALLENGING DAYS
June 27, when Venus turns direct.

July—Cancer

LUNAR HIGHLIGHTS
July 3 features a full moon in Capricorn, your opposite sign, and should bring news concerning a business or romantic partnership or a career matter. Or all of the above! Pluto forms a close conjunction to this moon, suggesting that power issues may be involved or that transformative change is upon you.

The new moon in your sign on July 19 comes around just once a year and is usually a powerful time. This new moon ushers in new personal opportunities. Several days before the new moon occurs, it would be to your advantage to make a list of what you would like to experience, achieve, or have in the next year. Post the list where you will see it often. If you're really motivated, create a wish board of photos and pictures that illustrate your desires.

FINANCES, OTHER STUFF
On July 3, Mars enters Libra, your solar fourth house. This transit brings plenty of activity into your home and personal environment. You may start a home-beautification project, repaint rooms, buy new furniture, put down new flooring. Mars now forms a beneficial angle to your financial area, suggesting that money flows in more easily now, and you're able to pay off bills.

Mercury enters your financial area on June 25, ushering in discussions about finances, perhaps with a college-bound child or your partner. On July 14, Mercury will turn retrograde in Leo, in this same area of your chart. So before then, make your travel plans, sign contracts, seal deals.

CAREER
Reread the Big Picture section for what you can expect with Uranus transiting Aries. Right now you may be experiencing the tumultuous part of this equation in your career. If things seem uncertain or your professional life is beset with sudden and unexpected changes, just try to go with the flow. The less resistance you exert, the more likely it is that you'll come through this transit with a better job and a more rewarding career.

ROMANCE
With Venus now moving toward your sign, it's time to tie up loose ends in your own psyche. What are you really looking for in a relationship? If you're involved in a relationship now, does it suit you? Are you happy? What would you change if you could? These basic questions beg for answers. If you've got the answers already, then skip this section!

BEST DAYS, CHALLENGING DAYS
Saturn went direct in Libra, your solar fourth house, on June 25, so now you're reaping the benefits. Your home environment should be more solid and grounded, your home-improvement projects are coming along. Even if you meet

with some delays or restrictions during this transit, don't worry about it. Once Saturn enters Scorpio on October 5, you'll be in a much better place.

July 14: Mercury turns retrograde in Leo, your financial area. Ouch.

August—Cancer

LUNAR HIGHLIGHTS
With three lunations this month, life is likely to get wild and crazy. Let's take a closer look. The full moon of August 1 in Aquarius falls in your solar eighth house. Expect news concerning taxes, insurance matters, a will, or a partner's income. Mars forms a wide, beneficial angle to this full moon, indicating that your life at the beginning of August is likely to be hectic.

The new moon in Leo on August 17 falls in your financial sector. Saturn forms a beneficial angle to it, so it looks as if any financial decisions you'll be making around this time are solid. New financial opportunities that come your way could involve working with other people or with groups, and the opportunities look positive.

The full moon in Pisces on August 31 should suit you. Pisces is a fellow water sign and brings imagination, deeper intuition, and a lot of compassion. This full moon occurs in your solar ninth house, so news you hear could be connected to publishing, higher education, overseas travel, your worldview. Neptune forms a wide conjunction to this full moon, an aspect that indicates your ideals are somehow factored into the equation.

FINANCES, OTHER STUFF
The biggest news? On August 8, Mercury turns direct in your financial area. Now you can safely move forward again with investments, sign contracts, do whatever you weren't doing during the retrograde. On the eighth, Venus enters your sign, where it will be until September 6. During

this period you're very much in your element, things flow your way—romantically, creatively, in every way.

Once Mars enters fellow water sign Scorpio on August 23, you'll be moving ahead on projects about which you're passionate and will be looking for the absolute bottom line in your investment strategies.

CAREER
With Venus in your sign for three weeks and Mercury finally moving in direct motion, you should take advantage of the situation by pushing your professional agenda forward. It will be easier now to gather the support you may need for an ambitious project or idea. Once Mars enters Scorpio on the twenty-third, your life could be jammed in fast motion.

ROMANCE
Whenever Venus transits your sign, your self-confidence soars, your sex appeal is at its peak, and you're in the flow. In fact, this period should be one of the most romantic and creative for you all year. If you're not involved when the transit begins, then you may meet someone special before the transit ends. If you're in a relationship already, then your relationship will be on a roll and may take a more serious/committed turn.

BEST DAYS, CHALLENGING DAYS
August 7, when Venus enters your sign, should be one of the best days this month.

September—Cancer

LUNAR HIGHLIGHTS
The new moon in Virgo on September 15 should be quite positive for you, Cancer. Virgo is an earth sign compatible with your water-sign sun, and this new moon brings new opportunities with communication. You might start a blog,

build a Web site, write a book, do public speaking, land a teaching job. Not only does it fall in your solar third house of communication, but Mercury—the planet symbolic of communication—forms a close conjunction to this new moon.

The full moon in Aries on September 29 should bring career news. Whatever it is, the news seems to come out of the blue, catching you by surprise. This could be a chaotic time of the month too, since Uranus is closely conjunct to this full moon, which tends to bring sudden upsets, but also excitement and unusual occurrences.

FINANCES, OTHER STUFF
On September 6, Venus enters Leo and your financial area. At the same time, Jupiter in Gemini is forming a beneficial angle to Venus and your money house. Does it get much better than this? Some possibilities: you get a handsome bonus, a royalty check, a raise. One way or another, additional income comes out. So even if you're spending more as well, you're covered!

On August 31, Mercury entered Virgo, where it will be until September 16. During this period your attention to details is remarkable, and you're able to speak well and clearly about anything.

CAREER
During Venus's transit of Leo—September 6 to October 3—the planet forms a beneficial angle to your career area. Jupiter does, too. Again, any time you have the influence of these two planets working in harmony with each other the benefits and payoffs can be gratifying. But you have to uphold your end, Cancer. You may be feeling so good about things that you decide to kick back and chill. Instead, take advantage of this opportunity—pitch your ideas, expand your business, push ahead.

ROMANCE
With Venus in Leo, you're undoubtedly feeling fired up and passionate about a special someone. You could be ex-

periencing possessiveness and jealousy as well, and if so, then step back, detach emotionally from the situation, and figure out what's really bothering you. Mars is in Scorpio right now—until October 6—so your feelings are exacerbated by the intensity of this fellow water sign. Your sexuality is heightened during this transit.

BEST DAYS, CHALLENGING DAYS
The full moon in Aries on September 29 could be a challenging day. But there's other good stuff happening this month that can offset it. If you feel rushed and harried on or around the time of this full moon, reach for more positive thoughts and take time out for yourself.

October—Cancer

LUNAR HIGHLIGHTS
October's new moon in Libra occurs on the fifteenth, in your solar fourth house. This moon should bring new opportunities related to your domestic and personal environment. You might move, for instance, and thanks to a beneficial angle from Jupiter, the move could be to a larger, more beautiful place. Your environment could expand in some way—a child moves back home, a parent moves in, you get a roommate, you add an additional room to your home.

The full moon in Taurus on October 29 should be very much to your liking. Taurus is an earth sign compatible with your water-sign sun and is undoubtedly a comfortable moon for you. Leave your social calendar wide open just before and after this full moon, as the social invitations are going to pour in, Cancer, and you'll have your choice of festivities to attend. Pluto forms a close and beneficial angle to this full moon, so you're in the power seat.

FINANCES, OTHER STUFF
Mercury and Venus both enter two signs this month. Mercury transits fellow water sign Scorpio from October 5 to

29, and then it enters Sagittarius. Venus transits Virgo from October 3 to 28, then it enters Libra. The transit that is likely to benefit you financially is Mercury's through Scorpio. This transit brings a deep intuitive bent to your conscious mind and enables you to make quick decisions. Follow your hunches during this transit and you won't go wrong.

CAREER

On October 6, Mars enters Sagittarius and your solar sixth house. It forms a beneficial angle to your career area and acts as your professional booster rocket until November 16. Take advantage of the energy by getting projects in motion, garnering the support you need to implement an idea, and pitching your ideas and agenda.

With Venus in compatible earth sign Virgo from October 3 to 28, your communication skills are heightened, and others find you and your ideas appealing.

ROMANCE

You'll enjoy both of these Venus transits. The first, through Virgo, suggests that romance may be as close your neighborhood! Or you may meet a special someone in the course of your regular day. If you're involved already, then you and your partner may be socializing with neighbors and relatives. Or perhaps you're involved in some sort of communication project together.

When Venus transits Libra, your home becomes the place for congregating. You may have a party, beautify rooms, add color and art to your living quarters. Your love life should be quite satisfying, too.

BEST DAYS, CHALLENGING DAYS

Mars enters Sagittarius on October 6. This day could be as good or bad as you make it! If you have fire-sign planets in your natal chart, then you'll probably love it. Regardless, your physical energy should be powerful. Circle October 5. Saturn enters Scorpio. Read about it under the Big Picture section.

November—Cancer

LUNAR HIGHLIGHTS
Okay, buckle up! November could be a wild month.

On November 13, there's a solar eclipse in Scorpio, your solar fifth house. This solar eclipse has repercussions for romance, love, creativity, children, what you do for fun and pleasure. New opportunities surface in any of these areas. If you're not involved, then this solar eclipse could bring the right person into your life at exactly the right time. If you've considered starting a family, this eclipse would bring about a pregnancy. Creatively, you'll be on a roll, for sure.

The lunar eclipse two weeks later, on November 28, falls in Gemini, your solar twelfth house. This one could brings news that will delight you. It expands your personal unconscious so that you're better able to understand your own motives—and those of others.

FINANCES, OTHER STUFF
Okay, Mercury retro alert. It's the last one this year, occurs in Sagittarius, and runs from November 6 to 26. You undoubtedly know the drill on these retrogrades by now, but refresh your memory by reading more about it in the Big Picture section for your sign. In terms of finances, it means: not a good time to apply for mortgages or loans, don't sign contracts, don't make any financial deals, don't buy large-ticket items.

Of course, you can't live your life according to what Mercury is doing. If your washing machine breaks down at the beginning of the retrograde period, you probably don't want to wait until the end to buy a new washer!

CAREER
By now you certainly have a clear idea how Jupiter in Gemini and Uranus in Aries are affecting your career. If you're delighted with the effects, then read no further. If you're not, then perhaps it's time to consider how your beliefs may be impacting your career. Do you believe, for

instance, you don't deserve a better job? Or that you will never get to work at what you love? You get the idea here. Brainstorm and dig within yourself to ferret out the negative beliefs. Then turn them around into positive beliefs. As you begin to do this, your experience will change.

ROMANCE
This is a huge area in November. Venus enters Scorpio on November 21, so the period from then to December 15 should be a very romantic and creative period. You're due for great fun, your muse will be up close and personal, and your love life should be intense. In addition, Saturn is now in Scorpio, forming a beneficial angle to your sun. It's possible that a relationship takes a more serious and committed turn. On November 10, Neptune in fellow water sign Pisces turns direct, and your compassion and idealism come into play in a major way.

BEST DAYS, CHALLENGING DAYS
The Mercury retrograde period could be challenging: November 6–26.

December—Cancer

LUNAR HIGHLIGHTS
With the new moon in Sagittarius on December 13, you have ample new opportunities in your work. This could entail landing a new job, a promotion, perhaps even a move to another state or country. On or around this new moon would be a great time to think about your goals for the coming year and to look back at all you have experienced and achieved this year.

The hype about 2012 and that December 21 date is probably really at a fever pitch about now. Ignore the doomsayers. Move forward, Cancer.

The full moon in your sign on December 28 should be a welcome relief. You can retreat into yourself or get off with your partner or other family members and enjoy that quiet time between Christmas and New Year's Eve. However, Pluto is directly opposed to this full moon, so there could be some general lunacy unfolding in the larger world.

FINANCES, OTHER STUFF
On December 15, Venus enters Sagittarius, your solar sixth house. This transit, which lasts into January 2013, should bring about a festive atmosphere in your workplace. People will be in more generous moods, the spirit of giving will prevail. Be careful about overspending on gifts during the holidays. Or, at any rate, pay with cash so you don't have to face the credit card blues in January.

CAREER
Between December 10 and 31, Mercury is in Sagittarius, forming a beneficial angle to your career area. After the fifteenth, Venus will be there too. The combination of planets and aspects indicates that it would be a good time to make a last-minute pitch for—well, whatever. Take your pick. A raise? A project? An idea? If you aren't satisfied with your job/career, then this period favors sending out résumés, adding your name to craig'slist, getting out the word.

ROMANCE
With both Venus and Mercury in Sagittarius, you may be in a flirtatious mood for much of December. One of these flirtations at work could develop into something more. If you're involved already, then these two transits could portend a trip over the holidays, some romantic getaway for two.

BEST DAYS, CHALLENGING DAYS
December 28, the full moon in your sign, may be as peaceful or as chaotic as you desire. It will reflect your own emotional state.

Happy New Year!

6

Leo

The Big Picture in 2012

Welcome to 2012, Leo. This year is marked by leadership, independence, and an entrepreneurial spirit. It's the year for fresh starts, new beginnings, new experiences and people. Let's take a closer look.

Pluto, the snail of the zodiac, starts off the year in Capricorn, in your solar sixth house, where it has consistently been since November 2008. You're accustomed to its energy now. Its transit, which lasts until 2024, is bringing profound and permanent change globally, evident in the economic challenges that now face the U.S. Most institutions are in the throes of great change—the health-care industry, the petroleum and insurance industries, mortgages/lending, housing, aviation, even the Internet. You name it, and Pluto's fingerprint can be found.

On a personal level, this planet's transit through your daily work area has been altering your work schedule and bringing profound and permanent change. You're more aware of your own needs and motives now, particularly as they pertain to your career ambitions. You may be discovering that your attitudes and beliefs about your work are changing. If you change jobs during this long transit, it's likely that you'll find work that is much different from what you were doing when this transit began.

Neptune entered Pisces and your solar eighth house on April 4, 2011. But by early August 2011, it had slipped back into Aquarius. On February 3, 2012, it enters Pisces again and won't move on until January 2026. This transit forms a challenging angle to your sun, so its initial impact can create confusion. For hints about what this may mean for you, look back to that period in 2011 when Neptune was in Pisces.

Neptune symbolizes our higher ideals, escapism, fiction, spirituality, and our blind spots. It seeks to dissolve boundaries between us and others. One possible repercussion of this transit is prolonged religious wars, which proliferated during Uranus's transit in Pisces from early 2003. On a personal level, though, Neptune's transit through your solar eighth house suggests that you may try to integrate your spiritual beliefs more readily into other areas of your life. There may be some confusion concerning a partner's finances, about wills, inheritances, taxes. It's a wonderful placement for the study and investigation of psychic phenomena and for intuitive development. You could embark on some sort of spiritual quest that takes you to sacred sites overseas. You may meet people you have known in past lives.

Uranus entered Aries and your solar ninth house in March 2011. This transit probably has already attracted new and unusual people into your life and will continue to do so. It may be altering the landscape of your belief system and spiritual views in new, unprecedented ways. You may have opportunities to travel abroad that occur suddenly and without warning. By all means, take advantage of these opportunities. They will broaden your worldview and could lead to unexpected new relationships and opportunities.

Since Uranus is forming a beneficial angle to your sun until 2019, your life is apt to be more exciting and unpredictable. Your need for greater freedom will cause you to get rid of any relationships or situations that are restrictive. You are urged to reach for and embrace the new, the innovative, the different.

Saturn begins the year in Libra, in your solar third house. It has been there since the summer of 2010 and will be there until October 2012. This transit brings greater structure to your creative endeavors, your relationship with your kids, and everything you do for fun and pleasure. Instead of taking a vacation just to get away, for example, you might travel for research or on a spiritual quest with a group of likeminded individuals.

Once Saturn enters water sign Scorpio on October 5, the transit won't have the same level of comfort. It will be in your solar fourth house of the home, so you may discover certain elements in your domestic life that are restricting your freedom in some way. A parent may need additional help and support. An adult child could move home. However the specifics unfold for you, you will have to make better and more efficient use of your time.

One of your best periods this year falls between June 11, 2012, and June 25, 2013, when Jupiter transits compatible air sign Gemini and your solar eleventh house. This transit should expand your social venues—you join new groups, make new friends, link up with individuals who share your passions and interests. You may do more public speaking, make become involved in publicity and promotion for your company's products or your own services. If you're self-employed, you could see a marked expansion to overseas markets.

Between January 1 and June 11, Jupiter transits earth sign Taurus and your career area. This transit has been going on since June of 2011, so you already should have seen professional expansion. That trend will continue. You may find that your career options broaden or that you launch your own business, and it takes off beyond your wildest dreams.

They say that timing is everything, so with that in mind let's look at some specific areas in your life in 2012.

ROMANCE/CREATIVITY

The most romantic and creative time for you all year falls between December 15 and January 9, 2013, when Venus transits Sagittarius and your solar fifth house. If you're not involved before this transit begins, you probably will be before the transit ends. If you're not, it won't matter because you're having too much fun. Your creativity soars during this transit too, with your muse up close and personal. This would be an excellent period to travel with a partner.

Another good period: September 6 to October 3, when Venus is moving direct in your sign. Things really seem to flow your way then in many areas, but particularly with romance and creative ventures. The best time for serious involvement and deepening commitment in an existing relationship occurs when Venus transits Aquarius, your seventh house of partnerships, which occurs between January 1 and 14. You and your partner may decide to move in together, get engaged, or get married. Just be sure that you don't do any of this under a Mercury retrograde period. Take a look under the appropriate section below to find out when Mercury will be retrograde this year.

Other good backup dates: October 6 to November 16, when Mars transits fellow fire sign Sagittarius. This stirs up a lot of activity with a partner.

CAREER

Usually Venus and Jupiter transits to your career area are the times to look for. This year, lucky you, Jupiter in Taurus transits your career area from January 1 to June 11. Venus transits it between March 5 and April 3. So this second period, when the two planets are traveling together, is the time to circle. Use this period for pitching ideas, socializing with peers and bosses, asking for a raise, applying for a promotion, or for launching your own business. Use this period for pushing your professional agenda forward. You'll find all the support you want or need.

Another nice period is when Mercury joins Jupiter in Taurus, between May 9 and 24. Your communication skills are especially strong then, and you have just the right amount of stubbornness to take things to the finish line.

Between November 16 and December 25, Mars in Capricorn links up with Pluto, and both planets form a beneficial angle to your career area. The energies of this powerful duo should be used carefully. You can achieve a great deal professionally, but you don't want to alienate people with an overbearing attitude.

BEST TIMES FOR

Buying or selling a home: November 21 to December 15, when Venus is in Scorpio and your solar fourth house; October 5 to 29, when Mercury transits the same sign and house.

Family reunions: Any of the dates above or when Venus is in your sign between September 6 and October 3.

Financial matters: The period from October 3 to 28, when Venus transits Virgo and your solar second house.

Signing contracts: When Mercury is moving direct!

MERCURY RETROGRADES

Every year Mercury—the planet of communication and travel—turns retrograde three times. During this period it's wise not to sign contracts (unless you don't mind renegotiating when Mercury is moving direct), to check and recheck travel plans or, better yet, don't travel, and to communicate as succinctly as possible. Refrain from buying any large-ticket items or electronics during this time too. Often computers and appliances go on the fritz, cars act up, data is lost ... you get the idea. Be sure to back up all files before the dates below:

March 12–April 4: Mercury retrograde in Aries, your ninth house—higher mind, overseas journeys, worldview.

July 14–August 8: Mercury retrograde in your sign.

November 6–26: Mercury retrograde in Sagittarius, your solar fifth house of love and romance and creativity.

ECLIPSES

Solar eclipses tend to trigger external events that bring about change according to the sign and house in which they fall. Lunar eclipses trigger inner, emotional events according to the sign and house in which they fall. Any eclipse marks both beginnings and endings. The solar and lunar eclipse in a pair falls in opposite signs. If you're interested in detailed information on eclipses, take a look at Celeste Teal's excellent and definitive book, *Eclipses: Predicting World Events & Personal Transformation.*

If you were born under or around the time of an eclipse,

it's to your advantage to take a look at your birth chart to find out exactly where the eclipses will impact you.

Most years feature four eclipses—two solar, two lunar, with the set separated by about two weeks. In November and December 2011, there were solar and lunar eclipses, so this year the first eclipses fall during May and June.

May 20: Solar eclipse at 0 degrees Gemini. This one should bring in new opportunities to meet people, join groups, and reach for and attain your dreams.

June 4: Lunar eclipse in Sagittarius, your solar fifth house. This should be a positive eclipse for your love life!

November 13: Solar eclipse in Scorpio, in your solar fourth house. New opportunities surface in your domestic life.

November 28: Lunar eclipse, Gemini. Jupiter forms a five-degree conjunction to the eclipse degree, suggesting that news you receive around this time will be cause for celebration!

LUCKIEST DAY OF THE YEAR
Every year there's one day when Jupiter and the sun meet up, and luck, serendipity, and expansion are the hallmarks. This year that day falls on May 13, with a conjunction in Taurus.

January—Leo

LUNAR HIGHLIGHTS
The full moon in Cancer on January 9 brings news concerning a parent, your parenting style, the way you nurture others. It occurs in your solar twelfth house of the personal unconscious, of all that is hidden, so insights into your own motives are also possible. Mars in Virgo forms a close, beneficial angle to this moon and brings a lot of activity, forward movement, and a need to tend to details.

The new moon in Aquarius on January 23 should usher in new partnership opportunities—romantic and business.

The business part of this equation is intriguing in light of the fact that expansive Jupiter is now transiting your career area. Read more about it under the appropriate section below.

FINANCES, OTHER STUFF

With Uranus in fellow fire sign Aries until March 2019, your beliefs are in a state of flux—but in a positive way! You may be discovering a new independence in yourself. Perhaps the opinions of others are no longer so important to you. You may have the self-confidence now to launch your own business, try new investments, new kinds of relationships. Your goals may be changing in radical and exciting ways.

With Venus in Pisces between January 14 and February 8, your partner's income could be spiking upward. Your dealings with banks, insurance companies, and taxes should improve.

CAREER

From now until June 11, Jupiter transits your career area. It's been there for six months already, so you should be experiencing an expansion of your professional life, responsibilities, and recognition. Some possibilities: a new job or career that is more satisfying, a promotion that comes with a hefty raise, more international travel. Or you might pen a novel or book or go to college or grad school.

From January 8 to 27, Mercury transits ambitious Capricorn and your solar sixth house. During this period you may be communicating more frequently with coworkers and employees, could be socializing with them outside of work, and could find that you're more focused on your goals.

ROMANCE

The new moon in Aquarius on January 23 could bring about a new level of intimacy and commitment in an existing relationship. You and your partner could decide to move in together, get engaged, perhaps even get married.

Uranus forms a tight, beneficial angle to this moon, indicating unexpected surprises, news that comes out of the blue.

BEST DAYS, CHALLENGING DAYS
With Mars in Virgo and your solar second house from now until July 3, you are energetically pursuing earning as much money as quickly as you can. But Virgo is a detailed, precise sign, so slow down and don't overlook the fine print. Scrutinize how you feel about the way you earn your living. Do you feel positive most of the time? Negative? Indifferent? Your emotions are key.

February—Leo

LUNAR HIGHLIGHTS
The full moon on February 7 falls in your sign, Leo, and should bring personal news that delights you. The day after this full moon, Venus enters fellow fire sign Aries, joining Uranus in your solar ninth house. This combination of energies could bring about sudden events in romance. Read more about it below.

The new moon in Pisces on February 21 falls in your solar eighth house. Expect new financial opportunities for your partner and with mortgages and insurance. You may also have a chance to flex your creative muscles and use your imagination in new ways. This would be an excellent time to apply for a mortgage or loan.

FINANCES, OTHER STUFF
In addition to the financial information above, keep in mind that Mars is now retrograde in your money house and won't straighten out again until April 14. Your energy may not be quite up to par during this period, and you may not feel as compelled to take on additional responsibilities in your job to make ends meet. If you're experiencing a financial crunch, the wisest thing to do is figure out where

you can cut expenses. Set up a budget you know you can live with.

With Mercury in Pisces between February 13 and March 2, there should be a lot of discussion with a partner—business or romantic—about money, mortgages, finances generally.

CAREER

Jupiter continues its transit through Taurus and your career area, a major plus. This month, it gets an additional boost from Mercury in water sign Pisces and from Neptune, which enters Pisces on February 3. The combination of energies should bring your ideals up front and center in your professional life, and you have no shortage of ideas. The challenge may lie in expressing these ideas in a way that others can understand.

ROMANCE

With Venus transiting fellow fire sign Aries from February 8 to March 5, your love life should be humming along at a pace that suits you. You may get involved with someone who was born abroad or could be traveling overseas yourself and meet someone. Your passions run quite high during this transit. You could be more possessive or have a tendency toward jealousy.

BEST DAYS, CHALLENGING DAYS

February 3 could be somewhat challenging. Neptune enters Pisces that day, for a run that will last fourteen years. Whenever an outer planet changes signs, there's often an adjustment period. You may feel confused about certain elements or relationships in your life. Don't obsess about it. Just go with the flow.

March—Leo

LUNAR HIGHLIGHTS
March 8: the full moon in Virgo, in your solar second house, brings financial news. Mars is conjunct this moon, suggesting a lot of activity and movement concerning finances generally. With both Venus and Mars in earth sign Taurus, the news you hear around this time looks positive.

The new moon in fellow fire sign Aries on March 22 should be very much to your liking. Both Mercury and Uranus form close conjunctions, suggesting that opportunities surface quickly and unexpectedly, and you must be on your toes, ready to seize them. The possibilities? A new romantic relationship that embodies all the passion and excitement you're looking for; a chance to travel overseas, perhaps on a quest of some kind; new opportunities to trailblaze.

FINANCES, OTHER STUFF
Mercury enters Aries on March 2, joining Uranus in your solar ninth house, and retrogrades between March 12 and April 4. During this period, don't sign contracts or enter into financial negotiations like for a mortgage or loan, and have your travel plans in place before the retrograde begins. Reread the section on Mercury retrogrades under the Big Picture for your sign. In addition, Mars continues to move retrograde in Virgo and your financial area. All the more reason to be cautious with finances!

CAREER
With Venus and Jupiter traveling together in Taurus and your career area between March 5 and April 3, you've got both of the benefic planets in your professional court. These two energies attract what you need when you need it, and could increase your earnings and bring a huge element of luck into the picture. These two energies require vigilance on your part, so that you recognize opportunities when they surface—and seize them.

ROMANCE

With lovely Venus in Taurus, a sign that it rules, from March 5 to April 3, the chances are high for a flirtation or romance in your workplace. Whenever Venus and Jupiter travel together, magic is in the air, synchronicity abounds, you're in the flow. Never mind that Taurus is an earth sign that doesn't mix well with your fire-sign sun. This combination literally screams out for camaraderie and the promise of love, Leo. Make it so.

BEST DAYS, CHALLENGING DAYS

The Mercury retrograde in fellow fire sign Aries from March 12 to April 4 is a big ouch. Nothing you can't conquer, though, Leo! This one occurs in your solar ninth house, so you can expect some snafus in your entrepreneurial projects, higher education, publishing.

April—Leo

LUNAR HIGHLIGHTS

The Libra full moon on April 6 should be very much to your liking, Leo. Libra is an air sign compatible with your fire-sign sun, and this one could put you in a social, affable mood. Your neighborhood could have a block party, you may have more contact than usual with siblings and other relatives. If you're considering a move, you may find a neighborhood that is ideal for you and your family. Expect news related to communication or writing projects, education, your daily routine.

The new moon in Taurus on April 21 occurs in your career area. Combined with Jupiter in this same sign and house, new professional opportunities should surface. Mars forms a close and beneficial angle to this moon, suggesting a lot of activity around the time of this new moon.

FINANCES, OTHER STUFF
Well, Mars finally turns direct on April 14, in Virgo, your financial area. This should prove helpful in several regards. If any financial projects have been stalled since the first of the year, that trend should reverse itself. Mortgages and loans that have languished in limbo will now come through.

On the fourth, Venus enters compatible air sign Gemini, where it will be until August 7. The transit is lengthy because Venus is retrograde between May 15 and June 27. But while it's moving direct, your social contacts could yield business ventures and financial rewards. Your people skills are legendary, and now is the time to use them!

CAREER
The new moon in Taurus and your career area can't be overstated! Combined with Jupiter's continued transit through this same sign, new professional opportunities should be popping up like mushrooms after a hard rain! Mars turning direct again in Virgo, on April 14, proves helpful as well. Mars brings forward thrust and precision to your agenda and projects.

ROMANCE
Love could be closer than you think. With Venus entering Gemini on April 3, you may discover that you and a friend have more in common than you thought. Long discussions spark a romantic chord. Or you meet someone special through friends, a group to which you belong, or perhaps through your blog or through a social network like facebook.

BEST DAYS, CHALLENGING DAYS
Mercury turns direct on April 4, an added plus regardless of your sign. On the fourteenth, it enters Aries once again, a fellow fire sign. This transit, which lasts until May 9, should fire up your interests and your communication skills.

On April 10, Pluto turns retrograde in Capricorn, so certain elements of your daily work routine may slow down. Set up a regular exercise regimen and stick to it. It will help you deal with stress.

May—Leo

LUNAR HIGHLIGHTS
May 5's full moon in Scorpio could be emotionally intense. It falls into the area of your chart that rules your domestic environment. Pluto in Capricorn forms a wide but beneficial angle to this full moon, so there could be power plays and power issues surfacing around this time. But you're in the driver's seat, Leo, as long as you aren't totally overwhelmed by emotions.

On May 20, the new moon in Gemini is also a solar eclipse. You can expect new opportunities with friends, social groups, and opportunities to express yourself. You might start a blog, for instance, or build a Web site. Your facebook participation could surge for some reason. Or you might encounter people who help you to realize your dreams.

FINANCES, OTHER STUFF
On May 15, Venus turns retrograde in Gemini and remains that way until June 27. If, in your natal chart, Gemini is on the cusp of your second house (finances), then this retrograde could be more difficult for you than others. You might discover, for instance, that you made an error in your bank statement or with your stock portfolio. It's best not to buy large-tickets items during this period. That said, though, you can sometimes find terrific deals during a Venus retrograde, but may later discover something wrong with the item you bought.

Mars continues its transit through Virgo and your solar second house, so you may be burning the candle at both ends, perhaps to meet a deadline so you can get paid!

CAREER
Next month, Jupiter leaves Taurus and your career area, so take advantage of its largesse before it leaves. You enjoy an additional professional boost this month between May 9 and 24, when Mercury enters Taurus and your career area.

This period favors resilience in pursuing your goals, a mental resolve to do things your way, and excellent communication.

ROMANCE
Yes, your love life could experience some bumps and bruises between May 15 and June 27, when Venus is retrograde. But if you can maintain a clear vision of your relationship and speak from the heart always, the effects can be mitigated. If Gemini falls in your fifth house of romance in your natal chart, then the combination of Venus retrograde and the solar eclipse in Gemini should having your head spinning!

BEST DAYS, CHALLENGING DAYS
May 15. Venus turns retrograde. Buy your large-ticket items before then!

June—Leo

LUNAR HIGHLIGHTS
June 4 features a lunar eclipse in fellow fire sign Sagittarius. This one should be quite good for you. Expect exciting news in any or all of these areas: an overseas trip, an educational venture, a publishing project. Or you may have an opportunity to live and work abroad, to expand your business or services to another country. Whatever the news, it catches you off guard.

On June 19, the new moon in compatible air sign Gemini brings new opportunities to express yourself, to meet new and exciting friends, to join groups of like-minded individuals. You might have an opportunity to teach or to speak to a large group. Maybe you'll be running a workshop, Leo! Whatever these opportunities are, seize them, enjoy them.

FINANCES, OTHER STUFF
June 11, Jupiter enters Gemini, an air sign compatible with your fire-sign sun. This year-long transit—until June 25,

2013—should expand your life in any number of ways. It could expand your financial base, your love life, your creative output, your self-expression... you get the idea. For specific clues to how this transit could impact your life, look back twelve years, when Jupiter was last in Gemini.

On May 24, Mercury entered Gemini, where it remains through the first week of June. While it travels with Jupiter, your conscious mind is expansive, your mood is optimistic, you're soaring. Those feelings can help to attract more positive experiences.

CAREER
Between June 7 and 25, Mercury is in water sign Cancer, your solar twelfth house. It looks as if you're preparing for something big, which you'll present once Mercury transits your sign from June 27 to August 31. Mercury will be retrograde, though, in your sign, between July 14 and August 8, so plan your presentation on either side of those dates.

Uranus turns direct on June 25, in fellow fire sign Aries, which is sure to galvanize you in new directions professionally. Keep track of ideas you have after this date. You'll be able to use them down the road.

ROMANCE
For much of the month, Venus continues its retrograde movement through compatible air sign Gemini. This means bumps and bruises in your love relationships, but your inimitable optimism gets you through. On June 27, it turns direct again, and suddenly your romantic relationship straightens out and your social calendar heats up.

BEST DAYS, CHALLENGING DAYS
Circle June 19. The new moon in Gemini should be a beauty for you. Another great day: June 27, when Venus turns direct again. June 11: Jupiter enters compatible air sign Gemini, so your social circles and opportunities to realize your dreams should expand enormously during the next year.

July—Leo

LUNAR HIGHLIGHTS
The full moon in Capricorn on July 3 brings news about a work-related or professional matter. Pluto forms a beneficial angle to your career area, suggesting that you're in the power seat, Leo, exactly where you like to be!

The July 19 new moon in Cancer occurs in your solar twelfth house. This moon should usher in new opportunities related to your home and domestic environment, to your parents, or to any work you do behind the scenes. At the same time, Venus and Jupiter are both in compatible air sign Gemini, expanding your social circles and your love life.

FINANCES, OTHER STUFF
On July 3, Mars leaves your financial area and enters Libra and your solar third house. This should be something of a relief for you. You won't have to work as hard to make ends meet and should be able to balance your budget with greater finesse!

Mercury turns retrograde in your sign on July 14. Read about this in detail under the Big Picture for your sign. Keep in mind that it's smart not to sign any financial deals during this time.

CAREER
With Jupiter now in Gemini, your communication skills are greatly enhanced, and this, in turn, urges you to make your pitches, garner support from coworkers, to reach out to strangers and friends alike. Bosses and peers are impressed with your ability to communicate your ideas. However, Mercury is retrograde in your sign between July 14 and August 8, so be sure to do your pitching and reaching out before the fourteenth.

Mars enters Libra on July 3, joining Saturn in your solar third house. The combination suggests a period where greater structure is important to you. Your relationships and communications are more structured, for instance, and any association you have with siblings and other relatives may revolve around family reunions.

ROMANCE
With Venus now direct in Gemini, your love life should be humming along at a perfect pitch now. If you're not involved with anyone right now, then be sure to get out and about, accept all social invitations, do what you enjoy. Chances are good that you will meet someone special through your social contacts.

Uranus turns retrograde in fellow fire sign Aries on July 13 and remains that way until December 13. This long retrograde simply means there could be some snafus or delays with things that are important to you.

BEST DAYS, CHALLENGING DAYS
Challenging day? July 14, when Mercury turns retrograde in your sign.

August—Leo

LUNAR HIGHLIGHTS
This month features two full moons and a new moon, so buckle up, Leo, it may be a wild, unpredictable ride!

The first full moon occurs on August 1, in Aquarius, your opposite sign. There could be news about a partnership—business or romantic—or you may tap into a vein of creative ideas that you should jot down, even if they seem too *out there*. Mars forms a beneficial angle to this full moon, indicating that you're energized, in a social mood, and ready to get things done.

The new moon on August 17 falls in your sign, Leo. This one comes around just once a year and is worth preparing for. Make a wish list a few days before the seventeenth. Be honest and wildly imaginative. No limits. Create a wish board with visuals that depict your primary desires and hopes. Post it somewhere prominent, where you'll see it often. This new moon should usher in new personal opportunities, and they look to be quite serious and deserve your utmost attention.

The second full moon falls on August 31, in Pisces, your solar eighth house. This full moon should bring news concerning joint finances—those you share with your partner, a parent, child, sibling, whoever. If you've applied for a mortgage or loan, then this full moon could bring news about its status.

FINANCES, OTHER STUFF
It's always good news when Mercury turns direct, which happens on August 8. Since Mercury is in your sign, Leo, you should be overjoyed when it turns direct. Not only do your finances straighten out, but so do other areas of your life. On the thirty-first, Mercury enters your financial area, so it will be possible to talk about finances with greater openness, you may make money from something you write, and you could be taking workshops or seminars related to finances. That transit lasts until September 16.

CAREER
On August 23, Mars enters passionate, secretive Scorpio and your solar fourth house. This transit lasts until October 6 and may pit you against yourself! You may feel conflicted, for instance, between your responsibilities at home and those at work. Your career may be kind of nuts until you realize that the most you can do at any time is your best.

ROMANCE
Venus transits Cancer and your solar twelfth house between August 7 and September 6. If a relationship begins during this transit, it may be secretive or extremely private. You and your partner may decide you prefer spending time alone together than time together with your friends. But once Venus enters your sign on September 6, all bets are off. You're going to want your partner to meet your friends, your family, even your neighbors. There will be no keeping any of it under wraps.

BEST DAYS, CHALLENGING DAYS
August 8: Mercury turns direct in your sign.

August 17: this should be one of the best days this year. Several days on either side of this new moon in your sign should be pretty spectacular, too.

September—Leo

LUNAR HIGHLIGHTS
The new moon in Virgo on September 15 occurs in your solar second house. This moon should usher in new financial opportunities. You earn more, perhaps because you land a raise or take on a second job. Or perhaps you sell a novel or screenplay or launch your own business. However this new moon shakes out for you, an improved financial picture is the end result.

The full moon in fellow fire sign Aries on September 29 should be filled with excitement, sudden occurrences, and perhaps a tad of lunacy! Uranus forms a close conjunction to this full moon, usually indicative of abrupt, unexpected events. Jupiter forms a wide and beneficial angle to this moon, suggesting that the events that happen somehow expand your world.

FINANCES, OTHER STUFF
The new moon in Virgo on September 15 is the best harbinger for your finances this month. However, between September 6 and October 3, Venus transits your sign, so this period favors finances, romance, creativity. Others see you in a positive light, which in turn makes you feel more upbeat and optimistic about life.

Mercury is now moving through Virgo and your financial area. Between now and October 5, it's likely that you'll be communicating more about money and your personal values. You may decide to start a blog or build a Web site.

CAREER
With Mars in Scorpio, opposite your career area until October 6, you may feel conflicted about your professional responsibilities versus your responsibility to home and family. Try not to obsess about it; that will only make things worse. Instead, go with the flow and just try to do your best in all your endeavors. The Mars transit is mitigated somewhat by Venus's transit through your sign. Push your own agenda forward, pitch ideas. You'll find the support you need.

ROMANCE
Back to Venus in your sign. This transit marks one of the most romantic and creative periods for you all year. If you're not involved when the transit begins, that probably will change before the transit ends. If you're involved in a relationship, then things may go to a deeper level of commitment. Jupiter's transit through compatible air sign Gemini should be expanding your social networks, and it's possible that you meet a romantic interest through a friend or through a group to which you belong.

BEST DAYS, CHALLENGING DAYS
September 6 looks very nice indeed. Venus enters your sign that day.

October—Leo

LUNAR HIGHLIGHTS
The new moon in compatible air sign Libra on October 15 should be quite pleasant for you. It ushers in new opportunities in friendships, the arts, your daily routine, and with communication. Jupiter forms a close and beneficial angle to this new moon, suggesting luck and expansion in various areas of your life.

The full moon in Taurus on October 29 brings career news. If you have recently applied for a job, then around the time of this full moon you hear whether or not you got it. Chances are, you did. You also gain insight into your career path. Pluto forms a close, beneficial angle to this moon, suggesting powerful forces are at work. Positive forces!

FINANCES, OTHER STUFF
Mars enters fellow fire sign Sagittarius and your solar ninth house. This transit lasts until November 16 and energizes your life. You have more physical energy and may feel restless, eager to get out on the open road. The Mars transit also may prompt you to spend more—impulsive buying. Just be sure you've got the money in the bank to cover the bills!

Between October 3 and 28, Venus transits Virgo and your financial area. This transit should bolster your earnings, but also may prompt you to spend more. Obviously the message this month in terms of finances is that although more money is coming in, more money is also going out!

CAREER
Between October 5 and 29, Mercury transits Scorpio and your solar fourth house. During this period you're investigating, researching, doing the grunt work so that down the road a bit, you'll have everything lined up. In addition, Saturn enters Scorpio and your solar fourth house on October 5 and will be there for two and a half years. Read more about this in the Big Picture section for your sign. One thing about this transit, though, is that it enables you to dig deeply into whatever you take on.

ROMANCE
With Mars in Sagittarius between October 6 and November 16, your love life is ramped up big time! Your sexuality is greatly heightened during this period and so is your creativity. In fact, you and partner may undertake some sort of creative project together.

Travel with a partner is also a possibility during this transit. You may head for some exotic port neither of you has visited before.

BEST DAYS, CHALLENGING DAYS
October 28. Venus enters compatible air sign Libra, where it will be until November 21. This transit should bring ease and comfort into your daily life.

November—Leo

LUNAR HIGHLIGHTS
The solar eclipse in Scorpio on November 13 is like a double new moon. This one should usher in new opportunities in your domestic life, in the area of shared resources, in investigation and research, and to more deeply understand your own psyche. It behooves you to find where Scorpio falls in your natal chart. The house placement of the solar eclipse will reveal the area of your life that will be impacted.

The lunar eclipse on November 28 falls in compatible air sign Gemini, in your solar eleventh house. Jupiter falls close to the eclipse degree. Any news you hear around the time of this eclipse should be positive, and your mood is likely to be buoyant.

FINANCES, OTHER STUFF
Okay, Mercury retrograde alert! This one, in Sadge, begins on November 6 and ends on the twenty-sixth. By now you know the drill for these retrogrades. But read them over in the Big Picture section for your sign. Pertaining to finances, the retrograde cautions against signing any loan agreements.

Venus transits compatible air sign Libra until November 21, so there may be money made through the arts or through your connections with social networks and friends.

CAREER
Jupiter continues to expand your social contacts and your wishes and dreams. These contacts can be helpful to you professionally, so be sure that you don't become a hermit.

Get out and mingle; don't hesitate to spread the word about your company, products, services. With Venus in compatible air sign Libra, your grace under pressure is admired by bosses and coworkers alike.

ROMANCE
With Venus and Jupiter in air signs compatible with your fire-sign sun, your love life should be on a roll. You and your partner are undoubtedly feeling very warm and fuzzy about each other and may even decide to take your relationship to another, deeper level. Your ideas should mesh well, and once you discover how much you have in common, the fireworks should be steady!

BEST DAYS, CHALLENGING DAYS
Mercury turns direct on November 26, always a day to celebrate. So now you can hit the road without worrying about travel snafus! On November 16, Mars enters Capricorn and your solar sixth house. Your ambitions and goals should now snap into clarity, but the sixteenth could feel confusing and muddled.

December—Leo

LUNAR HIGHLIGHTS
The new moon in fellow fire sign Sadge on December 13 should be very much to your liking. It brings new opportunities in foreign travel, with foreign countries and foreigners. Other possibilities? New opportunities in higher education and publishing. On the day of this new moon, Uranus and Mercury form tight, beneficial angles to each other and a beneficial angle to your sun. Your ideas are cutting edge, and even if you're more impatient than usual, it helps you get stuff done!

The full moon in water sign Cancer on December 28 falls in your solar twelfth house. It's opposed by Pluto in Capricorn, so this could be a somewhat challenging day. Power issues surface. You're more in tune with your emotions, though, so try to go with the flow and not get upset.

FINANCES, OTHER STUFF
It's time to take stock of 2012. Have you reached your financial goals? What goals do you have for 2013 and your finances? You should grasp the larger picture between December 10 and 31, when Mercury transits fellow fire sign Sadge. You're eager to talk about your goals during this time, too. Between December 15 and early January 2013, Venus also transits Sadge, so you may have an opportunity to make money in overseas markets.

CAREER
As the holiday season approaches, people tend to be in more buoyant moods, so make your year-end pitches, talk about your ideas for 2013, and by all means don't fall for the hype surrounding December 21, 2012! Stick to what you know, and don't believe everything you hear.

Uranus turns direct in fellow fire sign Aries on December 13. Any dealings you have with foreign markets and companies should now move ahead more smoothly. Expect the unexpected, and be ready to seize opportunities as they surface.

ROMANCE
You're in for a treat from December 15 to early January 2013, when Venus transits Sadge. This period should be one of the most romantic and creative for you all year. And, lucky you, since it goes into next year, you'll be starting 2013 on the right foot.

BEST DAYS, CHALLENGING DAYS
December 13, with that new moon in Sadge, should be a magnificent day for you.

Happy New Year!

7

Virgo

The Big Picture in 2012

Welcome to 2012, Virgo. This year is marked by partnership, cooperation, patience, kindness, and understanding. It's a year for an important relationship to develop—in business, in your personal life, or even both! Let's take a closer look.

Pluto, the snail of the zodiac, starts off the year in Capricorn, in your solar fifth house, where it has consistently been since November 2008. You're accustomed to its energy now. Its transit, which lasts until 2024, is bringing profound and permanent change globally, evident in the economic challenges that now face the U.S. Most institutions are in the throes of great change—the health-care industry, the petroleum and insurance industries, mortgages/lending, housing, aviation, even the Internet. You name it, and Pluto's fingerprint can be found.

On a personal level, this planet's transit through that area of your chart that represents romance and love, enjoyment, children, and creativity will continue to transform these things at profound levels. On the creative front, you will become more aware of your needs and motives. Your muse will be whispering in your ear 24/7. If you've wanted to start a family, consider doing it during this transit. Everything you do for fun and pleasure will have a deeper aspect to it. In other words, instead of just taking a trip somewhere, there will be a purpose behind the trip—to learn something, to expose yourself to new venues, or perhaps you'll travel as part of a spiritual quest. Romantically, you may be attracting unusual, idiosyncratic individuals who give you plenty of personal freedom and encourage your self-expression.

Neptune entered Pisces, your opposite sign, on April 4, 2011. But by early August 2011, it had slipped back into Aquarius. On February 3, 2012, it enters Pisces again and won't move on until January 2026. This transit forms a challenging angle to your sun, so its initial impact can create confusion. For hints about what this may mean for you, look back to that period in 2011 when Neptune was in Pisces.

Neptune symbolizes our higher ideals, escapism, fiction, spirituality, and our blind spots. It seeks to dissolve boundaries between us and others. One possible repercussion of this transit is prolonged religious wars, which proliferated during Uranus's transit in Pisces from early 2003. On a personal level, though, Neptune's transit through your solar seventh house suggests that you may try to integrate your spiritual beliefs more readily into your partnerships—both business and personal. Your partnerships may also become more spiritual, idealistic, even more psychic. In fact, if you can focus on these three elements in your relationships, there's less apt to be confusion during this transit. Given the spiritual aspect of this transit, it's quite possible that a relationship develops with someone you knew in a past life.

Uranus entered Aries and your solar eighth house in March 2011. One repercussion of this transit is that unusual and exciting people are going to be entering your life and shaking things up. The biggest changes are likely to be to your partner's income.

Saturn begins the year in Libra, your solar second house. It has been there since the summer of 2010 and will be there until October 2012. This transit brings greater structure to your finances and values. It may also restrict your earnings in some way, or perhaps for a time you have to take on a part-time job. But try to use this energy in terms of structure—start a budget, out of every check you receive, pay yourself a percentage first, pay cash for purchases, avoid credit card debt. You know the drill here, Virgo. Make it happen.

Once Saturn enters compatible water sign Scorpio on October 5, the transit will have a greater level of comfort. It will be forming a beneficial angle to your sun, in your solar third house. You will find a strong structure for your intuition, perhaps through writing—a blog, Web site, novel, self-help book—and your relationship with siblings, other relatives, and neighbors will benefit.

One of your best periods this year falls between January 1 and June 11, when Jupiter transits fellow earth sign Taurus, your solar ninth house. This transit expands your worldview, spirituality, your personal philosophy. It highlights higher education, publishing, overseas travel, foreign cultures. It's possible that your company's products or your services/products expand to overseas markets. You may be traveling overseas more frequently, which opens your consciousness to new experiences, thoughts, ideas.

From June 11, 2012, to June 25, 2013, Jupiter transits Gemini, your career area. This is a big wow, Virgo, and it's smart to plan for it. Seeds planted during Jupiter's transit through Taurus can sprout fast during its transit through Gemini. You may change jobs, land a promotion and raise, change careers, start your own business, write a novel . . . well, there are many possibilities. The more focused you are, the clearer your intentions, the greater the possibilities with this transit.

They say that timing is everything, so with that in mind let's look at some specific areas in your life in 2012.

ROMANCE/CREATIVITY

The most romantic and creative time for you all year falls between March 5 and April 3, when Venus transit fellow earth sign Taurus. You feel more sensual and appealing, and your self-confidence soars. Other people pick up what you radiate and respond accordingly. If you're in a committed relationship, then you and your partner rediscover each other. Plan a trip out of town, to some secluded, romantic spot. Spend time together doing whatever you both enjoy.

Another good period: October 3 to 28, when Venus is moving direct in your sign. Things really seem to flow your way then in many areas, but particularly with romance and creative ventures. The best time for serious involvement and deepening commitment in an existing relationship occurs when Venus transits Pisces and your solar seventh house of partnerships, which occurs between January 14 and February 8. You and your partner may decide to move in together, get engaged, or get married. Just be sure that you don't do any of this under a Mercury retrograde period. Take a look under the appropriate section below to find out when Mercury will be retrograde this year.

Other good backup dates: August 23 to October 6, when Mars transits compatible water sign Scorpio, and between November 16 and December 25, when it transits Capricorn and the romance/love area of your chart.

CAREER

Usually Venus and Jupiter transits to your career area are the times to look for. This year, lucky you, Jupiter in Gemini transits your career area for more than a year, from June 11, 2012, to June 25, 2013. Venus transits this area from April 3 to August 7. However, it's retrograde between May 15 and June 27, so try not to start anything new during this period.

Another nice period is when Mercury transits your career area between May 24 and June 7. This is the time to pitch ideas, push your agenda forward, travel related to work, and socialize with peers. It also favors all professional communication.

Between November 16 and December 25, Mars in Capricorn links up with Pluto, and both planets form a beneficial angle to your sun. This period is when you should seek creative solutions. Brainstorm. Don't be afraid to try the untried.

BEST TIMES FOR

Buying or selling a home: December 15 to January 9, 2013, when Venus is in Sagittarius and your solar fourth house; December 10 to 31, Mercury transits the same sign and house.

Family reunions: Any of the dates above or when Venus is in your sign between October 3 and 28.

Financial matters: The period from October 28 to November 21, when Venus transits Libra and your solar second house.

Signing contracts: When Mercury is moving direct!

MERCURY RETROGRADES

Every year Mercury—the planet of communication and travel—turns retrograde three times. During this period it's wise not to sign contracts (unless you don't mind renegotiating when Mercury is moving direct), to check and recheck travel plans or, better yet, don't travel, and to communicate as succinctly as possible. Refrain from buying any large-ticket items or electronics during this time too. Often computers and appliances go on the fritz, cars act up, data is lost... you get the idea. Be sure to back up all files before the dates below:

March 12–April 4: Mercury retrograde in Aries, your eighth house—shared resources, mortgages, loans, insurance, partner's income.

July 14–August 8: Mercury retrograde in Leo, your solar twelfth house—personal unconscious, what's hidden.

November 6–26: Mercury retrograde in Sagittarius, your solar fourth house of the home.

ECLIPSES

Solar eclipses tend to trigger external events that bring about change according to the sign and house in which they fall. Lunar eclipses trigger inner, emotional events according to the sign and house in which they fall. Any eclipse marks both beginnings and endings. The solar and lunar eclipse in a pair falls in opposite signs. If you're interested in detailed information on eclipses, take a look at Celeste

Teal's excellent and definitive book, *Eclipses: Predicting World Events & Personal Transformation*.

If you were born under or around the time of an eclipse, it's to your advantage to take a look at your birth chart to find out exactly where the eclipses will impact you.

Most years feature four eclipses—two solar, two lunar, with the set separated by about two weeks. In November and December 2011, there were solar and lunar eclipses, so this year the first eclipses fall during May and June.

May 20: Solar eclipse at 0 degrees Gemini. This one should bring in new professional opportunities.

June 4: Lunar eclipse in Sagittarius, your solar fourth house. Positive eclipse for your family life.

November 13: Solar eclipse in Scorpio, your solar third house. New opportunities surface for communication.

November 28: Lunar eclipse, Gemini. Jupiter forms a five-degree conjunction to the eclipse degree, suggesting that professional news you receive around this time will be cause for celebration!

LUCKIEST DAY OF THE YEAR
Every year there's one day when Jupiter and the sun meet up, and luck, serendipity, and expansion are the hallmarks. This year that day falls on May 13, with a conjunction in Taurus.

January—Virgo

LUNAR HIGHLIGHTS
The full moon in Cancer on January 9 brings news concerning a friendship or a goal or dream that you have, and could bring insights about a parent or your own parenting style. It occurs in your solar eleventh house and forms a beneficial angle to your sun. You may feel a tad of nostalgia for the good ole days or for some aspect of your childhood. Jupiter is in fellow earth sign Taurus, so your worldview is undergoing profound expansion.

The new moon in Aquarius on January 23 should usher in new opportunities in your daily work routine and in the maintenance of your health. It would be an excellent time to join a gym, sign up for yoga classes, or to start a diet or new course of nutrition. With Pluto forming a wide and beneficial angle to Jupiter in Taurus, you should be feeling quite confident about all areas of your life.

FINANCES, OTHER STUFF
Energetic Mars begins the year in your sign, a major plus. Your physical energy should be good, and that energy spills over into everything you undertake. Between January 24 and April 14, it is moving retrograde, so that could be a somewhat sluggish period. Between April 14 and July 3, Mars is moving direct again in your sign, and you enjoy a resurgence of forward thrust.

Try to pay for everything in cash. It will make you more aware of what you spend.

CAREER
Your best career time will be from June 11, 2012, to June 25, 2013, when Jupiter transits Gemini and your solar tenth house. Until then, while Jupiter is in Taurus and your solar ninth house, nurture your ideas and goals carefully, with the full belief that everything will unfold beautifully. You may be doing more international travel related to your profession.

Between January 14 and February 8, Venus is in Pisces, your opposite sign, bringing harmony to your business partnerships. This is an excellent time to pitch your ideas and generally move your agenda forward. From January 8 to 27, Mercury transits ambitious Capricorn and your solar fifth house. During this period your creativity is at a peak.

ROMANCE
During Venus's transit through Pisces, you and your partner should enjoy a very nice period of camaraderie. This transit softens your heart, deepens your intuition, and brings you and your partner closer together emotionally. With Mars in your sign, your sexuality is heightened, too.

BEST DAYS, CHALLENGING DAYS
January 24 could be somewhat challenging. Mars turns retrograde on that date, suggesting that you may be irritable and feel sluggish.

February—Virgo

LUNAR HIGHLIGHTS
February 7 features a full moon in Leo, your solar twelfth house. This full moon brings news and insights into your own psyche and motivations. On or around this date, you have an opportunity to shine, to really strut your stuff. Don't be shy!

The new moon in Pisces on February 21 looks quite promising for a partnership—either business or romantic. New opportunities surface in both areas. Neptune is closely conjunct to this new moon, suggesting an element of idealism and creativity in any opportunities that come your way.

FINANCES, OTHER STUFF
Between February 8 and March 5, Venus transits fiery Aries, your solar eighth house. This transit should make it easier for you to obtain loans and mortgages, could bring a break in insurance or taxes, and could bring your partner a substantial raise. The eighth house governs other people's resources—those of your partner or spouse or anyone with whom you share expenses and resources.

Until October 5, Saturn continues its transit of Libra and your financial area. This transit has been going on for about two years now, so you should have a clear idea of its impact on your life. You're more serious about your finances now, may be learning how to stick to a budget, and the financial opportunities you have are grounded, serious, and could come to you through friends and acquaintances.

Uranus in Aries is opposed to Saturn, however, bringing a tension that is, at times, almost unbearable. You may feel a deep need to bust free.

CAREER

With Mercury transiting intuitive Pisces from February 13 to March 2, you're better able to follow your hunches and intuitive guidance. A partner may be helpful at this time too. Perhaps you and a business partner are better able to agree on the fundamentals of your cooperative venture.

ROMANCE

With Jupiter in fellow earth sign Taurus until June, you have many opportunities to expand your romantic options. These opportunities surface during foreign travel or while pursuing your educational interests. It's also possible to meet like-minded individuals in the arts and in publishing. Your resolve is strong now. Make it count.

BEST DAYS, CHALLENGING DAYS

On February 3, Neptune enters Pisces, your opposite sign. This lengthy transit is discussed in more detail in the Big Picture section for your sign. However, know that Neptune transits bring both confusion and heightened ideals. The voice of your higher self urges you to delve into your own creativity.

March—Virgo

LUNAR HIGHLIGHTS

The full moon in your sign on March 8 receives a friendly nod from Jupiter and another from Pluto, and Mars is widely conjunct. The combination of planets should make for an exciting, maybe even wild couple of days. News you receive should be positive and lift your spirits. Just be careful that you don't take on more than you can realistically handle.

The new moon in Aries on March 22 may not be your favorite unless you've got fire-sign planets. That said, this one should usher in new opportunities in resources you share with others. You may get a break on your taxes or insurance, your partner could land a plump raise, you may launch your own business or build a Web site. With Aries in this equation, there's always a chance for your great entrepreneurial spirit to shine forth.

FINANCES, OTHER STUFF
Between March 5 and April 3, Venus transits Taurus, joining Jupiter in that sign, and forms a beneficial angle to your sun. This transit should be good for your finances generally. You might, for instance, expand your business or services to overseas markets, travel abroad for business and combine it with pleasure. If you're starting a new business or signing contracts, be sure to get it done before the twelfth, when Mercury turns retrograde in Aries. Reread the Mercury retrograde section under the Big Picture for your sign.

CAREER
With both Jupiter and Venus in fellow earth sign Taurus, traveling together between March 5 and April 3, the repercussions for your career can only be positive. Even if there's a bit of excess occurring, you're placed to make professional strides. But there can be a tendency to think that things are moving along so well that you don't have to do much. Banish the thought! The more you act upon and flow with what's happening, the more beneficial this period is for your career.

ROMANCE
Again, it comes back to Venus and Jupiter traveling together through Taurus. Your love life should be spectacular during this period. Also, Neptune in Pisces is tossed into this mix, so that you're really looking for a relationship that fits your ideals and your highest hopes for yourself.

BEST DAYS, CHALLENGING DAYS
The full moon in your sign on March 8 will be as good or as challenging as you make it.

April—Virgo

LUNAR HIGHLIGHTS
On April 6, the full moon in Libra falls in your solar second house and brings financial news. Saturn is widely conjunct this new moon, suggesting that the news is serious, the kind of news that can change your life at fundamental levels. It sounds as if you come into some money, Virgo. Lottery? Inheritance? Pay raise? Tax break? Insurance settlement? All are possibilities.

The new moon in Taurus on April 21 is one to anticipate. There's plenty of forward thrust on or around the date of this new moon. It looks as if you have an opportunity to travel overseas, go to graduate school or college, or perhaps your novel is sold.

FINANCES, OTHER STUFF
The full moon in Libra on April 6 is the main financial indicator for the month. Keep in mind that Mercury turns direct on April 4, so you won't have to delay signing contracts for a loan, mortgage, whatever. Also, on the fourteenth, Mars finally turns direct in your sign, suggesting that things that had been delayed can now move forward again. Mars is your booster rocket, and when it's in your sign, you're in a good spot to make stuff happen.

CAREER
The professional indicators for this month look exceptionally nice. Between April 3 and May 15, Venus in Gemini transits the career area of your chart in direct motion. This transit brings out the best in your professional skills. Other people find you so clever and appealing that it's easy to gather the support you may need from coworkers and bosses.

With Mercury turning direct on April 4, you can finally move forward with projects, travel, pitches, and be assured that your ideas will be well received.

ROMANCE

With Venus now in Gemini and the career area of your chart, it's possible that an office flirtation heats up. Just be careful that you don't break hearts where you work, Virgo. Remember that once the romance is over, you still have to work in the same place as your ex.

If a relationship begins under this transit, the communication is apt to be strong and clear. That's always a good indication that you're on the right track.

GOOD DAYS, CHALLENGING DAYS

April 6. That full moon in Libra could go either way for you. It depends to some extent on how many air-sign planets you have in your natal chart and how social you are—that's the Libra part of the equation.

May—Virgo

LUNAR HIGHLIGHTS

The full moon in Scorpio on May 5 falls in your solar third house. This moon should bring news concerning a research project or investigation, about your siblings, your neighborhood, or a communication project. If you've been hunting for a new neighborhood in anticipation of a move, this full moon may help you find exactly the right location.

May 20 features a solar eclipse in Gemini, your career area. This eclipse should bring new professional opportunities and open new career doors. If you've been hunting for a new job, you may land the one you want on or around this date. Uranus forms a wide, beneficial angle to the eclipse degree, suggesting that opportunities surface suddenly and unexpectedly. All you have to do, Virgo, is be ready to seize them.

FINANCES, OTHER STUFF

Between May 15 and June 27, Venus is retrograde in Gemini, your career area.

During this period try not to purchase any large-ticket items—a car, computer, appliances. That said, it is possible to get some good deals during a Venus retrograde. We once bought a car during a Venus retrograde. It wasn't exactly what we wanted, but the price was right. A year later, we traded it in for close to what we had paid for it. In between, though, we discovered the car had been in an accident and had been repaired somewhere other than the dealer's garage, which canceled the warranty.

CAREER
The biggest career break this month comes with that solar eclipse on May 20. In addition, Mercury enters your career area on May 24, so your conscious mind is sharp, your communication skills are heightened. With Mars still in your sign, you've got plenty of get-up and go and are eager to move forward with your projects and ideas. This forward thrust continues until July 3. Make good use of it!

ROMANCE
Venus continues to be retrograde until June 27, which can cause some bumps and bruises in a relationship. Any relationship that begins during this Venus retrograde may not last forever, but it certainly should be interesting, particularly with Mars in your sign as well. Just take each day as it comes. Live moment to moment.

GOOD DAYS, CHALLENGING DAYS
May 15 could be challenging. It's the day that Venus turns retrograde in Gemini. Next month, Jupiter enters Gemini, and you're in for a whirlwind of expansion in your career.

June—Virgo

LUNAR HIGHLIGHTS
The lunar eclipse in Sagittarius on June 4 falls in your solar fourth house. This eclipse could bring news about your do-

mestic environment, your parents, the early part of your life. If your home is on the market, this eclipse could bring news about an offer. Or perhaps you close on a new home. Regardless of how events shake out, the eclipse should bring interesting turns of events.

June 19 features the second new moon in Gemini, in your career area. This one should bring new professional opportunities—a new job, new career path, new boss. Perhaps you launch your own business or quit your job to freelance. With Jupiter now in Gemini and your career area as well, you're in for a wonderful year professionally.

FINANCES, OTHER STUFF

Mercury transits compatible water sign Cancer from June 7 to 25. This transit brings an intuitive flow to your conscious mind that enables you to make decisions quickly, by just checking with your feelings. During this period leave your social calendar open; the people you meet can be helpful professionally and some of them may become lifelong friends.

On the twenty-fifth, Mercury enters Leo, a fire sign, and your conscious mind is suddenly inflamed with passions. This transit lasts until August 31, and Mercury will be retrograde between July 14 and August 8. Plan your travel on either side of those dates.

CAREER

Jupiter is the planet of luck and expansion. While it's moving through your career area, you're in the right place at the right time and meet exactly the right people. There can be excesses with this transit, which is the one thing you should guard against. Don't assume so much responsibility that you become overburdened. Learn to pace yourself, be sure to express your gratitude and appreciation, and take nothing for granted! Just because you now have Jupiter in your career court, it's a mistake to figure you don't have to make any effort.

ROMANCE
The best day this month for romance? June 27, when Venus turns direct again. Things could still be a bit tense between you and your partner even after this happens. But once Venus stabilizes, you and your honey are back on track.

BEST DAYS, CHALLENGING DAYS
Saturn turns direct in Libra on June 25. This movement should be very good for your finances. Checks that were delayed now arrive, and perhaps a raise is in the stars!

July—Virgo

LUNAR HIGHLIGHTS
On July 3, the full moon in fellow earth sign Capricorn brings news about a romantic relationship, a creative project, or about your children. It could also bring news about whatever you do for fun and pleasure. Pluto forms a close conjunction with this moon, suggesting that the news you hear is transformative, powerful.

The new moon in compatible water sign Cancer on July 19 attracts new social opportunities and opportunities connected to your home and family. People you meet on or around the time of this new moon are important in a larger scheme of things, and you may feel a deep intuitive connection with them.

FINANCES, OTHER STUFF
Mercury entered Leo and your twelfth house on June 25, and on July 14 it turns retrograde. By now you know the best way to navigate these retrograde periods. But in the event you need to refresh your memory, reread the Big Picture section on Mercury retrogrades. In terms of your finances, be sure to have contracts signed before the retrograde begins. Ditto for travel plans.

Between July 3 and August 23, Mars transits Libra and your financial area. This transit brings a lot of forward thrust in terms of money. You could take a second job, for instance, or be working longer hours to meet some sort of deadline. Or perhaps your precision and skills earn the praise of your boss, and you receive a raise.

CAREER
Despite Jupiter's expansive efforts on your behalf, the Mercury retrograde could throw a wrench into plans. What you're proposing at work, for example, may not get the attention it deserves. Or your pitch is delayed for some reason. Try not to obsess about the small snafus you encounter. Things will straighten out once Mercury turns direct on August 8.

ROMANCE
With Venus now moving direct, it continues its trek through Gemini, traveling with Jupiter through your career area, until August 7. The interesting thing about the Venus/Jupiter combination is that they support each other, urging you to seek new, expansive relationships. If you become involved during this transit, communication will be important in the relationship and may even dominate your priorities.

BEST DAYS, CHALLENGING DAYS
July 3. You'll feel the distinct change in energy when Mars enters compatible water sign Cancer. Your intuition should ramp up; you'll feel more in the flow of life.

August—Virgo

LUNAR HIGHLIGHTS
August could be a wild ride! There are two full moons and a new moon this month, and with that kind of lunar activity, you will be hopping, for sure.

On August 1, the full moon in air sign Aquarius occurs in your solar sixth house. This full moon could create a little lunacy in your daily work schedule. Both Mars and Aries form beneficial angles to this moon, suggesting that news you hear occurs suddenly, unexpectedly. Jupiter forms an exact and beneficial angle to this full moon, so the news looks positive. Even the lunacy looks positive!

The new moon in Leo on August 17 falls in your solar twelfth house. This one should usher in new opportunities to delve into your own psyche, your own unconscious. What you discover about yourself enables you to showcase your skills and talents.

On August 31, the full moon in Pisces, your opposite sign, highlights a partnership—business or romantic. Neptune is widely conjunct this moon, so there may be some confusion about this partnership, or you're acting from a place of idealism.

FINANCES, OTHER STUFF

On August 8, Mercury turns direct, always a welcome change. So sign your contracts, finalize your travel plans, apply for your loans, mortgages. With Saturn now direct in your financial area, you should be getting back on track with money—living within your budget, paying with cash, paying down debt—and visualizing more money coming in.

CAREER

Uranus turns retrograde on July 13. This movement tends to taken Uranian energy inward, so you may have unusual thoughts and ideas. Be sure to record them for future use. Uranus in Aries and Jupiter in Gemini are moving in favorable angles to each other, suggesting that professional matters continue to expand, but in unforeseen ways.

ROMANCE

On August 7, Venus enters compatible water sign Cancer. Your social calendar quickly gets crowded, and you have your pick of parties and festivities. Get out and about as much as possible. You could meet interesting romantic prospects through friends and any groups to which you belong. This transit lasts until September 6.

BEST DAYS, CHALLENGING DAYS
Mercury turning direct on August 8 is cause to celebrate!

September—Virgo

LUNAR HIGHLIGHTS
The new moon in your sign on September 15 is one to anticipate. This moon occurs only once a year and sets the tone for the next twelve months, so it's worthwhile to prepare for it. Make a wish board that visually depicts what you would like to experience and achieve in the course of the next year. Do some sort of ritual about these dreams and goals. Then release your desires and trust that the universe will be your greatest ally in bringing them about.

September 29 features a full moon in Aries, your solar eighth house. Uranus is closely conjunct to this moon, so the combination should be quite powerful. Possibilities? Unexpected events that come out of the blue, encountering unusual individuals, a flood of eccentric, perhaps even brilliant ideas. Expect a lot of excitement.

FINANCES, OTHER STUFF
This Aries full moon brings focus to resources you share with others—a spouse, partner, child. There could be some disagreement about who is spending what and when. But just take a few deep breaths and detach emotionally from the situation, if you can. This moon is apt to make you restless and impatient, which will be reflected in the people around you.

CAREER
Venus transits Leo from August 31 to September 16 and forms a beneficial angle to Jupiter in your career area. Things should go very much your way now, with other people looking to you for answers, insights, guidance. Other people find you and your ideas appealing too, which makes it easier to gain acceptance for your various projects and

ideas. With Mercury, your ruler, now in your sign, everything you say sounds brilliant and cutting edge. Your precision and attention to details are remarkable. Once Mercury enters Libra after September 16, you may be more consciously focused on financial matters.

ROMANCE
Pluto continues its trek through Capricorn and the romance area of your chart. This long transit—until 2024—is altering your romantic relationships at a profound level. It's also changing what you do for fun and pleasure. You may find that you're more focused on making your time count! You could be attracting romantic interests who reflect your new needs and desires.

GOOD DAYS, CHALLENGING DAYS
With Mercury in your sign until September 16, you're on a definite roll, Virgo. Make it count.

October—Virgo

LUNAR HIGHLIGHTS
With the new moon in Libra on October 15, your finances are highlighted in a very good way. This new moon should attract new financial opportunities. Your income increases—perhaps through a raise, the repayment of a loan, by paying off a car or mortgage. Jupiter forms a wide, beneficial angle to the moon, so the opportunities that surface will expand your income in significant ways.

The October 29 full moon in fellow earth sign Taurus should be quite splendid for you, too. There could be news about a trip abroad, about some new creative project you're involved in, or even about an educational goal you have. Taurus ramps up your resolve to manifest your desires, whatever they may be.

FINANCES, OTHER STUFF
The big financial news this month centers around the new moon in Libra and your money area. In addition, Mars enters fire sign Sagittarius on October 6, so between then and November 16, you've got a handle on the bigger picture of your domestic situation. Certain things are becoming more clear to you, and these things could involve money—how others spend what you earn (teenagers? a partner?) and how you spend what you earn. Take stock, Virgo. If you don't like what you see, take steps to change it.

CAREER
With Venus in your sign between October 3 and 28, you're in rare form. You seem to know exactly where you're headed professionally—and personally. It's as if the various aspects that constitute your personality are all on the same page. It's a nice change, isn't it? Also, on October 5, Saturn enters Scorpio for a run of about two and a half years. Scorpio, as a water sign that's compatible with your earth-sign sun, will help to stabilize your conscious life and bring structure to where structure is needed.

ROMANCE
With Venus in your sign between October 3 and 28, you're in one of the most romantic and creative periods all year. Your personal relationships should hum along at a pleasing pace, your muse is up close and personal, and you're feeling happy with where you are. When you're happy in this way, your life in general seems to work better!

BEST DAYS, CHALLENGING DAYS
The best days? October 3 to 28, when Venus is in your sign.

November—Virgo

LUNAR HIGHLIGHTS
The solar eclipse in Scorpio on November 13 should be positive for you. New opportunities surface related to education, consciousness, your daily routine. You might, for instance, have a chance to attend a workshop or seminar on consciousness and self-improvement; could launch a research or investigation project; and may have an opportunity to alter your daily routine from the ground up.

The lunar eclipse in Gemini on November 28 occurs in your career area. This should be quite an interesting eclipse for you. Jupiter is closely conjunct to this moon, suggesting that your feelings are expansive and positive, so it looks as if news you hear around this time is good. The news is related to your career and communication.

FINANCES, OTHER STUFF
Between October 28 and November 21, Venus transits Libra and your financial area. You could get a raise, a second job that pays well, or could find a new earning venue that surprises you. With this transit, you may also be tempted to spend more, but it's likely you'll be earning more as well.

Mars enters Capricorn, a fellow earth sign, on November 16. This transit, which lasts until December 15, should ramp up your love life. Your sexuality is highlighted. Since Mars is traveling with Pluto, you're in a powerful position to call the shots.

CAREER
Mercury transits Sagittarius between October 29 and December 31. It is retrograde between November 6 and 26, in your solar fourth house. During this transit you may feel conflicted about your responsibilities at home and your responsibilities at work. You'll be inclined to discuss it at some length with people involved. This transit expands your conscious mind and pumps you up, Virgo, creating excitement about some new idea, relationship, or situation.

ROMANCE
Venus transits Scorpio between November 21 and December 15 and will be forming a beneficial angle with Mars for much of this time. The combination should add spice and excitement to your love life. If you're not involved at this time and would like to be in a relationship, then be sure to get out and about, opening up your options. Go to places you don't usually go. Try new things. Be adventurous.

BEST DAYS, CHALLENGING DAYS
November 6: Mercury turns retrograde in Sagittarius, the last retrograde of 2012!

December—Virgo

LUNAR HIGHLIGHTS
On December 13, the new moon in Sagittarius falls in your solar fourth house. This moon brings new opportunities in your domestic situation, with foreign travel and business dealings, and in publishing and higher education. You may move, someone could move into your home or out of it, your family expands (a birth!) or there is some other change in your family.

The full moon in Cancer on December 28 sets you up nicely for New Year's Eve. Keep your social calendar open around this time, and go with the flow. Do what feels right and pleasant. Follow your intuition.

FINANCES, OTHER STUFF
Now is the time to look back on 2012 and see how far you have come, how you have achieved your goals and dreams. Take stock. Then look forward to 2013. What would you like to achieve in the coming year? How much would you like to earn next year? Create a wish board for 2013. Post it somewhere you'll see it often.

CAREER
With Jupiter in Gemini and your career area until June 2013, it's possible to make significant professional strides. If you're looking for a new job or career path, then that can happen too. Be clear about your desires and intentions, maintain an upbeat, positive attitude, and let the universe do its work in bringing about the manifestations of your desires.

ROMANCE
From December 15 to early January 2013, Venus transits Sagittarius and your solar fourth house. This transit brings plenty of passion into your love life. You could get involved with someone at work or with someone you meet through work. Again, be clear about your desires and intentions regarding romance and love. The clearer your intentions, the quicker the universe responds.

BEST DAYS, CHALLENGING DAYS
Mars enters Aquarius on December 25, so there could be a definite shift in your physical energy. By year's end, all planets are moving in direct motion, i.e., functioning as they should.

Happy New Year!

8

Libra

The Big Picture in 2012

Welcome to 2012, Libra. It's a year of innovation, intellectual curiosity, research, communication. It's also a year when your closest partnerships in business and in romance undergo abrupt change. Let's take a closer look.

Pluto, the slowest-moving planet in the zodiac, starts off the year in Capricorn, in your solar fourth house, where it has consistently been since November 2008. You're accustomed to its energy now. Its transit, which lasts until 2024, is bringing profound and permanent change globally, evident in the economic challenges that now face the U.S. Most institutions are in the throes of great change—the health-care industry, the petroleum and insurance industries, mortgages/lending, housing, aviation, even the Internet. You name it, and Pluto's fingerprint can be found.

On a personal level, this planet's transit through that area of your chart that represents home and family, will continue to transform these things at profound levels. You may start a family, or your kids leave home as adults. One of your parents moves in with you or needs additional help and support. You move. Get married or divorced. The specifics that unfold with this transit depend on your age and circumstances. But profound change is certain.

Neptune entered Pisces and your solar sixth house on April 4, 2011. But by early August 2011, it had slipped back into Aquarius. On February 3, 2012, it enters Pisces again and won't move on until January 2026. This transit forms an angle to your sun that demands an attitude adjustment with your daily work routine. It is a challenging angle, so its initial impact can create confusion. For hints about what this may mean for you, look back to that period in 2011 when Neptune was in Pisces.

Neptune symbolizes our higher ideals, escapism, fiction, spirituality, and our blind spots. It seeks to dissolve boundaries between us and others. One possible repercussion of this transit is prolonged religious wars, which proliferated during Uranus's transit in Pisces from early 2003.

On a personal level, though, Neptune's transit through your solar sixth house indicates that you will try to integrate your ideals and spiritual beliefs more readily into your daily work routine. Since the sixth house also deals with the maintenance of your health, you may be trying alternative therapies for health stuff—anything from acupuncture to homeopathy. If you are diagnosed with any ailment, get a second opinion. Neptune lends itself to plenty of confusion, and a misdiagnosis is possible during this transit.

Uranus entered Aries and your solar seventh house in March 2011. One repercussion of this transit is that unusual and exciting people are going to be entering your life and shaking things up. Your business and personal partnerships are about to undergo radical and unexpected changes.

Saturn begins the year in your sign. It has been there since the summer of 2010 and will be there until October 2012. This transit brings greater structure to your life, but can also indicate delays, restrictions. You are urged to live up to your responsibilities and obligations.

Once Saturn enters water sign Scorpio on October 5, your attention turns toward finances—what you earn, what you spend, your budget, your values. This transit is apt to be emotionally intense, as is the nature of Scorpio, but also intuitive, psychic. You may have hunches about how to earn more money, about creating a financial niche for yourself. Follow those hunches.

One of your best periods falls between June 11, 2012,

and June 25, 2013, when Jupiter transits fellow air sign Gemini. This transit provides an expansive foundation for what will follow when Jupiter enters Cancer and your solar tenth house of career in 2013. Every seed you plant during this period, every thought you change, every belief you fine-tune will produce results down the road, but will also broaden your outlook about what is possible in your life overall.

It highlights higher education, publishing, overseas travel, foreign cultures. It's possible that your company's products or your services/products expand to overseas markets. You may be traveling overseas more frequently, which opens your consciousness to new experiences, thoughts, ideas.

From January 1 to June 11, when Jupiter transits earth sign Taurus and your solar eighth house, everything connected to mortgages, loans, taxes, and insurance will go your way. Nice change, right? Also, your partner's income should expand in a major way. Your own psychic and intuitive abilities will deepen. Other people will be ready and willing to share their time, expertise, and money with you.

They say that timing is everything, so with that in mind let's look at some specific areas in your life in 2012.

ROMANCE/CREATIVITY

The most romantic and creative time for you all year falls between October 28 and November 21, when Venus transits your sign. Think: appeal, seduction, popularity, artistic flow. You feel more sensual, your self-confidence soars. Other people pick up what you radiate and respond accordingly. If you're in a committed relationship, then you and your partner rediscover each other. Plan a trip out of town, to some secluded, romantic spot. Spend time together doing whatever you both enjoy.

Other good periods: April 3 to May 15 and June 27 to August 7, when Venus is moving direct in fellow air sign Gemini. Your communication abilities are ramped up; you're in your creative groove, Libra. The best time for serious involvement and deepening commitment in an existing relationship occurs when Venus transits Aries and your solar seventh house of partnerships. This happens between February 8 and March 5. You and your partner may decide to move in together, get engaged, or get married. Just be sure that you don't do any of this under a Mercury retrograde period. Take a look under the appropriate section below to find out when Mercury will be retrograde this year.

Other good backup dates: September 16 to October 5, when Mars transits your sign.

CAREER

Usually Venus and Jupiter transits to your career area are the times to look for. Jupiter doesn't transit that area this year, but in 2013 it will, so now is the time to sow the seeds for whatever you desire professionally in 2013.

Between August 7 and September 6, Venus transits Cancer and your career area. This is the time to pitch your ideas and garner support among coworkers for your projects. Others are open and receptive to your insights and ideas, and it's much easier to move ahead with specific projects. A raise or promotion could be in the offing, too. Fortunately, Mercury turns direct on August 8, so you enjoy the full benefit of Venus's transit.

Even though Jupiter doesn't transit your career area until 2013, during its transit through Taurus it forms a beneficial angle to your career area. Your professional responsibilities expand, your worldview deepens and broadens, and the people you meet and draw into your professional sphere will be experts.

Another nice period is when Mercury transits your career area between June 7 and 25. This is the time to pitch ideas, push your agenda forward, travel related to work, and socialize with peers. It also favors all professional communication.

Between July 3 and August 23, Mars transits your sign, linking up with Saturn in your sign too.

BEST TIMES FOR
Buying or selling a home: November 16 to December 25, when Mars transits Capricorn and your solar fourth house. Between January 8 and 27, Mercury transits the same sign and house.

Family reunions: Any of the dates above or when Venus is in your sign between October 28 and November 21.

Financial matters: The period from November 21 to December 15, when Venus transits Scorpio and your solar second house.

Signing contracts: When Mercury is moving direct!

MERCURY RETROGRADES
Every year Mercury—the planet of communication and travel—turns retrograde three times. During this period it's wise not to sign contracts (unless you don't mind renegotiating when Mercury is moving direct), to check and recheck travel plans or, better yet, don't travel, and to communicate as succinctly as possible. Refrain from buying any large-ticket items or electronics during this time too. Often computers and appliances go on the fritz, cars act up, data is lost ... you get the idea. Be sure to back up all files before the dates below:

March 12–April 4: Mercury retrograde in Aries, your seventh house—partnerships.

July 14–August 8: Mercury retrograde in Leo, your solar eleventh house—groups, friends.

November 6–26: Mercury retrograde in Sagittarius, your solar third house of communication, travel, siblings.

ECLIPSES
Solar eclipses tend to trigger external events that bring about change according to the sign and house in which they fall. Lunar eclipses trigger inner, emotional events according to the sign and house in which they fall. Any eclipse marks both beginnings and endings. The solar and lunar eclipse in a pair falls in opposite signs. If you're interested in detailed information on eclipses, take a look at Celeste

Teal's excellent and definitive book, *Eclipses: Predicting World Events & Personal Transformation.*

If you were born under or around the time of an eclipse, it's to your advantage to take a look at your birth chart to find out exactly where the eclipses will impact you.

Most years feature four eclipses—two solar, two lunar, with the set separated by about two weeks. In November and December 2011, there were solar and lunar eclipses, so this year the first eclipses fall during May and June.

May 20: Solar eclipse at 0 degrees Gemini. This one should bring in new opportunities for foreign travel, education, publishing, and expressing your spiritual beliefs and worldview.

June 4: Lunar eclipse in Sagittarius, your solar third house. News that arrives around this time is positive.

November 13: Solar eclipse in Scorpio, your solar second house. New financial opportunities.

November 28: Lunar eclipse, Gemini. Jupiter forms a five-degree conjunction to the eclipse degree, suggesting that news you receive around this time will be cause for celebration!

LUCKIEST DAY OF THE YEAR

Every year there's one day when Jupiter and the sun meet up, and luck, serendipity, and expansion are the hallmarks. This year that day falls on May 13, with a conjunction in Taurus.

January—Libra

LUNAR HIGHLIGHTS

The full moon in Cancer on January 9 brings news concerning your career. Mars forms a close and beneficial angle to this full moon, suggesting lots of activity and forward thrust. Your intuition, particularly regarding career matters, should be quite strong. Power issues could surface, though, so be sure not to blow things out of proportion.

The new moon on January 23 falls in fellow air sign

Aquarius and promises a new romantic relationship, new venues for pleasure and fun, and cutting edge ideas. It occurs in your solar fifth house of romance and pleasure. Circle this date. This new moon should be quite good for you.

FINANCES, OTHER STUFF
Mercury transits Capricorn and your solar fourth house between January 8 and 27, so you're going to be more goal oriented and determined to make 2012 the best year ever. Your goals may start at home, within your domestic environment, but will impact other areas of your life too. You may decide to revamp your work schedule in some way to accommodate these new goals.

Saturn is still in your sign, urging you to meet your responsibilities and commitments, something you typically don't have any problem doing. On October 5, Saturn will enter Scorpio and your financial area, so between now and then be sure to stick to your budget and continue to save your money. With Jupiter in Taurus until June 11, your partner may land a plump raise or you may get a break on insurance, taxes.

CAREER
The big career news this month is the new moon in Cancer, your career area. But there're some other things going on too that we should look at. Between January 14 and February 8, Venus transits Pisces and forms a beneficial angle to the career sector of your chart. This would be an ideal time to push your professional agenda forward, to pitch your ideas, submit your manuscripts. Others are receptive to you and your ideas, and you shouldn't have any trouble gaining support.

ROMANCE
An office flirtation may heat up between January 14 and February 8, with Venus's transit through Pisces and the area of your chart that governs your daily work routine. Also, for part of this time, Mercury will be in Capricorn, an earth sign compatible with Pisces, so there will be good

communication between you and a romantic interest. Mars remains in Virgo and your solar twelfth house until July 3, stirring up your unconscious, bringing old relationship and sexuality issues to the surface.

BEST DAYS, CHALLENGING DAYS
That new moon in your career area on January 23 is a day to anticipate. There could be new opportunities headed your way for a few days on either side of the new moon.

February—Libra

LUNAR HIGHLIGHTS
The full moon in Leo on February 7 should be exciting for you. As a fire sign, Leo is compatible with your air-sign sun and encourages you not to be shy about your skills and talents. There could be news about a friendship or a group to which you belong or news about something that enables you to achieve your dreams.

The new moon in Pisces on February 21 should attract new work opportunities that allow you to express your ideals in a more open fashion. If you've been looking for a job, this new moon could bring the right one your way. Your intuition deepens, so be sure to follow your hunches.

FINANCES, OTHER STUFF
Neptune enters Pisces on February 3, a lengthy transit that lasts for fourteen years. Read more about it in the Big Picture section for your sign. It forms a beneficial angle to your financial area, which suggests that your ideals will become more and more important to you and that you'll strive to integrate them into the way you earn your living. Between February 13 and March 2, Mercury joins Neptune in Pisces. This transit suggests an intuitive bent to your mind that can prove quite valuable in the way you earn and invest your money.

CAREER

Between February 8 and March 5, Venus transits Aries, your opposite sign. This transit favors partnerships—business and personal. If you're in contract negotiations, then things turn out in your favor. You win the finer points you wanted in the negotiation. If you're in business for yourself, then you may find exactly the right partner for a venture. Aries is an entrepreneurial sign, so you're the trailblazer now.

ROMANCE

With Venus in Aries between February 8 and March 5, your love life with your significant other should be passionate and exciting. You could feel somewhat possessive and jealous too, so be careful to keep those negative passions in check. Also, Venus is traveling with Uranus now, which can bring about sudden, unexpected events. Be on your toes, Libra!

BEST DAYS, CHALLENGING DAYS

February 3, when Neptune enters Pisces, could feel a bit strange. You might be disoriented or confused about certain issues. You could feel as if your head is stuffed with cotton! The feeling will pass.

March—Libra

LUNAR HIGHLIGHTS

The full moon in Virgo on March 8 occurs in the most secretive part of your chart. Mars forms a seven-degree conjunction, so you can expect a lot of activity internally. Your psyche and your unconscious are bubbling with issues, dreams, stuff that's coming up, seemingly out of nowhere. Just go with the flow.

The new moon in Aries on March 22 occurs in your partnership area. This should attract new partnership opportunities—in romance and business. Both Mercury and Uranus form close conjunctions to this new moon, so it's likely that sudden, unexpected events will be part of this lunar equation. Expect a lot of discussions, too.

FINANCES, OTHER STUFF

The financial focus this month is on resources you share with others. Your romantic partner could land a significant raise, you might inherit money, get a tax or insurance break, or sell an artistic project. Venus transits Taurus and your solar eighth house from March 5 to April 3, bringing luck and serendipity into the financial arena. Now would be a great time to apply for a mortgage or a loan. Just be sure to do it on either side of the Mercury retrograde in Aries, which runs from March 12 to April 4.

CAREER

Things may slow down between March 12 and April 4, when Mercury is retrograde in Aries, your opposite sign. Your business partner may be reluctant to commit time and energy to a project you hold dear. Your boss may not be as receptive to an idea as you had hoped. You get the idea here. During the retrograde period, don't tackle anything new. Don't launch new projects. Just bide your time and wait until after April 4 to move forward again.

ROMANCE

With Uranus continuing its journey through Aries and your solar seventh house, there can be upsets in existing relationships. However, there's also the possibility of tremendous excitement and daring, with many unexpected twists and turns in the relationship. Go with the flow. Try not to second-guess the universe about what's going on. With Mercury retrograde in the partnership area from March 12 to April 4, misunderstandings can develop. Be sure to communicate as clearly and precisely as possible.

BEST DAYS, CHALLENGING DAYS

Reread the drill for Mercury retrograde under the Big Picture section for your sign. Follow the suggestions so that you can mitigate the impact of the retrograde. March 12, the day the retrograde begins, could be a confusing day.

April—Libra

LUNAR HIGHLIGHTS
The full moon in your sign on April 6 should light up your social calendar and bring news of a personal nature that should lift your spirits. Saturn forms a wide conjunction to this moon, suggesting that the news you hear or the insights you gain are solid.

The new moon in Taurus on April 21 brings new opportunities for your partner's earnings or with insurance and tax issues. It's also possible that you have a chance to delve into metaphysics, perhaps through a workshop or seminar on some facet of the field that interests you.

FINANCES, OTHER STUFF
Venus enters fellow air sign Gemini on April 3 and will be there until August 7. This long transit is due to the fact that Venus will be retrograde between May 15 and June 27. On either side of those dates, though, your financial picture should improve, you may have an opportunity to travel overseas, and your communication abilities really shine. This would be a favorable time for starting a blog or building a Web site.

CAREER
With Venus in fellow air sign Gemini, your communication abilities bring you to a new level of professional recognition. You may travel abroad for business or do business with foreign countries. Your business or services could easily expand to foreign markets. Once Jupiter enters Gemini on June 11, you're in for a real treat. Your worldview will expand appreciably, and once that happens, everything else begins to expand, too.

ROMANCE

A romance is possible with someone from a different country or perhaps occurs while you're traveling. If you're not in a committed relationship now, keep your options open. Others find you attractive and interesting during Venus's transit through Gemini, so capitalize on it, Libra!

BEST DAYS, CHALLENGING DAYS

Mercury turns direct on April 4. It's safe to pack your bags and hit the road again.

May—Libra

LUNAR HIGHLIGHTS

The full moon in Scorpio on May 5 falls in your financial area. Expect news about your finances, research, and motives—yours or other people's. Pluto forms a wide, beneficial angle to this full moon, suggesting that power issues may surface, but you're in a perfect spot to deal with them.

The new moon on May 20 is a solar eclipse in Gemini, the equivalent of a double new moon in your solar ninth house. New opportunities should surface in terms of higher education, publishing, foreign travel. Your business or service could expand to overseas markets, you may have an opportunity to travel overseas for business or pleasure, and a new writing project could be headed your way.

FINANCES, OTHER STUFF

With Venus turning retrograde in Gemini on May 15, be sure to get your financial ducks in order before that date. If you're in the market for a mortgage or car loan, settle things before May 15 or after June 27. Avoid purchasing large-ticket items during the retrograde period.

Between May 9 and 24, Mercury transits Taurus and your solar eighth house, so the period between May 9 and

14 would be ideal for applying for mortgages, loans. You'll have the presence of mind to negotiate for a good deal.

CAREER
Until July 3, Mars continues its journey through Virgo and forms a beneficial angle to your career area. Your precision and attention to details during this period are nothing short of remarkable. Your physical energy, particularly as it relates to career matters, is excellent. You're highly motivated.

ROMANCE
Romance during Venus's retrograde may be challenging at times. You and your partner may not see eye to eye on certain aspects of your relationship. If you're not involved, then stay clear of involvement until after June 27. But since it's impossible to live life entirely by what the stars are doing, don't hold back if you meet someone interesting. Just understand that the relationship may not last forever. So enjoy it moment to moment.

BEST DAYS, CHALLENGING DAYS
May 15. Challenging. Definite change in energy.

June—Libra

LUNAR HIGHLIGHTS
June 4 features a lunar eclipse in Sagittarius, your solar third house. This eclipse brings news about a sibling or something in your daily routine, and the news looks positive. Saturn forms a strong and beneficial angle to the eclipse degree, suggesting that the news isn't whimsical and should benefit you.

June 19 features the second new moon this year in Gemini, in your solar ninth house. This one looks especially good, bringing new opportunities for foreign travel, education, publishing, and with communication. Just eight days before this new moon, Jupiter enters Gemini for a year-long run that should prove to be quite terrific for you!

FINANCES, OTHER STUFF
Jupiter transits fellow air sign Gemini from June 11, 2011, to June 25, 2013. This period should be expansive and lucky for you. Read more about it in the Big Picture section for your sign. It's to your advantage to look at your natal chart and find out where Gemini falls. If, for instance, Gemini is on the cusp of your second house, then you'll reap financial benefits from this transit—but could also be spending more. If Gemini is on the cusp of your tenth house, then your career will benefit.

CAREER
Between June 7 and 25, Mercury transits Cancer and your solar tenth house. This transit favors all your professional endeavors. Pitch your ideas, push your own agenda forward, socialize with coworkers, do whatever you need to do during this period to advance yourself. This isn't to say that you should be pushy or obnoxious, just clear cut in your communications. Have you priorities in line. Know what you desire.

ROMANCE
Venus turns direct on June 27. Any delays you've been experiencing in your life, any disagreements, challenges and so on should now begin to straighten out. Next month, Mars enters your sign, Libra, so you'll have more physical energy and will feel revved up and excited about the direction in which your love life—and your life generally—is headed.

BEST DAYS, CHALLENGING DAYS
You'll breathe more easily after June 27, when Venus straightens out. Another day to watch for is June 25, when Saturn in your sign turns direct again. This movement should improve the structures in your life and enable you to make more concrete and realistic goals.

July—Libra

LUNAR HIGHLIGHTS
The full moon in Capricorn on July 3 occurs in your solar fourth house. Lots of activity connected to your home and domestic environment. Pluto is closely conjunct to this moon, so the goals you're setting or the rules you're laying down are serious, transformational. This might be a good time to quit a habit—smoking, overeating, whatever it is. You might want to start an exercise regimen if you don't have one already.

The new moon in Cancer on July 19 is a beauty for your career. Some possibilities: new job, new career path, new ideas about what you'd like to be doing professionally, new professional contacts, you launch your own business. You get the idea here. Be ready for a whole new chapter in your career.

FINANCES, OTHER STUFF
Mars transits your sign, Libra, from July 3 to August 23. During this period, you've got more physical energy, more get-up and go. Your focus should be quite powerful, and you'll act as a magnet to attract the right people at the right time. You may be more motivated than ever to increase your earnings and could take a second job, land a significant raise, or go into business with someone else.

CAREER
The Mars transit through Libra and the transits of Jupiter and Venus through Gemini are all helpful to you this month. However, Mercury turns retrograde in Leo on July 14 and remains that way until August 8. So get to your professional endeavors and pitches on either side of those dates. During the retrograde, tend to unfinished business rather than starting something brand new.

ROMANCE
Be sure that during the Mercury retrograde period you communicate clearly, succinctly. The possibility of misunderstandings is greater during a retrograde period. That

said, with Mars in your sign, your sexuality will be heightened, and you'll be in a social frame of mind.

BEST DAYS, CHALLENGING DAYS
Challenging: July 14, when Mercury turns retrograde in Leo, and July 13, when Uranus turns retrograde in Aries. The first impacts your friendships and communication, the second impacts your partnerships, both business and personal.

August—Libra

LUNAR HIGHLIGHTS
It's a hectic month and may contain a tad of lunacy too, so buckle up, Libra. With two full moons and a new moon, you're going to be busy. August first features a full moon in fellow air sign Aquarius, your solar fifth house of romance. This full moon should bring news about or insight into a romantic relationship or news about what you do for fun and pleasure. News about your children is also possible. Mars in your sign and Jupiter in Gemini form beneficial angles to this full moon, suggesting a lot of activity and expansion, serendipity, synchronicity, and luck.

The new moon on August 17 falls in compatible fire sign Leo and attracts new friendship opportunities as well as new opportunities to reach for and achieve your dreams. Saturn and Mars form strong, beneficial angles to this new moon. You're in the right time and place.

On August 31, the full moon in water sign Pisces brings news about your daily work routine. There could be some confusion about your daily work—perhaps you don't have all the information you need, or perhaps there's some deception that has to be dug out and exposed.

FINANCES, OTHER STUFF
Mercury turns direct on August 8, so everything starts straightening out, even your finances. Just as important

is that on August 23, Mars enters Scorpio and your financial area. This transit, which lasts until October 6, brings heightened activity around your earnings—what you earn, how much you spend, and your attitudes toward money. If you've been hoping for a raise, now you display all the talents and skills you have to prove that you're worth it! Of course, people with whom you work already know your worth.

CAREER
August 7 to September 6 marks an important time for you professionally. Venus transits Cancer and your career area, so things really begin to turn your way. Other people find you and your ideas appealing, your intuitive grasp of relationships proves helpful, and your charm wins over even the skeptics.

ROMANCE
Back to Venus. With this planet transiting your career area for three weeks, you may be easily distracted by an office flirtation. Decide early on what your priorities are—romance or career. You can have both, but your professional focus is important now. Maybe keep the two separate?

In addition, Mars is in passionate Scorpio until October, so your sexuality is heightened. Another distraction?

BEST DAYS, CHALLENGING DAYS
Circle August 8. Mercury turns direct in Leo. In another few months, Saturn will be leaving your sign and entering Scorpio. The exact date is October 5. Keep this in mind as you continue to maintain your budget and save money.

September—Libra

LUNAR HIGHLIGHTS
The new moon in Virgo on September 15 occurs in your solar twelfth house, the most secretive part of your chart.

Mercury forms a close conjunction with this new moon, suggesting that opportunities which surface may be concerned with communication—writing, public speaking. You may have an opportunity to enter therapy, if you're so inclined, or may start a blog or Web site about inner motives, the unconscious, synchronicity.

The full moon in Aries on September 29 occurs in your opposite sign, your solar seventh house. This moon should bring news about a partnership—romantic or personal. Since Uranus is closely conjunct, the news catches you by surprise. Pluto forms a challenging angle to this full moon, so there could be power issues or deeply transformative events that occur around the end of September.

FINANCES, OTHER STUFF

Mars entered Scorpio and your financial area on August 23 and won't move on again until October 6. During this period you spend a lot of time working, thinking about money and what you earn, and what your priorities are. You're after a bottom line regarding your finances—a bottom line that you hope to earn this year, a bottom line in what you spend. Is your budget working? With Venus in compatible fire sign Leo until October 3, your natural charm works very much in your favor. You seem to have your finger on the public pulse and may be able to translate that into increased earnings.

CAREER

From September 16 to October 6, Mercury is in your sign, so you're the one with the golden tongue. Words simply pour out of you—a wellspring of wisdom, humor, and good will. Your aesthetic and artistic tastes are heightened, and it's easy to convince others about the validity of your ideas and projects. Use this time period to pitch new ideas, ask for a raise or promotion, or even to look for a new job, if that's what you're after.

ROMANCE

With Venus in Leo between the dates mentioned above, your next romantic adventure may be with someone you now regard as a friend. The friendship could take a new, unexpected turn, perhaps as a result of a prolonged conversation about the meaning of life and the universe! You're somehow more on stage during this period, your confidence heightened.

BEST DAYS, CHALLENGING DAYS

The full moon in Aries on September 29 could catch you off guard. Just be vigilant for surprises.

October—Libra

LUNAR HIGHLIGHTS

The new moon in your sign on October 15 happens just once a year and sets the tone for the next twelve months. It's worth preparing for—make a wish list, a wish board, some sort of visual depiction of your desires. Jupiter forms a close, beneficial angle to this new moon, indicative of expansion and luck. New personal opportunities surface, and you're in the right time and place.

The full moon in Taurus on October 29 falls in your solar eighth house of shared resources. This moon brings news about a partner's income or an inheritance, insurance or tax matter. Pluto forms a strong and beneficial angle to this full moon, suggesting that you're in a strong position to get what you want.

FINANCES, OTHER STUFF

With Saturn still in your sign, now traveling with Venus, your financial situation should be more stable than it has been recently. Venus sometimes urges us to spend on extravagant items. If you do so, just be sure you've got money in the bank to pay for the item. You seem to be keeping to your budget and may discover that around the time of the new moon, you land a raise.

Mercury transits Scorpio and your financial area between October 5 and 29, so there seems to be a lot of discussion about money, your earnings, your budget.

CAREER
With Jupiter continuing its transit of fellow air sign Gemini and Venus in your sign between October 28 and November 21, you're in good shape professionally during the latter part of the month and on into November. Also, the new moon in your sign could bring new professional opportunities. Mainly, Libra, you just have to be alert and vigilant during this period, prepared to seize the opportunities as they manifest themselves.

ROMANCE
In your love life, the time to anticipate falls between October 28 and November 21. This will be one of the most romantic and creative times for you all year. Everything flows your way. Other people are intrigued by you and your personality, your talents. You can do no wrong, Libra! However, things may run so smoothly that you'll be tempted to kick back and let the good times roll. Resist that urge. Use this period wisely.

BEST DAYS, CHALLENGING DAYS
Pluto's long transit through Capricorn could make some professional matters uncomfortable. You may feel a constant tug-of-war between responsibilities at home and your professional responsibilities. On October 5, Saturn enters Scorpio for a run of two and a half years. Read about it in the Big Picture section for your sign.

November—Libra

LUNAR HIGHLIGHTS
The solar eclipse in Scorpio on November 13 is like a double new moon—so double the new opportunities that come your way. There are a few caveats, though, with solar eclipses—namely that you may have to give up something before you can take advantage of the opportunities. At any rate, for this eclipse, expect new opportunities to surface in your daily life. You may have an opportunity, for example, to go to college or grad school. Or you may meet new friends in the neighborhood where you live. Or perhaps you have a chance to write a book, start a blog, a Web site.

The lunar eclipse in Gemini on November 28 brings excellent news. It could involve a proposal or book you've written, a journey overseas, publishing, higher education, even business in foreign countries.

FINANCES, OTHER STUFF
Venus continues its trek through your sign until November 21. This can have wonderful financial repercussions, but also terrific surprises related to your personal life, career, marriage/relationship. Any area, really.

Between November 6 and 26, Mercury is retrograde in Sagittarius, the last retro of the year. This one impacts your daily life, usually routines, your communication, your relationships with siblings—and the other areas usually associated with Mercury retros, like travel and finances. You know the DONTs by now. If you can't recall them, reread the Big Picture section for your sign.

CAREER
With Mercury retrograde for part of the month, it's smart to tackle the old, not to start anything new. Clear up loose ends. Revisit projects you've shelved. People you knew in the past may resurface and could help you out in some way. With Saturn now out of your sign, you breathe more easily, for sure. It forms a beneficial angle to your career area, bringing stability.

ROMANCE
Yes, until November 21, you are in one of the most romantic and creative times of the year. Enjoy it. Socialize. Don't keep to yourself. If you're unattached, then get out and be seen, keep your social options open. With your love life on the rise, everything else in your life looks brighter, too.

BEST DAYS, CHALLENGING DAYS
November 6 could be challenging. Mercury turns retrograde in Sagittarius.

December—Libra

LUNAR HIGHLIGHTS
The new moon in Sagittarius on December 13 falls in your solar third house, so expect new opportunities related to communication, travel, your daily routine, your conscious mind. You may have a chance to take a seminar or workshop of some kind—writing, the raising of consciousness, intuitive development.

The full moon in Cancer on December 28 falls in your career area. Around the time of this full moon, you should expect career news. Perhaps you land a promotion, a raise, or a job for which you've applied. Saturn in Scorpio forms a beneficial angle to this new moon, indicating that the news or insights you gain are on solid footing. Pluto is opposed to this moon, though, so there could be struggles with power issues. You want one thing, your boss wants something else, that sort of thing.

FINANCES, OTHER STUFF
With Saturn now in your financial area, you may be looking for the bottom line in your finances. Are you pleased with the way you earn your living? Do you want to be doing some other kind of work? Can you stick to a budget? How can you earn more money? Those are the kinds of questions you probably will be asking yourself. Until Decem-

ber 15, Venus travels with Saturn in Scorpio, and this could bring about an ease of restrictions you may be experiencing. Think of this transit as a bonus.

CAREER
The big career news this month is the full moon in your career area on December 28. Until December 15, Venus forms a beneficial angle to your career area, so this adds to the opportunities and general ease you'll experience. Also, people are usually in more optimistic moods around the holidays, which can work to your advantage in pitching ideas and moving your professional agenda forward. Until December 25, Mars transits Capricorn, and you could feel some tension between your life obligations and those of your career.

ROMANCE
From December 15 until early January 2013, Venus transits compatible fire sign Sagittarius and lights up your love life. The people around you tend to be in more gregarious, generous moods, just as you are. On December 13, Uranus turns direct in Aries, in your partnership area, a major plus for your closest relationships. Now you and your partner can use Uranus's energy to forge new pathways in your relationship, to come together for a joint creative project. You may even decide, on the spur of the moment, to move in together or get married.

BEST DAYS, CHALLENGING DAYS
By December 13, all the planets are in forward motion, i.e., functioning just as they should. So your holidays should be very nice indeed!

Happy New Year!

9

Scorpio

The Big Picture in 2012

Welcome to 2012, Scorpio. It's a year for perseverance, revision, laying foundations, creating goals and strategies, learning organization, and being methodical. There are changes coming up this year, but let's take a closer look.

Your ruler, Pluto, starts off the year in Capricorn, in your solar third house, where it has been since November 2008. You're accustomed to its energy now. Its transit, which lasts until 2024, is bringing profound and permanent change globally, evident in the economic challenges that now face the U.S. Most institutions are in the throes of great change—the health-care industry, the petroleum and insurance industries, mortgages/lending, housing, aviation, even the Internet. You name it, and Pluto's fingerprint can be found.

On a personal level, this planet's transit through that area of your chart that represents your conscious mind suggests a kind of dogged persistence for answers. You're not after the small stuff, the minutiae. Your quest is like a sweeping epic that spans the gamut—what happens when we die? Does the soul survive? Are we reincarnated?

Pluto's transit through Capricorn helps you to solidify your life goals, grounds your dreams, and both changes and strengthens relationships with siblings and other relatives.

Neptune entered Pisces and your solar fifth house on April 4, 2011. But by early August 2011, it had slipped back into Aquarius. Neptune symbolizes our higher ideals, escapism, fiction, spirituality, and our blind spots. It seeks to dissolve boundaries between us and others. One possible repercussion of this transit is prolonged religious wars, which proliferated during Uranus's transit in Pisces from early 2003. February 3, 2012, it enters Pisces again and won't move on until January 2026.

On a personal level, this transit forms a beneficial angle to your sun and brings idealistic and inspirational elements into your love life, creativity, and with all activities you pursue for fun and enjoyment. With this transit, for instance, you may embark on a spiritual quest with your romantic partner or get involved in charity work or with a nonprofit organization, or your creative endeavors may take off in a new direction.

Uranus entered Aries and your solar sixth house in March 2011. One repercussion of this transit is that unusual and exciting people are going to be entering your life and shaking things up. Your daily work routine is about to undergo radical and unexpected changes.

Saturn begins the year in Libra, your solar twelfth house. It has been there since the summer of 2010 and will be there until October 2012. This transit brings greater structure to your unconscious, your psyche, and everything you do behind the scenes. Since the twelfth house governs institutions, it's possible that you may have more dealing with hospitals, nursing homes, and the like during this transit.

Once Saturn enters your sign on October 5, you're urged to live up to your responsibilities and obligations. You may have more responsibility than you normally do, but that's rarely a problem for a Scorpio. It's possible that you encounter delays and restrictions that limit your freedom in some way, but the purpose is to strip your life of situations and relationships that no longer serve your best interest. This transit represents a major life cycle and can be beneficial once you live up to your end of the bargain.

One of your best periods falls between January 1 and June 11, when expansive Jupiter transits Taurus and your solar seventh house. Your partnerships in business and romance broaden, and you may do more overseas traveling with a partner. Your partnerships generally will be easier, but there can be such excessive optimism that you're unrealistic in your expectations.

From June 11, 2012, to June 25, 2013, Jupiter transits Gemini and your solar eighth house. Your partner's income may rise, it should be easier to obtain mortgages and loans, and you may get a lucky break with insurance and taxes. Again, though, feelings of optimism may be excessive, which could cloud your judgment.

They say that timing is everything, so with that in mind let's look at some specific areas in your life in 2012.

ROMANCE/CREATIVITY

The most romantic and creative time for you all year falls between November 21 and December 15, when Venus transits your sign. Not only do others find you more appealing, seductive, and radiant, but you feel that way about yourself too. If you're in a committed relationship, then you and your partner rediscover each other. Plan a trip out of town to some secluded, romantic spot. Spend time together doing whatever you both enjoy. If you're single and looking, then be sure that during this period you do a lot of what you enjoy. The happier you are, the more likely it is that you will attract the right person.

Another good period: January 14 to February 8, when Venus transits fellow water sign Pisces and your solar fifth house. During this transit, you're really in your element, psychically aware, with vivid dreams that provide information and insights. Romantically, things hum right along to your satisfaction, and you're in such a beautiful place within yourself it's easy to have fun!

A deepening commitment in an existing relationship is possible between March 5 and April 3, when Venus transits Taurus and your solar seventh house of partnerships. You and your partner may decide to move in together, get engaged, or get married. Just be sure that you don't do any of this under a Mercury retrograde period. Take a look under the appropriate section below to find out when Mercury will be retrograde this year.

Other good backup dates: October 5 to 29, when Mars transits your sign.

CAREER
Usually Venus and Jupiter transits to your career area are the times to look for. Jupiter doesn't transit that area this year. So let's look for Venus transits.

Between September 6 and October 3, Venus transits Leo and your career area. During this period bosses and peers are receptive to your ideas, and you could find yourself in a position where you're called upon to show what you can do. Wow them, Scorpio. With Venus in Leo and your career area, let them hear you roar.

Another good career period falls between February 8 and March 5, when Venus transits Aries and forms a beneficial angle to your career area. During this period don't hesitate to be bold, a trailblazer. Your daily work schedule may be hectic, but you can get a lot done. Put your best effort into it.

November 14 to 26 is another period to circle. Your co-ruler, Mars, is in your sign. It favors research, investigation, intuitive work and development. You're a powerhouse of energy, and nothing is insurmountable!

Another strong period is when Mercury transits your career area between June 25 and August 31. This is the time to pitch ideas, communicate what you think and feel about projects, and to express your ideas. However, Mercury is retrograde between July 14 and August 8, so that's when you rethink, revise, review.

BEST TIMES FOR
Buying or selling a home: January 27 to February 13, when Mercury transits Aquarius and your solar fourth house.

Family reunions: The above dates or when Venus is in your sign between November 21 and December 15.

Financial matters: The period from December 15, 2012,

to January 9, 2013, while Venus transits Sagittarius and the money area of your chart.

Signing contracts: When Mercury is moving direct!

MERCURY RETROGRADES

Every year Mercury—the planet of communication and travel—turns retrograde three times. During this period it's wise not to sign contracts (unless you don't mind renegotiating when Mercury is moving direct), to check and recheck travel plans or, better yet, don't travel, and to communicate as succinctly as possible. Refrain from buying any large-ticket items or electronics during this time too. Often computers and appliances go on the fritz, cars act up, data is lost . . . you get the idea. Be sure to back up all files before the dates below:

March 12–April 4: Mercury retrograde in Aries, your solar sixth house—daily work, health.

July 14–August 8: Mercury retrograde in Leo, your solar tenth house—career.

November 6–26: Mercury retrograde in Sagittarius, your solar second house of finances.

ECLIPSES

Solar eclipses tend to trigger external events that bring about change according to the sign and house in which they fall. Lunar eclipses trigger inner, emotional events according to the sign and house in which they fall. Any eclipse marks both beginnings and endings. The solar and lunar eclipse in a pair falls in opposite signs. If you're interested in detailed information on eclipses, take a look at Celeste Teal's excellent and definitive book, *Eclipses: Predicting World Events & Personal Transformation*.

If you were born under or around the time of an eclipse, it's to your advantage to take a look at your birth chart to find out exactly where the eclipses will impact you.

Most years feature four eclipses—two solar, two lunar, with the set separated by about two weeks. In November and December 2011, there were solar and lunar eclipses, so this year the first eclipses fall during May and June.

May 20: Solar eclipse at 0 degrees Gemini. This one should bring in new opportunities for communication and with mortgages, loans, taxes, and insurance.

June 4: Lunar eclipse in Sagittarius, your solar second house. Financial news that arrives around this time is positive.

November 13: Solar eclipse in your sign. New personal opportunities for you, Scorpio.

November 28: Lunar eclipse, Gemini. Jupiter forms a five-degree conjunction to the eclipse degree, suggesting that news you receive around this time will be cause for celebration!

LUCKIEST DAY OF THE YEAR
Every year there's one day when Jupiter and the sun meet up, and luck, serendipity, and expansion are the hallmarks. This year that day falls on May 13, with a conjunction in Taurus.

January—Scorpio

LUNAR HIGHLIGHTS
The full moon on January 9 falls in Cancer, a fellow water sign. Mars forms a close and beneficial angle to this full moon, promising a lot of activity and forward thrust. You could hear news about an educational endeavor, a publishing project, your domestic situation/environment, or a trip abroad.

January 23 features a new moon in Aquarius and your solar fourth house. This one should usher in new opportunities related to your home and domestic environment. You might sell your home and move, start a home-based business, join a community of like-minded individuals in an alternative living situation. Uranus forms a close, beneficial angle to this new moon, so be prepared for the unexpected (in a good way!)

FINANCES, OTHER STUFF

Your communication abilities are particularly strong between January 8 and 27, when Mercury is in compatible earth sign Capricorn. You feel quite strongly about your financial goals this year and should be able to communicate clearly about them—your expectations, your uncertainties, your strategies. With Mars in compatible earth sign Virgo until July 3, you're very precise about details.

CAREER

Your career goals for 2012, like your goals for other areas of your life, may be in flux. But that's okay. Fine-tuning is something we do constantly. Just don't stick to a particular plan because you think you have to. See how the plan feels intuitively. If it makes you feel good, then move in that direction. With Venus in fellow water sign Pisces between January 14 and February 8, you may feel more like hanging out with friends, a lover, and doing things you truly enjoy. Try to turn that sense of enjoyment toward your work.

ROMANCE

Aren't you the lucky one! Romance starts early for you this year. In fact, between January 14 and February 8, while Venus transits water sign Pisces and your solar fifth house, you're in for a treat. Your love life hums along in high gear, you feel as if you're in the flow. Whether you're in a relationship or not, your overall feelings during this period should be quite optimistic, and your intuition is strong, powerful. If you aren't involved, you probably will be before the transit is over. If not, well, you're having too much fun to care!

BEST DAYS, CHALLENGING DAYS

January 14 looks very nice. It's when Venus enters fellow water sign Pisces, setting you up for a romantic and creative period.

February—Scorpio

LUNAR HIGHLIGHTS
The February 7 full moon in Leo brings news concerning a career matter, situation, or relationship. It also enables you to shine in some way, Scorpio, so don't hesitate to strut your stuff. Others see you as an example of how to get the job done—whatever the job may be.

On February 21, the new moon in fellow water sign Pisces ushers in a whole new period in your love life and with your creativity. Neptune forms a close conjunction with this new moon, so you may be looking for a partner who fits your ideals. If you're involved in a relationship already, then things may be moving to a whole new level in the romance department!

FINANCES, OTHER STUFF
With Jupiter in Taurus, your opposite sign, until June, you feel the excesses of the largest planet. Yes, Jupiter represents luck and good fortune, but Jupiter's energy is also excessive, and when in opposition to your sun it can create excessive feelings, excessive expenditures, excessive everything. You might, for instance, take on more than your share of responsibility in some area and suddenly realize you are overwhelmed. Pace yourself in all areas during this opposition, which ends on June 11.

Mercury transits Aquarius and your solar fourth house from January 27 to February 13. This transit should bring unusual discussions into your domestic environment. You have many unusual and cutting edge ideas during this transit, which can be used in some way for creative fodder.

CAREER
Between February 8 and March 5, Venus transits Aries and your solar sixth house and forms a beneficial angle to your career area. During this period be sure to record your unusual ideas. Think about niches that your product or services can fill in the market. You're in an entrepreneurial frame of mind now, so this type of thinking should be easy

for you. Your daily work routine—how you utilize your time, what you spend your time on, what you think and believe about what you're doing—is vital now.

ROMANCE
If you think you've got your love life all figured out, think again. With Venus in Aries between February 8 and March 5, you're on a trajectory that screams, *Let's do something different.* What's different is who you're attracted to and who is attracted to you. If life is all about vibration, then the vibes you're emitting during this time frame are that you're looking for excitement, something totally outside your usual framework. Even if you're involved in a relationship already, then something shifts between you and your partner. You may become more possessive, jealous, passionate, and impatient to have things the way *you* want them rather than how your partner wants them.

Independence, Scorpio. That's key to this transit.

BEST DAYS, CHALLENGING DAYS
February 8 and February 13 should be days that you notice. They signal a heightening of your intuition.

March—Scorpio

LUNAR HIGHLIGHTS
The full moon in compatible earth sign Virgo occurs on March 8 and falls in your solar eleventh house. This one should ramp up your social life in a major way, so keep your options open during the first part of the month. Mars forms a wide conjunction to this moon, a sure sign of heightened activity and perhaps even a tad of chaos!

On March 22, the new moon in Aries is accompanied by both Uranus and Mercury in Aries. Expect new opportunities to emerge in your daily work routine which will be anything but routine. Any time Uranus is involved in the equation, events happen suddenly, without warning, so to take advantage of these opportunities you simply have to be ready to seize them.

FINANCES, OTHER STUFF
Mercury enters Aries on March 2 and will be there until May 9, the result of a retrograde between March 12 and April 4. So let your entrepreneurial spirit shine until the twelfth. Then gather up the projects and issues you've put on hold and complete them. Try not to start anything new during the retrograde period—don't apply for a mortgage or loan, for instance. With Mars retrograde in Virgo until April 14 and in that sign until July 3, you may be more precise and detailed now about your finances.

CAREER
Saturn in Libra will be in your solar twelfth house until October 5. It forms a beneficial angle to your career area, suggesting a solidness to your professional goals and plans. It turned retrograde on February 7 and will remain that way until June 25. During the retrograde period, you may be revisiting some of your strategies and goals.

Then you've got Uranus in Aries, also forming a beneficial angle to your career area, in your solar sixth house, but the two planets—Saturn and Uranus—are opposed to each other. So this combination can work in several ways. You may feel compelled to do things in unusual, innovative ways, but there may be a constant tug to conduct business as usual. Or you implement these new, innovative techniques, and they are outrageously successful. Which is it going to be, Scorpio?

ROMANCE
Between March 5 and April 3, Venus is in Taurus, your opposite sign. A close partnership is your focus during this period, and things between you are heating up—sexually, romantically. If you're not involved during this transit, then it could translate into creative endeavors with another person. Through that creativity, romance blossoms.

On February 3, Neptune entered fellow water sign Pisces, where it will be for the next fourteen years. This transit brings an idealism and spirituality to all your romantic relationships.

BEST DAYS, CHALLENGING DAYS
March 22. That new moon in Aries is exciting and unpredictable and could spell a hectic day. Just try to go with the flow! In fact, whenever you feel overwhelmed, find your calmest center, enter it, and offer no resistance to whatever transpires.

April—Scorpio

LUNAR HIGHLIGHTS
April 6 features a full moon in Saturn, your solar twelfth house. This one could feel strange and unsettling. Any news you receive may have the same feel to it. Try not to obsess about the news, whatever it is. Simply examine your emotions for the reason you feel as you do. Saturn forms a wide conjunction to this moon, which tends to make things seem harsher than they actually are.

April 21 looks most interesting for you, Scorpio. The new moon in Taurus, your opposite sign, ushers in new partnership opportunities—in business and romance. Mars in Virgo is friendly toward this new moon, so you can expect a swirl of activity around any opportunities that surface. You may also exert discretion with a new romantic interest and could be asking yourself if the individual has the traits you value.

FINANCES, OTHER STUFF
Venus transits Gemini and your solar eighth house from April 3 to August 7. That's a long transit for this planet and is due to a retrograde period between May 15 and June 26. During the retrograde don't purchase large-ticket items—unless you don't mind returning them at a later date. On

either side of the retro period, however, your partner or spouse could land a nice raise, and it should be easier to obtain a loan or mortgage. You may also attend a workshop dealing with metaphysical topics.

Mercury turns direct on April 4, so if you're applying for a mortgage or loan, do it after that date.

CAREER
The new moon in Taurus and Jupiter's transit through that sign until June 11 could be harbingers of an uptick professionally. It all depends on how you use Jupiter's expansive energy. It's to your advantage to take a look at your natal chart to find out where Taurus falls, so you'll have a better idea of how the new moon and Jupiter's transit impact you personally.

ROMANCE
With Venus in chatty Gemini from April 3 to August 7, the path is cleared for a relationship in which communication is not only important, but could be the foundation of the attraction. You may feel mentally restless during this transit, as if there's something you're forgetting or that you should say. You and your partner should try to get away for a few days, step out of your routine, and embrace whatever comes your way.

BEST DAYS, CHALLENGING DAYS
April 4. Mercury turns direct. Go out and celebrate!

May—Scorpio

LUNAR HIGHLIGHTS
Buckle up for this one, Scorpio. It could be a wild month. On May 5, the full moon in your sign brings news of a personal nature. The news proves transformative at some level, and your intense emotions are powerful. Both Pluto and Mars, the ruler and coruler of your sign, form wide,

beneficial angles to this full moon, so it looks as if you're in the power seat. But because moons represent our inner worlds, our emotions, you're able to pivot what you feel in a more positive and uplifting direction.

A solar eclipse in Gemini on May 20 holds repercussions for your joint finances. Your partner or spouse or anyone with whom you share finances could land a raise. You might get a break on insurance or taxes, on a loan or mortgage. There will be a second new moon in Gemini next month, so what doesn't surface with this solar eclipse may surface next month.

FINANCES, OTHER STUFF
Between May 9 and 24, Mercury transits Taurus, your opposite sign. This transit suggests that you may be incredibly stubborn about something. Scorpios can be plenty stubborn, but Taurus wins the prize on this score. If you really feel strongly that your position is correct for you, then stick to it. But if you're uncertain, don't be stubborn just to make a point.

Venus turns retrograde on May 15 in Gemini, in your solar eighth house. This movement indicates delays or snafus with things like mortgages, loans, insurance, taxes. It's best not to buy big-ticket items during a Venus retro, although some good deals can be found. Trust your instincts in that regard.

CAREER
Next month, expansive Jupiter enters Gemini and forms a beneficial angle to your career area. This transit lasts until June 25, 2013, and should facilitate your professional life. Things will seem to flow your way. You'll be in the right place at the right time, and you will be the right person for the right job. You get the idea. So plan now for what you would like to manifest in your professional life. Then step out of the way and let the universe bring it to you.

ROMANCE
Between May 15 and June 27, Venus is retrograde in Gemini. This movement can lead to bumps in any relationship, so it's important to take things in stride, to remain levelheaded when others are not. You don't want to blurt something that you may regret later and not be able to take back.

Mars is now moving direct in Virgo, an earth sign compatible with your water-sign sun, so this should help you out with your physical and sexual energy.

BEST DAYS, CHALLENGING DAYS
May 15, a small ouch day! Venus turns retrograde.

June—Scorpio

LUNAR HIGHLIGHTS
On June 4, there's a lunar eclipse in Sagittarius, your financial area. News about money comes your way, and you look pretty happy about it. Uranus forms a wide and beneficial angle to the eclipse degree, so the news seems to come out of nowhere.

June 19 features the second new moon in Gemini, your solar eighth house. The opportunities that surface could be similar to what occurred around the time of the solar eclipse on May 20. But this time you won't have to relinquish something to benefit. Saturn forms a beneficial angle to this new moon, so opportunities look solid.

FINANCES, OTHER STUFF
On June 7, Mercury enters fellow water sign Cancer, so you tend to feel more at home in your life and with yourself. Your intuition, which is considerable to begin with, really deepens. Your best bet between June 7 and 25 is to follow your hunches on all things. You won't go wrong.

Once Venus turns direct again on June 27, financial issues should straighten out. Then you can head out to the nearest store and buy that large-ticket item you've been eyeing.

CAREER
The really good period professionally is going to happen in September, between September 6 and October 3. That's when Venus will be transiting your career area. Until then, however, plant your seeds carefully. Take on projects that you know you can see through to the end. Pace yourself. Fulfill your responsibilities, show yourself—and everyone else—that you're the person who is rising through the ranks and shining.

ROMANCE
Venus turns direct on June 27, so romantic issues should clear up after that date. Now you get to enjoy Venus in Gemini until August 7. Jupiter will be traveling with Venus from June 11 to early August, and the combination should result in some positive expansion in your universe—with romance, money, your career, family, wherever you place your energy and attention.

BEST DAYS, CHALLENGING DAYS
June 27 is a day to circle: that's when Venus turns direct again. Another good day? Circle June 11, when Jupiter enters Gemini. In fact, take a look at your natal chart to find Gemini. That area will experience the greatest expansion during the next year.

July—Scorpio

LUNAR HIGHLIGHTS
On July 3, the full moon in Capricorn brings news about a sibling, your neighborhood or a neighbor, a communication project. Within your daily life, there can be some sort of news too that could involve a goal that you hold or a goal that is changing. Pluto forms a close conjunction to this full moon, so its impact will be powerful.

The new moon on July 19 falls in Cancer, your solar ninth house. The moon should bring new opportunities for foreign travel, higher education, publishing, one of your parents, or about something or someone you nurture. Saturn forms a challenging angle to this new moon, so be on your toes, Scorpio. Strive to go with the flow.

FINANCES, OTHER STUFF
On July 3, Mars enters Libra and your solar twelfth house, and it will be there until August 23. This transit stirs up your psyche, issues you may have buried. Now you have to confront and resolve these issues. Since Mars is in Libra, a social sign, you may be focused on relationships and the arts. Mars is now forming a beneficial angle to Venus in Gemini, your solar eighth house. The combination should ramp up activity in resources you share with others—a partner, spouse, even a child.

CAREER
Between July 14 and August 8, Mercury is retrograde in Leo, your career area. OK, by now you know what you should and shouldn't do to make this transit easier for yourself. But the bottom line is that things probably will go haywire, and you simply have to make the best of them and understand this too shall pass. Work on projects already in the works. Try not to start something new. Communicate as clearly and succinctly as possible.

ROMANCE
You could meet someone special through friends, a social function, or at a seminar or workshop dealing with metaphysical topics. With Mercury's retrograde motion, though, between the dates mentioned above, it's smart to wait before you really leap into this new relationship.

In a current relationship, there could be misunderstandings or miscommunications. A typical example would be that you and your partner agree to meet for lunch somewhere. But one of you gets held up in traffic or lost and because your cell phone is dead you can't check in with your partner. So he leaves. Then you're in a huff about it.

BEST DAYS, CHALLENGING DAYS
July 14. Circle it in red. Mercury turns retrograde.

August—Scorpio

LUNAR HIGHLIGHTS
It's a busy month astrologically—two full moons and a new moon. Let's take a closer look. On August 1, the full moon in Aquarius occurs in your solar fourth house. Both Mars and Uranus form beneficial angles to this full moon, so there's a lot of activity and a suddenness to events. Excitement rules the day, Scorpio, and if you feel overwhelmed at any point, just retreat and spend a little time alone.

The new moon in fire sign Leo occurs on August 17 in your career area and should bring new professional opportunities. You land a new job, get a promotion or raise, or even find a new career path. Saturn and Mars form exact and beneficial angles to this new moon, so the offers and opportunities that surface are solid and give you the opportunity to show that you're the best one for the job.

The full moon in fellow water sign Pisces on August 31 brings news and insights about a romantic relationship or about something you're doing for fun and pleasure. If you have kids, then the news you hear may concern them. Neptune forms a wide conjunction with this moon, and Pluto forms a close and beneficial angle to it. The combination suggests news and events that involve power issues and idealism.

FINANCES, OTHER STUFF
Mercury turns direct on August 8, which should help to straighten out your finances and career issues. In addition, Venus enters fellow water sign Cancer on August 7, which should bring a deeper intuitive flow to everything you do. This transit lasts until September 6. Keep in mind that Jupiter in Gemini impacts your shared resources—your part-

ner's finances, in other words—and helps to expand that person's earnings. In turn, it helps you out.

CAREER
The new moon in Leo on August 17 spells big career opportunities. With Jupiter still in Gemini and forming a beneficial angle to your career area, expansion rules the day. You feel as if your life is exceptionally lucky right now—and it is. Just be sure that you're vigilant, so that when opportunities surface, you're ready to seize them.

ROMANCE
Between August 7 and September 6, Venus transits fellow water sign Cancer and your solar ninth house. This transit brings an intuitive flow to your romantic relationships. You feel more grounded within yourself, so are better able to communicate what you feel, when you feel it. If you're traveling abroad, then romance may find you on the road!

BEST DAYS, CHALLENGING DAYS
August 8: circle it. Mercury turns direct that day.

September—Scorpio

LUNAR HIGHLIGHTS
September 15 features a new moon in compatible earth sign Virgo and promises new opportunities with friends, social groups, and in achieving your wishes and dreams. Mercury is within five degrees of this new moon, suggesting that you may have an opportunity to write a book, start a blog or Web site, or to do public speaking. In fact, your involvement with groups may be as a result of public speaking. Perhaps you're invited to teach a workshop.

September 29 features a full moon in fire sign Aries, your solar sixth house. This one should bring news about your daily work. You might receive kudos from a boss for a job well done or hear of a job opening that sounds like it's made to order for you. Uranus is closely conjunct this moon, so there will be a suddenness and unpredictability to events around this time.

FINANCES, OTHER STUFF

Next month there will be a lot of activity in your financial area when Mars enters Sagittarius. But in September things look fairly quiet, steady, even, just the way you like them. Mercury enters Libra and your solar twelfth house on September 16, and between then and October 5 you may be doing a lot of communicating through emails, blogs, your Web site, the phone. Even though this transit occurs in the most hidden part of your chart Libra is part of the equation, and it's a social sign. So leave room for other people in your life, Scorpio. Plan some social activities with people you enjoy.

CAREER

Finally. You've got a three-week period here where everything goes your way. Between September 6 and October 3, Venus transits Leo and your career area. This period favors pitching ideas, garnering support you may need for a project, finding a new job, selling a manuscript or screenplay . . . you get the idea. With Venus in your professional court, you're in the flow, in the groove.

ROMANCE

Venus in Leo also has romantic repercussions, Scorpio. A flirtation at work may heat up and become something more serious, you could have a fling with your boss (not advised!), or you may be traveling for business and meet your soul mate. It all depends on where you place your energy and attention.

BEST DAYS, CHALLENGING DAYS

September 6: Venus enters Leo and your career area. You now have an opportunity to shine.

October—Scorpio

LUNAR HIGHLIGHTS
October 15 features a new moon in Libra, with a close and beneficial angle from Jupiter. Opportunities that come your way with this new moon may include: new friendships, a new romantic relationship, artistic appreciation, a chance to flex the muscles of your creativity, and new opportunities in communication.

The full moon of October 29 occurs in your opposite sign, Taurus, and should bring news about a partnership—either romantic or business. You may be incredibly stubborn on or around the time of this full moon, but it's probably exactly what a situation calls for. Pluto forms a close, beneficial angle to this full moon, so powerful emotions will be stirred.

FINANCES, OTHER STUFF
On October 6, energetic Mars enters Sagittarius and your financial area. This transit, which lasts until November 16, ramps up the activity and your attention on finances. You may be trying to stick to a budget and have to pay closer attention to what you spend. Or perhaps you're working longer hours to meet a deadline with a bonus promised at the end. However this transit works out specific to you and your situation, Mars now forms a beneficial angle to your career area as well. Promotion in store for you, Scorpio? A significant raise? Buy a lottery ticket.

CAREER
Mars in Sagittarius will be a boost to your career; as stated above, it forms a strong, beneficial angle to your career area. In addition Venus transits compatible earth sign Virgo between October 3 and 28, so the social contacts you make during this period could prove helpful professionally. You've got another bonus this month, too, when Mercury transits your sign between October 5 and 29, deepening your innate intuition to the point where you can act on your hunches without worrying about whether you've made the right decision.

ROMANCE
Venus transits Virgo between October 3 and 28, so during this period it's possible that a friend becomes something more to you. Or perhaps a romance begins at some sort of social function that you attend. Be sure to keep your social calendar wide open during this period. If you're already in a relationship, then this transit could see you and your partner socializing more than usual, getting out and enjoying yourselves with people of like minds.

BEST DAYS, CHALLENGING DAYS
On October 5, Saturn enters your sign and will be there for about two and a half years. Read more about this in the Big Picture section for your sign. You probably will feel a shift in energy on the fifth.

November—Scorpio

LUNAR HIGHLIGHTS
The new moon in your sign on November 13 is actually a solar eclipse, Scorpio, and should be quite positive for you. New personal opportunities should surface around the date of this eclipse, and all you have to do is be ready to seize them. The possibilities depend on what it is you desire, where you place your attention and focus, and how you have been living your life up until now.

The lunar eclipse on November 28 falls in Gemini and should bring positive and uplifting news about money, insurance, taxes, mortgages, loans. You could also hear positive news about a communication project or your partner's income. Uranus forms a close and beneficial angle to the eclipse degree, suggesting that your emotional reaction will be unusual.

FINANCES, OTHER STUFF
Okay, hold onto your hat. The winds that will blow with the next and last Mercury retrograde of 2012 sweep through

your financial area. Big ouch. There are ways to mitigate the effects, however. The Mercury retro period falls between November 6 and 26, twenty days' worth of communication snafus. So what you need to do is make sure you've got everything lined up financially before Mercury gets mischievous. Your bank statements should be in order, your insurance and tax documents should be in good shape, your will should be up to date. Reread the Mercury retrograde sections under the Big Picture for your sign.

CAREER

By now the hype over 2012 should be in full force, broadcast 24/7 on the cable news, running rampant on the Internet. Who has time to pay attention to career matters? But this is precisely the time to pay attention to what's happening in your professional life. With Mercury retrograde between November 6 and 26, tackle work you've put on a back burner rather than starting new projects.

ROMANCE

On November 16, Mars enters Capricorn, which it transits until December 25. Between November 6 and 26, Mercury is retrograde. From November 21 to December 15, Venus is in your sign. So let's take a look at all the elements here. First, Venus's transit through your sign marks one of the most romantic and creative periods for you all year. For part of this time, though, Mercury will be retrograde, so there could be some communication snafus. The Mars transit through Capricorn could ramp up your sexuality, Scorpio. On the romance front, it's going to be an interesting month.

BEST DAYS, CHALLENGING DAYS

November 6. Tough day. Mercury turns retrograde in Sagittarius, your financial area.

December—Scorpio

LUNAR HIGHLIGHTS

The new moon on December 13 calls in Sagittarius, your financial area. This one should bring new financial opportunities—a raise, a job that pays better, a second job that supplements your income. It also forms a beneficial angle to your career area, so there could be some professional opportunities that come your way as a result of this new moon.

The full moon on December 28 is in fellow water sign Cancer and should bring news about an educational or publishing goal you may have or about an upcoming trip abroad. There could also be news about your parents or anyone else whom you nurture or who nurtures you. Saturn in your sign forms a beneficial angle to this full moon, suggesting that the news you hear is serious, solid. This is the last lunation of 2012.

FINANCES, OTHER STUFF

The media hype about 2012 is probably at full blast right now. The best way to navigate the hype is to ignore it. This should be fairly easy to do if you simply pivot your attention elsewhere. On December 10, this gets a bit easier, when Mercury (conscious mind) enters Sagittarius and your financial area. Now your focus is on money—perhaps what you're spending for the holidays, whether you should be paying with cash or credit cards, what you should buy for whom. On the thirty-first, Mercury enters Capricorn, an earth sign that's compatible with your water-sign sun. This transit takes you into the new year, filled with goals and wishes and dreams that you hope to realize in 2013.

CAREER

Professional matters may seem to slide during the holidays, especially with all the 2012 media hype. Until the fifteenth, though, Venus is in your sign, which means things roll your way with little effort on your part. People are more generous; they see you and your ideas as bright lights of clarity and are eager to hear more of your ideas. With Saturn now in your sign, you're urged to fulfill your obligations and responsibilities and do so with great dedication and resolve.

ROMANCE
If romance comes your way during December, it's sure to be a fascinating and exciting relationship. Until the twenty-fifth, Mars is in Capricorn and your solar third house. This transit heightens your sexuality and your ability to communicate what you think and feel. On the twenty-fifth, Mars enters Aquarius and forms a beneficial angle to Venus, which by then is in Sagittarius. The combination of energies leads to satisfying experiences in love and romance.

BEST DAYS, CHALLENGING DAYS
On December 13, Uranus turns direct in Aries, so every planet is now functioning at optimum level. Start making your new year's resolutions!

Happy New Year!

10

Sagittarius

The Big Picture in 2012

Welcome to 2012, Sagittarius. It's a year of freedom, variety, versatility, and no restrictions. Well, there may be restrictions, but you'll certainly do your best to get rid of them.

Your ruler, Jupiter, moves through two signs this year—Taurus from January 1 to June 11 and Gemini from January 11 to June 25, 2013. Both transits will expand and broaden your life and worldview in some way.

During Jupiter's transit through Taurus, you may find that your daily work schedule is so jammed that you're working longer hours just to get things done. Or you're becoming more efficient in the way you use your time. You may take new steps to safeguard your health—a new exercise regimen, for instance, or a new diet or nutritional program.

When Jupiter transits Gemini, your opposite sign, your business and romantic partnerships expand. You might get engaged or married; you and your partner could go into business together; your relationship could move into a deeper level of commitment.

Pluto starts off the year in Capricorn, where it has been since November 2008. You're accustomed to its energy now. Its transit, which lasts until 2024, is bringing profound and permanent change globally, evident in the economic challenges that now face the U.S. Most institutions are in the throes of great change—the health-care industry, the petroleum and insurance industries, mortgages/lending, housing, aviation, even the Internet. You name it, and Pluto's fingerprint can be found.

On a personal level, this planet's transit through your financial area suggests a profound and irrevocable change in your finances. If you're in debt, your debt could deepen or you could wipe it out. You might get a significant raise or promotion, inherit money, or land an insurance settlement. To a great extent, the way things shake out during this transit depends on where your finances are when the transit begins.

Neptune entered Pisces on April 4, 2011. But by early August 2011, it had slipped back into Aquarius. Neptune symbolizes our higher ideals, escapism, fiction, spirituality, and our blind spots. It seeks to dissolve boundaries between us and others. One possible repercussion of this transit is prolonged religious wars, which proliferated during Uranus's transit in Pisces from early 2003. February 3, 2012, it enters Pisces again and won't move on until January 2026.

On a personal level, this transit forms a challenging angle to your sun and brings idealistic and inspirational elements into your home and domestic life. The challenge lies in a certain confusion that rides tandem with Neptune transits. Just try to channel the energy into your spiritual pursuits and studies and activities connected with your ideals.

Uranus entered Aries in March 2011. One repercussion of this transit is that unusual and exciting people are going to be entering your life and shaking things up. Your love life may change from second to second, your creativity will be in high gear. You should enjoy this one, Sadge.

Saturn begins the year in Libra. It has been there since the summer of 2010 and will be there until October 2012. This transit forms a beneficial angle to your sun and should bring greater structure to your friendships and wishes and dreams. Then on October 5, Saturn enters Scorpio and your solar twelfth house. This transit should help to bring greater structure to your unconscious, your psyche, and everything you do behind the scenes. Since the twelfth house governs institutions, it's possible that you may have more dealings with hospitals, nursing homes, and the like during this transit.

They say that timing is everything, so with that in mind let's look at some specific areas in your life in 2012.

ROMANCE/CREATIVITY

The most romantic and creative time for you all year falls between December 15 and January 9, when Venus transits your sign. Not only do others find you more appealing, seductive, and radiant, but you feel that way about yourself too. If you're in a committed relationship, then you and your partner rediscover each other. Plan a trip out of town, to some secluded, romantic spot. Spend time together doing whatever you both enjoy. If you're single and looking, then be sure that during this period you do a lot of what you enjoy. The happier you are, the more likely it is that you will attract the right person.

Another good period: February 8 to March 5, when Venus transits fellow fire sign Aries and your solar fifth house. During this transit you're really in your element—intuitive, aware, unafraid to try new things and new relationships and creative endeavors. Romantically, things hum right along to your satisfaction, and you're in such a beautiful place within yourself it's easy to have fun!

A deepening commitment in an existing relationship is possible between April 3 and August 7, when Venus transits Gemini and your solar seventh house of partnerships. You and your partner may decide to move in together, get engaged, or get married. Just be sure that you don't do any of this while Venus is retrograde between May 15 and June 27. Stay away from Mercury retrogrades too. See the section below to find out when Mercury will be retrograde this year.

Other good backup dates: October 6 to December 25, when Mars transits your sign.

CAREER

Usually Venus and Jupiter transits to your career area are the times to look for. Jupiter doesn't transit that area this year. So let's look for Venus transits.

Between October 3 and 28, Venus transits Virgo and your career area. During this period, bosses and peers are receptive to your ideas and you could find yourself in a position where you're called upon to show what you can do. Another good career period falls between March 5 and April 3, when Venus transits Taurus and forms a beneficial angle to your career area. During this period, be resolute in everything you take on. Let people know you're in for the long haul.

October 6 to November 16 is another period to circle. Mars is in your sign then, and you've got the physical energy and confidence to get things done. You're a powerhouse then, and nothing is insurmountable!

Another strong period is when Mercury transits your career area between August 31 and September 16. This is the time to pitch ideas, communicate what you think and feel about projects, and express your ideas.

BEST TIMES FOR

Buying or selling a home: February 13 to March 2, when Mercury transits Pisces and your solar fourth house.

Family reunions: The above dates or when Venus is in your sign between December 15 and January 9, 2013.

Financial matters: August 7 to September 6, when Venus transits Cancer and that area of your chart that governs shared financial resources.

Signing contracts: When Mercury is moving direct!

MERCURY RETROGRADES

Every year Mercury—the planet of communication and travel—turns retrograde three times. During this period it's wise not to sign contracts (unless you don't mind renegotiating when Mercury is moving direct), to check and recheck travel plans or, better yet, don't travel, and to communicate as succinctly as possible. Refrain from buying any large-ticket items or electronics during this time too. Often computers and appliances go on the fritz, cars act up, data is lost ... you get the idea. Be sure to back up all files before the dates below:

March 12–April 4: Mercury retrograde in Aries, your solar fifth house of creativity, love, and romance.

July 14–August 8: Mercury retrograde in Leo, your solar ninth house—your worldview.

November 6–26: Mercury retrograde in your sign!

ECLIPSES

Solar eclipses tend to trigger external events that bring about change according to the sign and house in which they fall. Lunar eclipses trigger inner, emotional events according to the sign and house in which they fall. Any eclipse marks both beginnings and endings. The solar and lunar eclipse in a pair falls in opposite signs. If you're interested in detailed information on eclipses, take a look at Celeste Teal's excellent and definitive book, *Eclipses: Predicting World Events & Personal Transformation.*

If you were born under or around the time of an eclipse, it's to your advantage to take a look at your birth chart to find out exactly where the eclipses will impact you.

Most years feature four eclipses—two solar, two lunar, with the set separated by about two weeks. In November and December 2011, there were solar and lunar eclipses, so this year the first eclipses fall during May and June.

May 20: Solar eclipse at 0 degrees Gemini. This one should bring in new partnership opportunities.

June 4: Lunar eclipse in your sign. Positive news that delights you should arrive around this time.

November 13: Solar eclipse in Scorpio. New opportunities to delve into your own psyche and for research and investigation.

November 28: Lunar eclipse, Gemini. Jupiter forms a five-degree conjunction to the eclipse degree, suggesting that news you receive around this time will be cause for celebration!

LUCKIEST DAY OF THE YEAR
Every year there's one day when Jupiter and the sun meet up, and luck, serendipity, and expansion are the hallmarks. This year that day falls on May 13, with a conjunction in Taurus.

January—Sagittarius

LUNAR HIGHLIGHTS
The full moon in Cancer on January 9 falls in that area of your chart known as shared resources. It refers to money, energy, and time you share with others, usually a spouse or partner. There should be new in this area and lots of activity to boot. You may feel rushed and harried around the time of this full moon, but like any true Sadge, you take it all in stride. To do that, you may hit the road!

The new moon in compatible air sign Aquarius on January 23 occurs in your solar third house. This new moon should usher in new opportunities in communication with your siblings or other relatives and in your daily life. Uranus forms a close, beneficial angle to this new moon, suggesting a sudden and unexpected quality to the opportunities.

FINANCES, OTHER STUFF
From January 8 to 27, Mercury transits Capricorn and the financial area of your chart. This transit has you talking and thinking about your money. You may be facing holiday credit card bills or perhaps are feeling a financial crunch and need to set up a budget. Or you've received an unexpected bonus or royalty check and are talking about that. With Uranus transiting fellow fire sign Aries for the next seven years, there will be sudden fluctuations in your income, probably for the better.

CAREER
Mars continues its transit through Virgo and your career area until July 3, revving up everything related to your profession. It will be retrograde between January 24 and April

4, however, so initiate projects on either side of those dates. During the retrograde period, tackle current projects and anything you've put on a back burner.

With Jupiter in Taurus and your solar sixth house until June 11, your daily work routine should be expanding by leaps and bounds. Perhaps you're taking on more responsibilities. Just be sure to pace yourself.

ROMANCE
Venus transits water sign Pisces and your solar fourth house from January 14 to February 8. This transit should bring a nice intuitive flow to your romantic relationships, and you and your partner may be cocooning during this transit, spending time together alone.

BEST DAYS, CHALLENGING DAYS
January 23, with the new moon in compatible air sign Aquarius, looks good for you. The energy holds for a few days on either side of the date.

February—Sagittarius

LUNAR HIGHLIGHTS
The full moon on February 7 is in Leo, a fellow fire sign, and should be filled with excitement and plenty of drama. There could be news about an educational or publishing endeavor in which you're involved or about an overseas trip or foreign client. It's a good time to strut your stuff, Sadge. Don't be shy about showing others what you're capable of doing and achieving.

The new moon in Pisces on February 21 occurs in your solar fourth house. This one may usher in new opportunities related to your home and family. If your home is on the market, then the new moon could bring the right buyer offering the right purchase price. Or there could be a new addition to the family—a birth, someone moves in.

FINANCES, OTHER STUFF
Mercury transits Aquarius and your solar third house between January 27 and February 13. This transit heightens your communication skills. You may start a blog, build a Web site, or open an online forum about a topic that interests you. Or perhaps you'll do it to publicize your services or products. Then, between February 13 and March 2, Mercury transits Pisces, and your conscious mind becomes more intuitive, inward-looking.

CAREER
Mars continues its retrograde motion through Virgo and your career area. So keep to your current path; try not to start anything new. On a brighter note, though, Venus transits fellow fire sign Aries between February 8 and March 5, so your capacity for enjoyment and joy is deepened considerably. You're looking for fun and pleasure in everything you do, and this translates into a better situation for you in your career. Other people respond to your feelings.

ROMANCE
With Venus in Aries and your solar fifth house between February 8 and March 5, you enjoy the most romantic and creative period all year. If you're involved in a relationship, then things between you and your partner should soar past your expectations. Your passions are powerful and you may feel somewhat possessive at times, but overall this is a terrific period for you and your partner. If you're not involved, then this transit urges you to get out and about, keep your options open, and focus on feeling joyful.

BEST DAYS, CHALLENGING DAYS
The entire three weeks when Venus is in fellow fire sign Aries should be very pleasant for you, Sadge. Enjoy it! On February 3, Neptune enters Pisces. Reread the section on this in the Big Picture for your sign.

March—Sagittarius

LUNAR HIGHLIGHTS
March 8 features a full moon in Virgo, your career area. This moon should bring professional news. You get a raise or promotion, land the job you wanted, are put in charge of a project that thrills you. Equally possible? Your novel sells, your skills are recognized in some way by peers. Mars forms a wide conjunction to this full moon, so there's going to be plenty of activity and chaos!

The new moon of March 22 falls in fellow fire sign Aries, your solar fifth house. This new moon promises a new romance, new creative ventures, and something new concerning your children. If you've thought about starting a family, this moon could help bring it about. Mercury and Uranus are closely conjunct this moon, so events and opportunities will have a sudden, unpredictable quality about them.

FINANCES, OTHER STUFF
Between March 5 and April 3, Venus transits Taurus and forms a beneficial angle to your financial area. This period looks favorable for all financial dealings—from discussions and negotiations about money to contractual dealings concerning finances. Mercury enters fellow fire sign Aries on March 2 and remains there until May 9. It will be retrograde between March 12 and April 4, so be sure your discussions and negotiations occur on either side of those dates.

CAREER
Get stuff squared away this month so that you're fully prepared to move full speed ahead after April 14, when Mars turns direct again in your career area. With Uranus transiting Aries now—and for the next seven years—there can be some major distractions professionally because you're more focused on changes in your love life. Be careful, Sadge.

ROMANCE
You may want to reread the section in the Big Picture on Uranus's transit and its repercussions for your love life. You're in for plenty of excitement and variety during Uranus's seven-year transit of Aries. You've had a taste of it since March of 2011, when the uninterrupted transit started. So whenever another planet joins Uranus in Aries, things move quickly. Mercury joins Uranus in Aries on March 2, for a transit that lasts until May 9. Mercury will be retrograde between March 12 and April 4, but on either side of those dates you can count on plenty of discussion and exchanges of ideas in your love life.

BEST DAYS, CHALLENGING DAYS
Mercury turns retrograde on March 12. Circle it. Have your ducks lined up ahead of time.

April—Sagittarius

LUNAR HIGHLIGHTS
The full moon on April 6 falls in compatible air sign Libra, your solar eleventh house. You probably are going to find your social calendar jammed around this time. Your inbox fills to bursting, your phone rings off the hook. News and invitations arrive steadily for several days on either side of this full moon.

The new moon on April 21 falls in Taurus, your solar sixth house. This one should usher in new daily work opportunities. You might, for instance, be moved into a larger office, given more responsibility, land a promotion. You might get the job you really want. Mars forms a close and beneficial angle to this new moon, suggesting heightened activity.

FINANCES, OTHER STUFF
The good news: Mercury turns direct on April 4, so it's safe to pack your bags and hit the road again. Sign contracts, apply for a mortgage or loan, get things moving again. You

may feel like you've had sludge in your veins, but the moment you move your life back on track, the better you feel.

Venus enters Gemini on April 3 and stays there until August 7. It's a long transit for this planet because between May 15 and June 27, Venus will be retrograde. Plan for this period now by buying large-tickets items on either side of those dates.

CAREER
If you're in business or considering going into business with someone else, then Venus's transit through Gemini could help to solidify the situation. You and your partner or potential partner could be discussing the finer points of your partnership while Venus is moving direct (see dates above). You may even seal the deal with a formal contract and a signing. Or this could just be a precursor to the actual forming of a partnership after Jupiter enters Gemini on June 11.

ROMANCE
The time to be vigilant occurs between May 15 and June 27, when Venus is retrograde in Gemini, your partnership area. This movement of Venus can create tensions in a relationship, misunderstandings, and a general feeling of unease. The best way to navigate this period is to keep your gripes and complaints to yourself!

BEST DAYS, CHALLENGING DAYS
April 4 is a day to celebrate. Mercury turns direct. Mars turns direct in Virgo, your career area, on April 14, just in time for tax day! This movement should accelerate professional matters.

May—Sagittarius

LUNAR HIGHLIGHTS
The full moon on May 5 is in Scorpio, your solar twelfth house. You receive news about research or an investigation in which you're involved. An issue you thought was resolved could surface again. Your motive or that of someone else may become glaringly apparent to you. Pluto forms a wide, beneficial angle to this full moon, indicating that powerful forces are at work.

May 20 features a new moon and solar eclipse in Gemini, your opposite sign. There will be a second new moon in Gemini next month. For this one, however, new partnership opportunities surface. If you're involved in a relationship, then the solar eclipse could take things to a whole new level, a deeper level of commitment. If you're not involved, this solar eclipse could attract a new romance.

FINANCES, OTHER STUFF
May 9 brings Mercury into resolute Taurus and your solar sixth house, where it forms a beneficial angle to your financial area. Between the ninth and the twenty-fourth, you may be in financial discussions—for a raise, a loan or mortgage, or even just a discussion with family members about sticking to a budget.

CAREER
With Mars now moving direct in your career area, it's time to push forward with projects and ideas you've had on hold. Pitch your ideas, garner support you think you need for projects that interest you. You get help from Jupiter in Taurus, which forms a strong angle to Mars in Virgo and seeks to expand all your professional options. Once Jupiter enters Gemini on June 11, your partnership area begins to expand. Wait until then if you're planning on going into business with someone.

ROMANCE

With Venus retrograde from May 15 to June 27, you could be experiencing some bumps in a romantic relationship or with a creative project. Don't obsess about things during this period, don't chew away at what may be going wrong. Try to focus on what is positive and uplifting about the relationship. Ultimately, that will serve you—and the relationship—much better.

BEST DAYS, CHALLENGING DAYS

The big ouch day? May 15, when Venus turns retrograde in your partnership area.

June—Sagittarius

LUNAR HIGHLIGHTS

June 4 features a full moon in your sign. This should bring news of a personal nature that delights you. Saturn forms a wide, beneficial angle to this eclipse degree, so the news you hear is solid, favorable for you.

On June 19, there's a second new moon in Gemini, your partnership area. This moon should bring opportunities similar to those that surfaced with the solar eclipse last month, but could even be better. Venus and Jupiter are also in Gemini. Even though they are in the early degrees of Gemini and the new moon occurs at 28 degrees, you should receive some of the benefits. Perhaps a romance begins or a creative project lands in your lap.

FINANCES, OTHER STUFF

Between June 7 and 25, Mercury transits Cancer and your solar eighth house. This transit could lead to discussions about mortgages, loans, taxes, insurance. It could also suggest that you're taking a workshop in any of these areas or in something more esoteric—life after death, reincarnation, ghosts and hauntings. There is a deeply intuitive flow to your conscious mind at this time, so trust your hunches.

On the twenty-fifth, Mercury enters Leo and your solar ninth house, a transit better suited to your fire-sign sun. Travel and education are highlighted between June 25 and July 14. After that, Mercury turns retrograde again, so more on that next month.

CAREER
Whether you are in business for yourself or working for a large company, partnership issues should improve considerably between June 11, 2012, and June 25, 2013, while Jupiter transits Gemini and your partnership sector. In addition, the new moon in Gemini on June 19 and the solar eclipse in Gemini last month should prove helpful to you professionally.

ROMANCE
When Venus turns direct on June 27, it's a relief for you. It's not as if the retro period was awful, just that things with you and your partner weren't as great as usual. While Mercury transits Cancer between June 7 and 25, you and your partner may not enjoy the kind of communication you would like. But once Mercury hits Leo on June 25, things shift. You can feel it too.

BEST DAYS, CHALLENGING DAYS
June 27, the day Venus turns direct, should be good for you. You feel unburdened, brighter, more optimistic.

July—Sagittarius

LUNAR HIGHLIGHTS
The full moon on July 3 is in Capricorn, your financial sector. This one brings news about money—a raise, an unexpected check or royalty payment, the repayment of a loan. Pluto forms a close conjunction to this full moon, suggesting power issues surface or you're in a powerful position as a result of the financial news.

The new moon on July 19 falls in Cancer, your solar eighth house, which is also one of the financial areas. This new moon could bring your partner, spouse, or anyone else with whom you share financial resources a raise. Or you may get a break in taxes, insurance, or on a mortgage or loan. New opportunities could surface with parents or with your parenting. Could there be a new addition to the family? Possibly.

FINANCES, OTHER STUFF

Since both moons this month deal with finances, which we've talked about already, let's take a look at what else is going on. On July 3, Mars enters Libra and your solar eleventh house, where it will be until August 23. This transit energizes your social life, and the contacts you make will prove valuable to you in many ways.

Mercury will be retrograde between July 14 and August 8, in Leo, your solar ninth house. By now you know how to mitigate the effects of a Mercury retrograde, but to refresh your memory, reread the appropriate section in the Big Picture for your sign.

CAREER

With Venus now direct in Gemini, traveling with Jupiter through your partnership area, your business partnerships should be expanding and your options multiplying. However, since Mercury is retrograde for much of the Venus transit, don't sign any contracts. Simply negotiate and iron out the details, but don't sign until after August 8, when Mercury turns direct again.

ROMANCE

With Venus and Jupiter traveling together through your partnership area, your romantic life should be humming along at a pace you just love. In an existing relationship, you and your partner may decide to deepen your commitment to each other by moving in together, getting engaged or married. If you're not in a relationship right now, then this combination of energies could trigger a lot of creative adrenaline that prompts you to seek a partner whose creative interests match your own.

BEST DAYS, CHALLENGING DAYS
The challenge this month? The Mercury retrograde that falls in Leo, between July 14 and August 8.

August—Sagittarius

LUNAR HIGHLIGHTS
There are three lunations this month, so it's likely you'll feel rushed and harried, but also grateful for the opportunities that flow your way. August 1 features a full moon in compatible air sign Aquarius, your solar third house. This one should bring news or insights about a communication project—something you're writing, a book, blog, Web site, term paper, thesis—and about a sibling or other relative. You may have a clearer idea now about the kind of neighborhood where you would like to live. The Aquarius part of the equation brings a cutting edge to your ideas.

August 17 boasts a new moon in fellow fire sign Leo, so this one should be quite spectacular for you, Sadge. Expect new opportunities to surface with foreign travel, expanding your business interests overseas, your educational or publishing goals, and your spiritual beliefs. Saturn in Libra forms an exact and beneficial angle to this new moon, so the opportunities that surface are solid, serious, and deserve your consideration.

On August 31, the full moon in Pisces falls in your solar fourth house, illuminating your domestic environment. You receive news or gain insights into a situation at home. One of your parents or a child or even your partner may need special attention now. Pluto forms a close, beneficial angle with this full moon, suggesting that the situation is powerful. But you grasp the larger picture.

FINANCES, OTHER STUFF
Once Mercury turns direct on August 8, continue with your financial negotiations, sign your contracts, apply for your mortgage or loan. On August 23, Mars enters Scorpio and forms a beneficial angle to your career area. Think of this transit, which lasts until October 6, as your booster rocket. Pitch, sell, brainstorm, investigate, research. Use the time well.

CAREER
Venus transits Cancer and your solar eighth house from August 7 to September 6, and during this period it also forms a beneficial angle to your career area. Your intuition should be strong and enables you to make quick decisions without having to dig around for left-brain facts. The Mars transit through Scorpio also helps in this regard. Your biggest challenge during these two transits is that you may think you've got things all figured out and don't have to check in with your intuition. Your best bet is to check your hunches first.

ROMANCE
Sometimes our romance is with a creative project. That could be true for you during Venus's transit of Cancer, a nurturing, intuitive sign. You may dig out a project you stuck away in a drawer months ago and decide to rework it and try to sell it. Whether it's a novel or an exhibit of photos or art, it's time to nurture your own talents, Sadge. Onward!

BEST DAYS, CHALLENGING DAYS
The best day? August 8. Mercury turns direct again.

September—Sagittarius

LUNAR HIGHLIGHTS
The new moon in Virgo on September 15 occurs in your career area. This one ushers in new professional opportunities—a promotion, a new job, a new career path altogether. Mercury is conjunct this new moon, suggesting that the new opportunities could involve communication—public speaking, writing, a Web site forum. Mars also forms a wide, beneficial angle to this moon, so buckle up for a wild ride, Sadge.

The full moon in Aries on September 29 is right in line with your energies. It occurs in your solar fifth house of romance, pleasure, and children. The opportunities that surface around the time of this new moon will occur suddenly, unexpectedly, and will prompt you to do something very different. Just be ready to seize the opportunities as they appear.

FINANCES, OTHER STUFF
Mercury enters Libra and your solar eleventh house on September 16 and remains there until October 5. This transit brings the gift of gab, Sadge. Even though your personality is such that you can make friends with any stranger, anywhere, this transit helps to soften any bluntness in your speech. Others are drawn by your magnetism. If you're in sales, this transit could bring a record period.

CAREER
On September 6, Venus enters Leo and your solar ninth house. This transit, which lasts until October 3, should give you ample opportunity to demonstrate and show off your various talents. Bosses and coworkers notice, and suddenly you're the talk of the office. Everyone wants to be your friend! You're tapped for a project, are sent overseas to open an new branch... you get the idea, right? You shine during this period.

ROMANCE
Venus's transit through fellow fire sign Leo between September 6 and October 3 should be wonderful for your love

life. It's possible that you meet a special someone while traveling or that you and your partner, if you're involved, travel abroad together. With Jupiter in Gemini, forming a strong angle to Venus, your love life is ripe for expansion. Perhaps you and your partner take the relationship to the next level. Or perhaps your new romantic interest has a line of work or hobbies that intrigue you. One way or another, your life is expanding.

BEST DAYS, CHALLENGING DAYS
On September 17, the snail of the zodiac, Pluto, turns direct in Capricorn. Things in your finances can move ahead full speed.

October—Sagittarius

LUNAR HIGHLIGHTS
The new moon on October 15 falls in Libra, your solar eleventh house. This one should usher in new friendships, group associations, and artistic interests. Jupiter forms a wide but beneficial angle to this new moon, so the opportunities should expand some facet of your life.

The full moon on October 29 falls in Taurus, your solar sixth house. The moon illuminates a work issue or concern, may make you stubborn about something, and could put you in the race for the long haul. Maybe that's where the stubbornness comes in?

FINANCES, OTHER STUFF
There's plenty of *other stuff* going on this month. First off, Saturn enters Scorpio on October 5. This transit is covered in the Big Picture section for your sign. Keep in mind it's a transit that lasts for two and a half years, and in Scorpio it plumbs the depths of your psyche. Also on the fifth, Mercury enters Scorpio, so for a few weeks Mercury and Saturn travel together. During this period you're looking at the depths of who you are and who you

may become. Mercury represents your conscious mind; Saturn represents authority and the laws of the physical universe.

CAREER
A nice bonus comes your way when Venus transits Virgo and your career area between October 3 and 28. Professional matters go your way now. Others like your ideas and your approach to your work and enjoy your company. Bosses and coworkers are in your court. You can do no wrong! Or at any rate if you do, you're quickly forgiven.

ROMANCE
Mars enters your sign on October 6 and doesn't leave until November 16. During this period your sexuality is heightened, your energy is remarkable, and you're a veritable powerhouse. If you're involved in a relationship, your partner may have trouble keeping up with you! If you're not involved, you aren't worried about it. You're too busy planning your next trip or creative project.

With Venus in your career area for most of October, it's easy to get involved with a coworker or boss.

BEST DAYS, CHALLENGING DAYS
October 5 may feel strange. With both Mars and Saturn entering Scorpio, there could be a lot of psychological stuff that surfaces. Just flow with it.

November—Sagittarius

LUNAR HIGHLIGHTS
The new moon in Scorpio on November 13 is actually a solar eclipse in that sign. Let's take a closer look. Solar eclipses are like double new moons—double the opportunities—but usually you may have to relinquish something first. This eclipse should bring about new opportunities for research and investigation and for getting to the absolute bottom

line of whatever you tackle. This eclipse should be positive for you.

The lunar eclipse two weeks later, on November 28, occurs in Gemini, your opposite sign. This one brings up emotions related to a business or romantic partner. There could be news, too, about this individual. It looks like a good eclipse for you, though, with expansive Jupiter conjunct by five degrees.

FINANCES, OTHER STUFF

Okay, between November 16 and December 25, Mars transits Capricorn and your financial area. You could get a raise or may take on a second job that helps you make ends meet, but regardless of how the details pan out, you will be putting a lot of energy into earning—and spending. Just pay cash for everything, Sadge, so you're aware of where your money goes.

CAREER

The best news? Mercury turns direct on November 26, in your sign. This movement will facilitate your professional matters and concerns and enable you to move forward again with projects, ideas, workshops. By mid-December every planet will be in direct motion, functioning at their optimum levels, so things are really going to improve—professionally and in every other area as well.

ROMANCE

Neptune turns direct in Pisces on November 10, which should sweeten up your home life. In addition, Venus enters Scorpio on November 21, so your sexuality is enhanced, and you're looking for really deep emotional experiences that speak to the Scorpionic soul. You find those experiences, too, and they prompt you to rethink a relationship.

BEST DAYS, CHALLENGING DAYS

The lunar eclipse in Gemini should be interesting. Whether it's positive or not depends on your attitude and beliefs, on where your current relationship is headed, and whether you're happy in this relationship.

December—Sagittarius

LUNAR HIGHLIGHTS

The new moon in your sign on December 13 is one to plan for. It happens just once a year and sets the tone for the next twelve months. Before it occurs, make a wish list for the upcoming year. Focus on what you would like to achieve and experience. Back these desires with emotion, visualize them happening, then let the universe do its job and manifest your desires. This new moon should be a good one for you.

The full moon in Cancer on December 28 occurs in your solar eighth house. This moon illuminates resources you share with others—specifically a spouse, partner, or someone else. Pluto is opposed to this moon, so there could be tension over power issues.

FINANCES, OTHER STUFF

Mars continues its journey through Capricorn and your financial area until December 25. During this period you may be working longer hours, perhaps to meet a deadline, or you may be juggling several different jobs. Your focus and energy are on earning money. On December 15, Venus enters your sign, so you earn a bonus or a raise, or the way you earn your daily bread may simply become easier and more fluid.

CAREER

People are usually in more generous moods around the holidays, so your professional life should be moving along at a pace and rhythm that suits you. With Venus in your sign from December 15 into early January 2013, others find you appealing, like your ideas and energy, and are more likely to support your endeavors.

There is probably a lot of media hype now about December 21, 2012, and a doomsday scenario. Ignore it. Keep to your path. Early in the month, start listing your new year's resolutions.

ROMANCE
Between December 15, 2012, and January 9, 2013, Venus is in your sign. This period should be one of the most romantic and creative times for you all year. And lucky you, Sadge, this energy takes you into 2013. If you're in a relationship when this transit begins, then things should only improve. If you're unattached, you probably won't be when the transit ends!

BEST DAYS, CHALLENGING DAYS
When Uranus turns direct in fellow fire sign Aries on December 13, every planet is moving in direct motion. Take advantage of it by setting your own life in motion!

Happy New Year!

11

Capricorn

The Big Picture for 2012

Welcome to 2012, Capricorn! It's a year for diplomacy, service, kindness, adjustments at home, and learning to balance your domestic and professional responsibilities. Your ruler, Saturn, occupies two signs this year—Libra and Scorpio. Saturn's transit through Libra brings additional professional responsibilities and a strong structure to all your career endeavors. Saturn's transit through Scorpio indicates stronger friendships and group affiliations and a good structure for attaining your wishes and dreams.

Pluto starts off the year in Capricorn, where it has been since November 2008. You're accustomed to its energy now. Its transit, which lasts until 2024, is bringing profound and permanent change globally, evident in the economic challenges that now face the U.S. Most institutions are in the throes of great change—the health-care industry, the petroleum and insurance industries, mortgages/lending, housing, aviation, even the Internet. You name it, and Pluto's fingerprint can be found.

On a personal level, this planet's transit through your sign portends deep and permanent change in your personal life. Possibilities? A birth, children leave home or return home; parents move in or out; you get married or divorced; you move; start a career or retire or land a nice promotion and raise. You get the idea. Pluto's changes are rarely sudden, but they usually work at deep levels and make us aware of just how special life is.

Jupiter transits Taurus from January 1 to June 11. This transit expands your romantic and love options. The things you do for fun and pleasure will broaden. If you've considered a family, then this transit may facilitate a pregnancy. If you have children already, then they expand your world in a significant way, perhaps through the friends they bring into your home. Foreign travel is a distinct possibility, particularly for pleasure. You might also return to school, get published, or expand your business interests to overseas markets.

Between June 11 and June 25, 2013, Jupiter transits Gemini and your solar sixth house of daily work and health. This transit expands your daily work schedule so that you may eventually feel you don't have enough time to accomplish everything you need to do in a given day. This transit also bolsters your communication abilities and suggests an addition of employees and coworkers and an expansion in whatever you do to maintain your health and well-being. A new exercise regimen, for instance, or a new nutritional program.

Neptune entered Pisces on April 4, 2011. But by early August 2011, it had slipped back into Aquarius. Neptune symbolizes our higher ideals, escapism, fiction, spirituality, and our blind spots. It seeks to dissolve boundaries between us and others. One possible repercussion of this transit is prolonged religious wars, which proliferated during Uranus's transit in Pisces from early 2003. February 3, 2012, it enters Pisces again and won't move on until January 2026.

On a personal level, this transit forms a beneficial angle to your sun and brings idealistic and inspirational elements into your conscious, daily life. You might start working for a charity or volunteer for an animal organization. Or you might donate your time to helping someone within your own community. Neptune's transit through Pisces should deepen your intuition and your spiritual beliefs and enable you to integrate both more readily into your life.

Uranus entered Aries in March 2011. The thing to remember with this transit is that it forms a challenging angle to your sun. To mitigate the impact of this transit, remember to think before you speak, to guard against blowing things out of proportion, and watch your temper!

They say that timing is everything, so with that in mind let's look at some specific areas in your life in 2012.

ROMANCE/CREATIVITY

The most romantic and creative time for you all year falls between March 5 and April 3, when Venus transits Taurus and the love/romance area of your chart. Not only do others find you more appealing, seductive, and radiant, but you feel that way about yourself too. You attract who and what you need when you need it. If you're single and looking, then be sure that during this period you do a lot of what you enjoy.

If you're in a committed relationship, then you and your partner rediscover each other. Plan a trip out of town, to some secluded, romantic spot. Spend time together doing whatever you both enjoy.

Another good time frame: October 3 to 28, when Venus transits fellow earth sign Virgo and your solar ninth house. During this transit you're more discriminating about your romantic interests and perhaps even a tad too critical. But you may share camaraderie with someone whose worldview and beliefs are similar to yours.

A deepening commitment in an existing relationship is possible between August 7 and September 6, when Venus transits Cancer and the partnership area of your chart. You and your partner may decide to move in together, get engaged, or get married.

CAREER

One of the most important dates falls on October 15, with a new moon in Libra and your career area. This transit promises new professional opportunities, and because Jupiter forms a beneficial angle to the new moon, the opportunities are expansive and lucky.

Between October 28 and November 21, Venus transits Libra and the career area of your chart. This is another lucky transit for career matters. Things go your way, Capricorn.

BEST TIMES FOR

Buying or selling a home: March 2 to 12, April 16 to May 9, when Mercury transits Aries and your solar fourth house.

Family reunions: The above date or when Venus transits fellow earth sign Taurus between March 5 and April 3.

Financial matters: September 6 to October 3, when Venus transits Leo and the shared resources area of your chart.

Signing contracts: When Mercury is moving direct!

MERCURY RETROGRADES

Every year Mercury—the planet of communication and travel—turns retrograde three times. During this period it's wise not to sign contracts (unless you don't mind renegotiating when Mercury is moving direct), to check and recheck travel plans or, better yet, don't travel, and to communicate as succinctly as possible. Refrain from buying any large-ticket items or electronics during this time too. Often computers and appliances go on the fritz, cars act up, data is lost ... you get the idea. Be sure to back up all files before the dates below:

March 12–April 4: Mercury retrograde in Aries, your solar fourth house of creativity, love, and romance.

July 14–August 8: Mercury retrograde in Leo, your solar eighth house of shared resources and your partner's income.

November 6–26: Mercury retrograde in Sagittarius and your solar twelfth house.

ECLIPSES

Solar eclipses tend to trigger external events that bring about change according to the sign and house in which they fall. Lunar eclipses trigger inner, emotional events according to the sign and house in which they fall. Any eclipse marks both beginnings and endings. The solar and lunar eclipse in a pair falls in opposite signs. If you're interested in detailed information on eclipses, take a look at Celeste Teal's excellent and definitive book, *Eclipses: Predicting World Events & Personal Transformation*.

If you were born under or around the time of an eclipse, it's to your advantage to take a look at your birth chart to find out exactly where the eclipses will impact you.

Most years feature four eclipses—two solar, two lunar, with the set separated by about two weeks. In November and December 2011, there were solar and lunar eclipses, so this year the first eclipses fall during May and June.

May 20: Solar eclipse at 0 degrees Gemini. This one should bring in new work opportunities and new opportunities for maintain your health.

June 4: Lunar eclipse in Sagittarius, your solar twelfth house. Positive news.

November 13: Solar eclipse in Scorpio. New opportunities for friendships and to achieve your goals and dreams.

November 28: Lunar eclipse, Gemini. Jupiter forms a five-degree conjunction to the eclipse degree, suggesting that news you receive around this time will be cause for celebration!

LUCKIEST DAY OF THE YEAR

Every year there's one day when Jupiter and the sun meet up, and luck, serendipity, and expansion are the hallmarks. This year that day falls on May 13, with a conjunction in Taurus.

January—Capricorn

LUNAR HIGHLIGHTS

The first lunation of the year falls on January 9, in Cancer, your opposite sign. This one should illuminate a concern or issue in a business or romantic partnership. Mars forms a close, beneficial angle to this full moon, suggesting increased activity and attention to detail around this time.

The new moon on January 23 falls in Aquarius, your financial area. It should usher in new opportunities for earning more money—a raise, a second job, even a new job that generates more income. Uranus forms a strong, beneficial angle to this new moon, so the opportunities may surface suddenly and unexpectedly.

FINANCES, OTHER STUFF
With Venus transiting Pisces between January 14 to February 8, you may discover opportunities in the course of your normal day to increase your earnings. It could come through an artistic or creative project, a home-based business or some other venue. Mars in Virgo forms a beneficial angle to your sun sign through July 3, suggesting that attention to details is important.

CAREER
Your ruler, Saturn, begins the year in Libra, where it has been for nearly two years. You should already have a clear idea how this transit impacts your life. It's transiting your career area, so even though you may be experiencing professional delays, you're fulfilling your obligations and responsibilities. Jupiter is in Taurus now, a fellow earth sign, and is joyously expanding your capacity for pleasure. So whatever you're doing in your career, it should be—first and foremost—fun!

ROMANCE
Let's talk a little more about Jupiter in Taurus. This transit, which lasts until June 11, is familiar to you already. Jupiter has been in Taurus for some time now, revving up your love life, increasing your options with creativity and whatever you do for fun and pleasure. Also, Venus is in compatible water sign Pisces, a gentle, intuitive sign, and this transit could attract a romance very close to home—perhaps in your neighborhood.

BEST DAYS, CHALLENGING DAYS
January 8 to 27 puts Mercury in your sign, Capricorn, so your communication skills are exceptionally strong, and so is your ambition!

February—Capricorn

LUNAR HIGHLIGHTS
February 7 features a full moon in Leo, your solar eighth house. This moon illuminates resources you share with others—the finances, energy, and times you share with others and vice versa. Usually it's about your spouse or partner's income. News about your partner's earnings? Perhaps. Other possibilities? News about a workshop you may attend on an esoteric topic or about taxes, insurance, wills.

The new moon in Pisces on February 21 should be quite pleasant for you, with new opportunities surfacing that match your ideals. Neptune is closely conjunct this moon, so that's where the idealism comes in. You may find the ideal neighborhood for you and your family, could discover you're going to have a new brother or sister, or new opportunities surface in your daily life.

FINANCES, OTHER STUFF
With Jupiter in Taurus now, many areas of your life are expanding. Your worldview and spiritual beliefs should be broadening, perhaps through foreign travel, foreign business dealings, or foreign-born individuals. You're learning how vastly different other cultures are from your own and how these cultural differences influence people's belief systems. It sounds obvious, but in the past certain nuances have escaped you.

CAREER
Jupiter's transit through Taurus has excellent repercussions for your daily work life. You may be assuming more

responsibility and get paid handsomely for it. You may be hiring more employees for your company, expanding your services/products to overseas markets, or perhaps moving to another country to establish services. With Saturn in your career area, one thing is for sure: your hard work is moving you toward success.

ROMANCE
Between February 8 and March 5, Venus transits Aries and your solar fourth house. This transit should bring passion and excitement into your love life. You may feel things you normally don't experience, and while it could be a bit confusing at times, you secretly enjoy these new feelings. Mars is retrograde in fellow earth sign Virgo until April 14, so you may be somewhat picky about who you get involved with or could find yourself being critical of your partner.

BEST DAYS, CHALLENGING DAYS
Between February 13 and March 2, Mercury transits Pisces, bringing a powerful intuitive flow to your conscious mind. You feel your way through situations and seem to have a better grasp of the people you encounter.

March—Capricorn

LUNAR HIGHLIGHTS
The full moon on March 8 falls in Virgo, a fellow earth sign, and Mars is widely conjunct. You can expect a lot of activity around this time, with news that somehow illuminates your spirituality and worldview or an educational, publishing, or travel issue. Because Virgo is part of the equation, a health report may be forthcoming too.

The new moon in Aries on March 22 occurs in your domestic environment and should bring new opportunities connected to your family. Mercury and Uranus form close conjunctions to this new moon, indicating that opportunities appear quickly and you have to be ready to seize them.

With Mercury as part of the equation, one potential opportunity could be with communication.

FINANCES, OTHER STUFF
On March 2, Mercury enters fiery Aries, so your communication ability is heightened with passion, enthusiasm, energy. Mercury will be traveling with Uranus until May 9, a long transit for this little planet, due to a retrograde period between March 12 and April 4. During this period don't sign contracts, be sure your travel arrangements are made on either side of this time frame, don't apply for a mortgage or loan, and be very clear in all your communication. Reread the section on Mercury retrogrades in the Big Picture for your sign.

CAREER
Mercury's retrograde applies across the board, so be aware of the dates. With work, it's smart to tackle current projects rather than moving on to something new. Saturn turned retrograde on February 7 in your career area, which could lead to professional delays until it turns direct again on June 25. They say that timing is everything, Capricorn!

ROMANCE
Despite Mercury's retrograde, your love life for most of this month looks very good. Venus joins Jupiter in Taurus between March 5 and April 3, bringing your focus squarely to romance, creativity, and your children. Whether you're attached or single, Venus and Jupiter traveling together promise expansion, luck, beauty, and plenty of private time with your creative muse!

BEST DAYS, CHALLENGING DAYS
The entire period when Venus and Jupiter travel together should be exceptionally pleasant for you. So mark these dates: March 5 to April 3!

April—Capricorn

LUNAR HIGHLIGHTS
The full moon in Libra on April 6 occurs in your career area. This moon illuminates a professional issue or concern, a professional relationship, or something else connected to your career. Saturn forms a wide conjunction to the full moon, suggesting a seriousness to the news or to what you discover.

April 21 features a new moon in Taurus, a fellow earth sign, and it occurs in your romance and creativity area. The possibilities are utterly delicious: a new romantic relationship, a new creativity project, a birth in the family. You've got Mars forming a beneficial angle to this new moon. It's your booster rocket.

FINANCES, OTHER STUFF
The best news is that Mercury turns direct on April 4. Wait a few days, then proceed with contract negotiations, applications for a mortgage or loan, and anything else you've put on hold. Venus transits Gemini between April 3 and August 7. The transit is long for Venus because it will be retrograde between May 15 and June 27. Before the retrograde begins next month, have your priorities in place—financially, with work, family, your personal life. If you need to buy large-ticket items—a computer, car, furniture—do it before May 15 or after June 27.

CAREER
Well, Saturn is still in Libra, in your career area. If professional matters aren't going the way you had hoped, don't get bummed out about it. It's a cycle, nothing more, nothing less. Things will improve after October 5, when Saturn enters compatible water sign Scorpio. Until then, fulfill your obligations and responsibilities; do your job as well as you can.

ROMANCE
Venus enters Gemini on April 3, and between then and May 15, your love life may involve flirtations at work, a re-

lationship with someone connected to your work, or someone you meet through work. Whether you're involved with anyone or not when the transit begins, communication will be a large and important part of any romantic relationship during this time. Mars in Virgo turns direct on April 14, so your sexuality and physical energy are heightened.

BEST DAYS, CHALLENGING DAYS
April 4 is a day to celebrate. Mercury turns direct.

May—Capricorn

LUNAR HIGHLIGHTS
May 5. The full moon in water sign Scorpio, a sign compatible with your earth-sign sun, brings news about a friendship, a group to which you belong, or about some dream or wish you have. Jupiter opposes this moon, which suggests that whatever you're feeling may be excessive, blown out of proportion to what is actually happening.

The new moon on May 20 is actually a solar eclipse in Gemini. Solar eclipses are like double new moons, so the new opportunities headed into your life are multiplied. Since this eclipse occurs in your daily work area, that's where the opportunities are likely to surface. But check your natal chart for where Gemini falls. That will tell the real story for you and this eclipse. Uranus forms a wide but beneficial angle to the eclipse degree, and by now you should know what that means—sudden, unpredictable events. Be ready to seize your opportunities as they happen.

FINANCES, OTHER STUFF
Mercury and Mars are now in direct motion, but Saturn, your ruler, is still retrograde and Venus turns retrograde on May 15. Between then and June 27, there could be some bumps and bruises in terms of finances. Nothing serious, nothing that you can't get a grip on. Just watch your bud-

get, and pay cash when possible so that you're more aware of what you spend and on what.

CAREER

With Venus turning retrograde in Gemini, the daily work area of your chart, on May 15, it's best to stick to what you know. You can be innovative with your ideas, of course, but don't try to implement them until after June 27. Venus retrograde sometimes results in physical discomforts—the AC/heat in your office or car, for instance, might conk out. Or you are moved to a smaller office that is less agreeable to you. Things like that. Capricorn, though, is made of hardy stuff, and nothing is insurmountable for you during this retrograde period.

ROMANCE

Be sure to communicate clearly with your partner. Avoid squabbles over silly things. In fact, avoid confrontations altogether if you can. The period to watch for—May 15 to June 27, that pesky Venus retrograde. Since Gemini is involved, it's a good idea to write down your gripes, get them out of your system. Then you're less likely to blurt out something you can't retract.

BEST DAYS, CHALLENGING DAYS

We don't want to overdo it with this Venus retrograde, but be aware that May 15 could be one of those scattered days, when it seems that not too much goes right.

June—Capricorn

LUNAR HIGHLIGHTS

It's a hectic month, Capricorn, and it gets off to a running start on June 4, with a lunar eclipse in Sagittarius, your solar twelfth house, the most hidden and private section of your chart. You may learn about someone else's true motives, and the discovery upsets you. Equally possible is that you're able to grasp the larger picture of your own motives and act accordingly. The eclipse is actually a positive one, so make the most of it. Just try to go with the flow.

June 19 boasts a second new moon in Gemini, which means new opportunities emerging in your daily work and in communication. Be sure to read the fine print, however.

FINANCES, OTHER STUFF

The big news this month is that Jupiter enters Gemini, where it will be until June 25, 2013. Your daily work routine is about to expand tremendously and could include a promotion, international travel, publishing, higher education. Your communication abilities and opportunities should also expand in some way, perhaps through public speaking or blogging, or perhaps you write a book or novel. Look at your natal chart to find out where Gemini falls. That house and the areas it rules will undergo the most expansion and luck.

CAREER

Saturn turns direct in Libra and your career area on June 25. Professional matters that have been delayed now move forward and are strengthened in foundations and structures. Jupiter forms a beneficial angle to Saturn, so with these two planets working in harmony, the expansion in your daily work translates into expansion in your career. You could change jobs or career paths, get a raise or promotion, or even go to law school! It all depends on where you place your focus and attention.

ROMANCE

Your love life continues to experience bumps and bruises until June 27, when Venus finally turns direct again. You might consider booking a getaway for you and your partner after that date. Pick someplace neither of you has been before, but which is romantic and idyllic. Until next month, Mars continues its journey through fellow earth sign Virgo and that section of your chart that rules foreign travel. So perhaps your trip should be to some exotic overseas location. You're in the mood for romance and seduction.

BEST DAYS, CHALLENGING DAYS

Between June 7 and 25, Mercury transits Cancer, your opposite sign. This brings your conscious focus to a partnership that you should nurture.

Neptune turns retrograde in Pisces on June 4. This movement suggests an inner searching and scrutiny of your ideals. The retrograde remains in effect until November 10.

July—Capricorn

LUNAR HIGHLIGHTS

The full moon on July 3 occurs in your sign and illumines a personal issue, relationship, or concern that you have. Pluto forms a close conjunction to this moon, significant in that it puts you in the power seat. Uranus forms a challenging angle to this full moon and an exact angle to Pluto, suggesting an unexpected quality to events and some power plays by others.

The new moon on July 19 falls in Cancer, your opposite sign. This moon should steer new relationship opportunities your way, or you and your partner decide to make a deeper commitment to each other. You might get engaged or married, move in together, buy a home. Saturn forms a challenging angle to this new moon, indicating some tension or strife. But like all challenges that come your way, you handle it with resolve.

FINANCES, OTHER STUFF

Mercury retro alert! This one extends from July 14 to August 8 and occurs in Leo, your solar eighth house. The eighth house rules shared resources—time, money, and energy you share with others, usually a spouse, but it could also be a parent, child, even a friend. It also rules taxes, insurance, mortgages, loans, wills. So this Mercury retro affects your finances. In the Big Picture section for your sign, reread the suggestions for navigating this retrograde period.

CAREER
With Mercury retrograde during the above dates, it's best to stick to current projects rather than starting something new. Or return to older projects and ideas and see if you can make them viable. Now that Venus is moving direct again, your daily work should be humming along at a pace that suits you. You may decide to start a blog or newsletter about your project/organization/services or products. Women prove helpful.

ROMANCE
Your creativity is racing full steam ahead, and you and a partner may decide to join forces to make things happen more quickly. If you do combine your talents, be sure that you agree on the basics. If you're not involved right now, don't fret about it. You've got plenty on your plate and may be having too much fun playing the field to worry about getting involved in a committed relationship.

BEST DAYS, CHALLENGING DAYS
July 14. Big ouch. Mercury turns retrograde.

August—Capricorn

LUNAR HIGHLIGHTS
With three lunations this month, it's going to be one crazy August, Capricorn. The action begins on August 1, with a full moon in Aquarius. This moon illuminates your finances in some way—something may be revealed suddenly and unexpectedly. Since Mars forms a wide, beneficial angle to this full moon, you can expect heightened activity, a lot of people coming and going, and an excess of forward thrust in all your activities.

On August 17, the new moon in Leo occurs in your solar eighth house. This moon should attract new opportunities for your spouse, partner, or anyone else with whom you share resources. He or she could land a raise or a better job or receive some payoff in stocks or royalties. You may get a break in taxes or insurance or have a chance to study an esoteric topic that intrigues you. Both Saturn and Mars form beneficial angles to this new moon, which means that the new opportunities are grounded, serious, and could involve working with groups. Mars brings forward motion.

The full moon in Pisces on August 31 should be a gentle, soft time for you. Your imagination and intuition are heightened, you have opportunities to hang out with your siblings and other relatives, and may be introduced to a new neighborhood that suits the needs of your family. Even if you aren't considering a move, you may change your mind.

FINANCES, OTHER STUFF

Mercury turns direct on August 8, always a reason to celebrate. Now you can apply for a mortgage or loan, refinance your home, pitch your ideas, send in your manuscript, move forward on everything. Once Mars enters Scorpio on August 23, you're after the absolute bottom line—in your finances, friendship, goals. The time to watch for, though, falls between November 16 and December 25, when Mars transits your sign. That's when your physical energy will be at its height.

CAREER

Venus transits your opposite sign, Cancer, from August 7 to September 6. During this period business partners are in your court, and you're nurturing those relationships, making sure everyone is happy and pleased with your arrangement. With Mercury turning direct on the eighth, you're filled with enthusiasm about moving forward with certain projects and ideas, and your enthusiasm is contagious. You won't have any trouble finding the support you may need.

ROMANCE

During the dates of the Venus transit cited above, you are nurturing your most intimate relationship—with a spouse or partner. It would be a great time to get away together, to break up your normal routine with an adventure to some intriguing spot neither of you has visited before. The mutual exploration of this place will bring the two of you closer together.

BEST DAYS, CHALLENGING DAYS
August 8, when Mercury turns direct again, is a day to circle! August 31 is another good date: Mercury enters fellow earth sign Virgo, strengthening your communication skills.

September—Capricorn

LUNAR HIGHLIGHTS
A new moon in fellow earth sign Virgo on September 15 should bring some interesting new opportunities to travel abroad, go to college or grad school, or expand your products or services to overseas markets. Mercury forms a wide conjunction to this moon, suggesting that new opportunities in communication could surface. Public speaking, teaching, writing a book, starting a blog are all possibilities. Mars forms a wide, beneficial angle to this new moon, and this prompts you to be ready to seize the opportunities as they manifest themselves.

The full moon on September 29 falls in Aries and illuminates your domestic environment. News is forthcoming about your home life, parents, your spouse, perhaps your children. Uranus is closely conjunct to this full moon, so it's likely that the news catches you completely off guard.

FINANCES, OTHER STUFF
Between September 6 and October 3, Venus transits Leo and your solar eighth house. This transit should facilitate obtaining a mortgage or loan, your spouse or partner could get a raise, and you could get a break on your taxes or on insurance payments. Venus in Leo gives you the opportunity to shine in some area of your life, Capricorn, so look your best!

CAREER

With Mercury now in Virgo, you may be traveling internationally and communicating with foreign investors or individuals who can help you to expand your products and services to overseas markets. Your worldview and spiritual beliefs are part of the picture, too. Perhaps you feel a need to integrate your beliefs more readily into your professional life.

Next month, Saturn leaves your career area and enters Scorpio and your solar eleventh house. This transit should enable your professional life to move ahead. No more delays!

ROMANCE

With Venus's transit through Leo from September 6 to October 3, you are more passionate. You may need more attention from your partner and could feel possessive or even jealous. Try to turn negative feelings around by focusing your attention elsewhere. Instead of giving your attention to what irritates you about your partner, find the things you appreciate. Demonstrate that appreciation in some way. Daily.

BEST DAYS, CHALLENGING DAYS

Between September 16 and October 5, Mercury transits Libra and your career area. This transit suggests discussions, travel, and an enhanced talent for making friends of strangers. You work a room with a master's touch.

October—Capricorn

LUNAR HIGHLIGHTS

October is full of change, with one of the major planets, Saturn, beginning a new transit on the fifth. But first, the lunar highlights. On October 15, a new moon in Libra looks quite good for your career. New professional opportunities certainly come your way now, particularly with Saturn out of your career area. If you've been job hunting, then you could be hired. If you've been considering a change in careers, a road opens up. If you intend to stay where you are, then a promotion and raise could be in the offing.

The full moon in Taurus on October 29 should be a good one. Taurus is a fellow earth sign, so its energy is compatible with your earth-sign sun. This full moon should bring news about a romantic relationship, a creative project, one of your kids, or something you do for fun and pleasure.

FINANCES, OTHER STUFF

On October 5, Saturn enters Scorpio and will be there for about two and a half years. During this time it forms a beneficial angle to your sun. As long as you fulfill your obligations and responsibilities, this transit should strengthen all your endeavors. As the ruler of your sun sign, its transit may impact you more profoundly than that of other planets. While it's in Scorpio, your investigative abilities should be more powerful, and you won't be satisfied with anything shallow.

Also on the fifth, Mercury enters Scorpio, where it will be until the twenty-ninth. While it travels with Saturn, your conscious mind will have a more serious bent to it, and your intuition should be considerably stronger. You may gravitate toward discussions about the ultimate esoteric questions: spirit contact, life after death, and the like.

CAREER

Your career should be expanding like crazy now. With Jupiter still in Gemini and forming a beneficial angle to your career area, you should be in the right place at the right time for the right job, promotion, raise. You name it, you desire it, you visualize it—and Jupiter tries to bring it to you. Between October 6 and November 16, Mars transits Sagittarius and forms a beneficial angle to your career area. Think of Mars as your booster rocket, the planet that gets you moving and makes things happen.

ROMANCE

With Venus in fellow earth sign Virgo between October 3 and 28, you enjoy slightly more than three weeks when everything seems to flow your way in romance, with your creative projects, with your kids. You and your partner may take off for a trip overseas for either business or pleasure or both. While Mercury is in Scorpio between October 5 and 29, you are passionate about everything—your romantic relationships, opinions and ideas, interests. Your passion proves contagious and draws your partner in.

BEST DAYS, CHALLENGING DAYS

You'll feel the shift in energy on October 5, when both Mercury and Saturn enter Scorpio, a sign that fits well with your earth-sign sun.

November—Capricorn

LUNAR HIGHLIGHTS

Eclipses always bring change of one kind or another, and the two eclipses this month are no exception. The solar eclipse on November 13 is in Scorpio and should usher in new opportunities in your daily life, with siblings and other relatives, even with neighbors. You could find the perfect neighborhood for you and your family and, as a result, decide to put your current home on the market.

Two weeks later, on November 28, the lunar eclipse falls in Gemini. Thanks to a close conjunction with Jupiter, it looks as if the news you hear brings a soaring optimism to your mood and expands your world in some way. This eclipse should be a good one for you.

FINANCES, OTHER STUFF

Mercury retro alert—last one this year. It extends from November 6 to November 26, and occurs again in a fire sign—Sagittarius. You know the drill now about what not to do. But here are some things you may want to consider doing. Take up meditation or yoga or both. With Mercury retrograde in your twelfth house, any activity that brings your attention inward is favored. If you're inclined, talk to a therapist, read Carl Jung, study the collective unconscious, or learn about synchronicity. Keep a synchronicity journal in which you record your experiences with meaningful coincidences.

CAREER
As 2012 winds down, the media hype over the end of the Mayan calendar is probably ramping upward. Ignore it. Go about your business, doing your work with your usual efficiency, and be sure to take time to be with the people you care about most. Once Venus enters Scorpio on November 21, shortly before Thanksgiving, your emotions will be more intense and passionate, and you can easily pour it into professional matters.

ROMANCE
On November 16, Mars enters your sign, where it will be until December 25. During part of this period, from November 21 until December 15, Venus will be in compatible water sign Scorpio. The combination of energies with these two planets will bring great intensity to your love life and heighten your sexuality and could trigger powerful passions. If you're not involved right now, then all this intensity may attract a romantic interest whom you meet through friends or through a group to which you belong. One way or another, the intensity needs an outlet, so it may be time to call upon your muse!

BEST DAYS, CHALLENGING DAYS
November 6 could be challenging. Mercury turns retrograde in Sagittarius, your solar twelfth house.

December—Capricorn

LUNAR HIGHLIGHTS

December's moons occur right before and after Christmas. The first, on December 13, is a new moon in Sadge, your solar twelfth house. This one should usher in new opportunities for foreign travel, in publishing and education, and with your own psyche. You may be digging into the past, uncovering power you have disowned over the years. Therapy could be good, but so are meditation and yoga.

On December 28, a full moon in Cancer should highlight a business or romantic partnership. This full moon receives a friendly nod from Saturn, so the opportunities that surface with a partner are serious, solid. Perhaps you and your partner decide to go into business together. Or you write a book together. If you're not married or deeply committed to each other, that may change with this moon. You might decide to move in together, get engaged or married, start a family.

FINANCES, OTHER STUFF

Mercury enters Sagittarius on December 10, and Venus follows on December 15. Combined with the new moon in Sadge on December 28, there's a lot of energy and focus on what is hidden in your life, within yourself. But that's just a solar chart. Look at your natal chart for a genuine picture of what's going on for you. Wherever you have Sagittarius in your chart, that's where the new opportunities will surface and where your conscious attention will be.

CAREER

With Mars in your sign until December 25, you've got plenty of physical energy to get things done. You may be a powerhouse during this period, ripping through whatever is on your desk, in your inbox, and on your computer. You're determined to get the job done, the way you want it done. Good. Ignore the media hype about December 21, 2012. Just throw yourself into your work, your home life, your love life, and do what Capricorn does best—move forward steadily.

ROMANCE
On December 15, Venus enters Sagittarius, where it will be into the early part of the new year. This transit suggests that you and your partner may be spending more time alone together. Perhaps you take a few days off, a long weekend, and head for parts unknown. If you're keeping the relationship secret for some reason, that won't last indefinitely. Once Venus enters your sign early next year, all bets are off. You'll be announcing your news to the rest of the world.

BEST DAYS, CHALLENGING DAYS
On Christmas Day, Mars enters Aquarius and your financial area. Maybe you get money for the holidays! Equally possible is that you come up with an idea for making more money, doing something you love.

Happy New Year!

12

Aquarius

The Big Picture in 2012

Welcome to 2012, Aquarius! It's a year of mystery and investigation, a year for delving into what is unseen and hidden, dealing with secrets, of looking beneath the surface.

Your ruler, Uranus, is in Aries this year and until March 2019. The bottom line with this transit is that it forms a beneficial angle to your sun, and you can expect sudden, unusual experiences. You'll meet unusual and exciting people in your daily life.

Saturn occupies two signs this year—Libra and Scorpio, which it enters on October 5. The first transit, through Libra, has been going on since late October 2009, so you should be accustomed to its energy by now. It forms a beneficial angle to your sun. Remember that Saturn in a fellow air sign enables you to build strong foundations in your life.

Neptune entered Pisces on April 4, 2011. But by early August 2011, it had slipped back into Aquarius. Neptune symbolizes our higher ideals, escapism, fiction, spirituality, and our blind spots. It seeks to dissolve boundaries between us and others. One possible repercussion of this transit is prolonged religious wars, which proliferated during Uranus's transit in Pisces from early 2003. February 3, 2012, it enters Pisces again and won't move on until January 2026.

On a personal level, there are several things you should keep in mind about this transit. Since it occurs in your second house of finances, your approach to how you earn your living, how much you earn and spend will be heavily influenced by your ideals and spiritual beliefs. Since Neptune often creates confusion, it's not a favorable time to speculate or gamble.

Pluto starts off the year in Capricorn and your solar twelfth house, where it has been since November 2008. You're accustomed to its energy now. Its transit, which lasts until 2024, is bringing profound and permanent change globally, evident in the economic challenges that now face the U.S. Most institutions are in the throes of great change—the health-care industry, the petroleum and insurance industries, mortgages/lending, housing, aviation, even the Internet. You name it, and Pluto's fingerprint can be found.

On a personal level, this planet's transit through Capricorn enables you to delve into your own psyche and get rid of beliefs that no longer serve you or which are limiting and restricting you in some way. Meditation, therapy, yoga, are all beneficial pursuits during this transit. Any work you do behind the scenes will be powerful and effective. Your professional goals may change dramatically, but you're equipped for the change. Pluto's changes are rarely sudden, but they usually work at deep levels and make us aware of just how special life is.

Jupiter's transit through Taurus from January 1 to June 11 expands your domestic life and personal environment. A birth is possible, a relative moves in, you add on to your house, or move to a larger home in a more upscale neighborhood. Foreign travel is a distinct possibility, particularly for pleasure. You might also return to school, get published, or expand your business interests to overseas markets.

Between June 11 and June 25, 2013, Jupiter transits fellow air sign Gemini and your solar fifth house of creativity, love and romance, enjoyment, and children. Your options in all these areas expand. If you've thought about starting a family, then this transit certainly helps make it possible. More foreign travel is likely. You might publish a novel, sell a screenplay, or have an opportunity express your creativity in new ways. This transit also bolsters your communication abilities and your intellectual interests.

Uranus entered Aries in March 2011. Remember that it forms a beneficial angle to your sun, so you'll undoubtedly enjoy the excitement it brings into your life.

They say that timing is everything, so with that in mind let's look at some specific areas in your life in 2012.

ROMANCE/CREATIVITY

The most romantic and creative time for you all year falls between April 3 and May 15 and June 27 and August 7, when Venus transits Gemini and the love/romance area of your chart. Not only do others find you more appealing, seductive, and radiant, but you feel that way about yourself too. You attract who and what you need when you need it. If you're single and looking, then be sure that during this period you do a lot of what you enjoy.

If you're in a committed relationship, then you and your partner rediscover each other. Plan a trip out of town, to some secluded, romantic spot. Spend time together doing whatever you both enjoy.

Another good time frame: October 28 to November 21, when Venus transits fellow air sign Libra and your solar ninth house. During this transit you're more social, which increases your chances of meeting someone special.

A deepening commitment in an existing relationship is possible between September 6 and October 3, when Venus transits Leo and the partnership area of your chart. You and your partner may decide to move in together, get engaged, or get married.

CAREER

One of the most important dates falls on November 13, when there's a solar eclipse in your career area. This transit promises new professional opportunities, and because Jupiter forms a beneficial angle to the eclipse degree, the opportunities are expansive and lucky.

Between November 21 and December 15, Venus transits Scorpio and the career area of your chart. This is another lucky transit for career matters. Things go your way, Aquarius.

BEST TIMES FOR
Buying or selling a home: May 9 to 24, when Mercury transits Taurus and your solar fourth house.

Family reunions: The above dates or when Venus is moving direct in Gemini between April 3 and May 15, and June 27 and August 7.

Financial matters: January 14 to February 8, when Venus transits Pisces and the financial area of your chart.

Signing contracts: When Mercury is moving direct!

MERCURY RETROGRADES
Every year Mercury—the planet of communication and travel—turns retrograde three times. During this period it's wise not to sign contracts (unless you don't mind renegotiating when Mercury is moving direct), to check and recheck travel plans or, better yet, don't travel, and to communicate as succinctly as possible. Refrain from buying any large-ticket items or electronics during this time too. Often computers and appliances go on the fritz, cars act up, data is lost ... you get the idea. Be sure to back up all files before the dates below:

March 12–April 4: Mercury retrograde in Aries, your solar third house of communication, siblings, your daily life.

July 14–August 8: Mercury retrograde in Leo, your solar seventh house of partnerships.

November 6–26: Mercury retrograde in Sagittarius and your solar eleventh house.

ECLIPSES
Solar eclipses tend to trigger external events that bring about change according to the sign and house in which they fall. Lunar eclipses trigger inner, emotional events according to the sign and house in which they fall. Any eclipse marks both beginnings and endings. The solar and lunar eclipse in a pair falls in opposite signs. If you're interested in detailed information on eclipses, take a look at Celeste

Teal's excellent and definitive book, *Eclipses: Predicting World Events & Personal Transformation.*

If you were born under or around the time of an eclipse, it's to your advantage to take a look at your birth chart to find out exactly where the eclipses will impact you.

Most years feature four eclipses—two solar, two lunar, with the set separated by about two weeks. In November and December 2011, there were solar and lunar eclipses, so this year the first eclipses fall during May and June.

May 20: Solar eclipse at 0 degrees Gemini. This one should bring in new love and romance opportunities as well as new opportunities to flex your creativity.

June 4: Lunar eclipse in Sagittarius, your solar eleventh house. Positive news.

November 13: Solar eclipse in Scorpio, your career area. New professional opportunities.

November 28: Lunar eclipse, Gemini. Jupiter forms a five-degree conjunction to the eclipse degree, suggesting that news you receive around this time will be cause for celebration! It relates to love, creativity, children, enjoyment.

LUCKIEST DAY OF THE YEAR
Every year there's one day when Jupiter and the sun meet up, and luck, serendipity, and expansion are the hallmarks. This year that day falls on May 13, with a conjunction in Taurus.

January—Aquarius

LUNAR HIGHLIGHTS
The first full moon of the year occurs in Cancer, that area of your chart that represents your daily work routine and the daily maintenance of your health. This full moon illuminates something in that area or with your parents or domestic environment. Mars forms a close, beneficial angle to this moon, suggesting swiftness and great energy infused into events.

January 23 features a new moon in your sign. This one is worth preparing for. It happens just once a year and sets the tone for the next twelve months. Make a wish list of what you desire to achieve or experience this year. Find visuals that depict these desires. Create a storyboard and post it where you'll see it often. This new moon should usher in new opportunities in any area of your life where you place your focus and attention. Uranus forms a close, beneficial angle to this new moon, suggesting a suddenness to events.

FINANCES, OTHER STUFF

Mars is currently in Virgo, your solar eighth house, where it will be until July 3. Between January 24 and April 14, Mars will be retrograde, so apply for mortgages and loans on either side of those dates. Be sure your insurance and tax payments are up to date. Your partner, spouse, or anyone else with whom you share financial resources may be working longer hours or could land a hefty raise.

Between January 14 and February 8, your financial situation improves, although you may feel an urge to spend more. Venus will be in Pisces, transiting your financial area.

CAREER

Between January 8 and 27, Mercury transits Capricorn and forms a beneficial angle to your career area. This transit helps you communicate in a way that clearly defines your goals, purpose, and intentions. You're a good communicator even on bad days; this transit simply strengthens your professional communications.

Right now, Saturn is still transiting Libra, your solar ninth house. This transit should be enabling you to explore your spirituality and worldview in depth, perhaps through other people—in groups, a seminar, or workshop. Once Saturn enters Scorpio on October 5 and begins to transit your career area, professional activities and relationships really begin to solidify.

ROMANCE

With Venus transiting intuitive, gentle Pisces from January 14 to February 8, your love life should be humming along, flowing at a pace that may feel a bit strange for you, Aquarius. Offer no resistance, though, and just go with whatever happens. If you're not involved now, follow your instincts about any romantic prospects. Your intuition is a powerful ally.

BEST DAYS, CHALLENGING DAYS
January 27: circle it. That day, Mercury enters your sign, where it will be until February 13. This transit should be excellent for you, with your mind zipping along borders that others simply don't have the courage to travel.

February—Aquarius

LUNAR HIGHLIGHTS
This month's full moon, on February 7, falls in your opposite sign, Leo. This moon should bring news or insight concerning a partnership—business or romantic. The news may not have you hopping around with joy, but at least you now know the score, Aquarius, and can move forward from there. Remember: your point of power lies in the present.

The new moon of February 21 is in Pisces, in your financial area. This one should bring you new financial opportunities—a new job, a raise at your current job, a second job, an unexpected royalty or insurance check. Neptune is closely conjunct this new moon, suggesting an element of confusion or that you may need more information before you make a decision.

FINANCES, OTHER STUFF
The big financial news is the new moon discussed above. Between February 13 and March 2, Mercury transits Pisces and your financial area, so it's likely you will be discussing your finances. You may set up a budget or savings plan, send out résumés, or make job applications. You could be talking to investors about launching your home-

based business or could be coming up with a business plan. One way or another, your finances are the focus during this transit.

CAREER
Expansive Jupiter remains in Taurus until June 11. This transit seeks to expand some area of your life. It behooves you to look at your natal chart and find out where Taurus appears. In a solar chart, Taurus rules your fourth house—your domestic environment—which means it's opposite your career area. This kind of opposition can result in increased responsibility for you, where you may take on more than you can effectively handle. Pace yourself during this transit.

ROMANCE
Between February 8 and March 5, Venus transits compatible fire sign Aries. Not only are your passions ignited, but romance may be closer than you think. You could meet that special someone through friends or through a group to which you belong. Venus will be traveling with Uranus during this period, suggesting that any relationship that begins will do so unexpectedly and suddenly and will catch both of you by surprise.

BEST DAYS, CHALLENGING DAYS
Between February 7 and June 25, Saturn is retrograde in Libra. You may become aware of the initial change in movement on or right after February 7. How? Your travel plans go could haywire, your trip might be delayed, a relationship develops fissures.

March—Aquarius

LUNAR HIGHLIGHTS
March 8 features a full moon in Virgo. Mars forms a wide conjunction with it, so this one triggers all sorts of activity with resources you share with others—and vice versa. You or your partner may apply for a mortgage or loan, draw up a will, inherit money. Virgo is a precise, efficient sign, so you're sure to read the fine print before signing any contract.

The new moon in Aries on March 22 should be much to your liking. Mercury and Uranus are both closely conjunct this new moon, so the opportunities headed your way could include: a writing/communication project; new friendships; new group associations; a new venue for self-expression. The opportunities come out of the blue, unexpectedly.

FINANCES, OTHER STUFF
The full moon in one of your financial areas brings news about a partner's resources/income. In addition, from March 2 to 12, Mercury is moving direct in Aries, so there will be a lot of discussion about finances and joint resources. If you're in the midst of a divorce or contract negotiations, be sure to get your paperwork in order before the twelfth, when Mercury turns retrograde, or after April 4, when it turns direct again. This Mercury retro is the first of the year. Refresh your memory by rereading the section about it under the Big Picture for your sign.

CAREER
Venus joins Jupiter in Taurus between March 5 and April 3. With these two planets traveling together, forming a beneficial angle to your daily work area, you're in the right place at the right time, and you're the right person for the job. You're resolute about the direction in which you're headed and are definitely in for the long haul. You outlast the competition through your sheer resilience.

ROMANCE
Feeling more sensuous? Sexier? Thank Venus in Taurus. While it travels with Jupiter through Taurus during the dates cited above, your love life should move along at a pace that suits you. Not too slowly, not too quickly, just right. You could hit a rough path during Mercury's retrograde, but don't obsess about it. Everyone around you feels the retrograde too. Be sure to communicate succinctly, clearly, as it's easy to be misunderstood.

BEST DAYS, CHALLENGING DAYS
March 12: Mercury turns retrograde in Aries. Ouch. There could be misunderstandings with friends.

April—Aquarius

LUNAR HIGHLIGHTS
You'll probably love the full moon in fellow air sign Libra on April 6. You're going to be socializing more around the time of this moon. Your inbox fills up, your cell rings constantly, people clamor for your company. Since this moon occurs in your solar ninth house, you could hear news about a trip abroad that you're planning, about an educational or publishing goal, or even about your spirituality.

April 12 boasts a new moon in earth sign Taurus. This one should bring new opportunities related to your home, domestic environment, or even your parents. Perhaps one or both of your parents move in with you or move closer to you. You might move or purchase a home. There could be a birth in the family. Mars forms a close, harmonious angle with this new moon, so things will be happening quickly.

FINANCES, OTHER STUFF
Mercury turns direct on April 4. It's safe now to hit the road, sign contracts, pitch ideas, apply for a mortgage or loan. Venus enters Gemini on April 3 and will be there until August 7. Its long transit is due to a retrograde be-

tween May 15 and June 27. While it's moving direct, you're extremely focused on pleasure, enjoyment, having fun. It's as if everything you do and undertake must first and foremost be pleasurable.

CAREER
Venus's transit through fellow air sign Gemini drives home the point that enjoyment should be your first priority. In your profession, that could translate into an infectious enthusiasm for current projects that wins you support from coworkers and bosses. You might even initiate some sort of office or company activity that spreads this sense of enjoyment. No telling what cutting edge ideas you may come up with, Aquarius. You're known for your vision.

ROMANCE
Back to Venus. One thing is for sure about its transit. April 3 to May 15 and June 27 to August 7 mark the most romantic and creative periods for you all year. Everything in these areas goes well for you. If you have children, then your relationship with them also proves to be excellent. We'll talk more about the retrograde period under May's roundup.

BEST DAYS, CHALLENGING DAYS
On April 10, Pluto turns retrograde in Capricorn. This isn't like a Mercury retro where everything goes haywire. It's more of a turning inward, using Pluto's profound lens to examine your motives, your own unconscious. It turns direct again on September 17.

May—Aquarius

LUNAR HIGHLIGHTS
The full moon on May 5 falls in Scorpio, in your career area. This one should bring news related to your career. It's powerful news, for sure, thanks to a beneficial angle from Pluto, and could be potentially transformative. If you

feel out of sort around the time of this full moon, just get off by yourself for a few moments and center your energy through deep breathing or some yoga postures.

May 20 features the first solar eclipse of the year, in Gemini. This one should usher in new opportunities in communication, networking, love life, and with creativity. Often with a solar eclipse you have to surrender something before you gain the promised opportunities. Uranus forms a wide, harmonious angle to the eclipse degree, so there will be a suddenness to events. Be ready!

FINANCES, OTHER STUFF
Venus turns retrograde on May 15. Between then and June 27, when it turns direct again, avoid buying any large-ticket items—computers, cars, jewelry. Expensive art work. Although it's sometimes possible to get a good deal on these items while Venus is retrograde, there may be something wrong or off with what you purchase. Best to avoid these purchases altogether.

CAREER
Between May 9 and 24, while Mercury transits Gemini, the gift of gab is yours. Trivia and facts are at your fingertips. You can talk circles around anyone. If you're in sales, you surpass your quota. But regardless of what you do, this transit brings stronger communication skills. Combined with your talent to spot trends before they become trends, you'll enjoy this transit and should be able to take away plenty of benefits.

ROMANCE
Yes, the Venus retrograde probably will impact your love life. It won't be something so serious that the relationship will end, but things between you and your partner may not go as smoothly as you would like. Try to keep your criticisms to yourself. Don't blurt something that you can't retract. You'll regret it later.

Mars continues its journey through Virgo, so you may be finding things about your partner that irritate you.

Virgo, after all, seeks perfection. Just bite your tongue, Aquarius.

BEST DAYS, CHALLENGING DAYS
May 15 could be a bit rough on your love life. But all will be rectified once Jupiter enters Gemini next month.

June—Aquarius

LUNAR HIGHLIGHTS
June 4 features a lunar eclipse in compatible fire sign Sagittarius. This eclipse brings news or stirs emotions related to friends, social groups, goals and dreams that you have. There could also be news in the areas that Sagittarius rules: publishing, higher education, foreign travel.

The second new moon in Gemini this year occurs on June 19, and this one should be a beauty for you, Aquarius. New opportunities come your way in the areas that Gemini rules—communication, writing—and with your daily work. New job description? Promotion? Raise? Brand new job? At the time of this new moon, Uranus and Venus form harmonious angles to each other, suggesting that opportunities are unexpected and may involve the arts.

FINANCES, OTHER STUFF
June 11: mark it. Jupiter enters Gemini for a transit that doesn't end until June 25, 2013. Lucky you, having Jupiter making such a beautiful angle to your sun for a full year. Every part of your life will expand in some way. You'll have a knack for meeting the right people at the right time. Also, Venus is traveling with Jupiter, and after the twenty-seventh, it is in direct motion, bolstering and supporting all the luck and expansion that Jupiter is bringing into your life.

CAREER
With Venus and Jupiter traveling together in Gemini, in that section of your chart that symbolizes your daily work routine, you are in for a treat. Everything you do in your daily work translates somehow into the larger picture of your career. Next month it gets even better, when Mars enters fellow air sign Libra and travels with Saturn in that sign. So plant your seeds now with care and focus and watch things begin to bloom quickly.

ROMANCE
With both Jupiter and Venus in your fifth house of romance and creativity, it doesn't get any better. Summon your muse; dive into the creative flow. You and your partner should get along exceptionally well while Venus travels with Jupiter. Things get especially good after Venus turns direct on June 27. Between then and August 7, your love life is in very good shape. If you're not involved now, you probably will be before this transit ends.

BEST DAYS, CHALLENGING DAYS
June 27 is the day to anticipate, when Venus turns direct. Mercury enters your opposite sign on June 25, bringing about discussions with a partner.

July—Aquarius

LUNAR HIGHLIGHTS
As you enter the second half of 2012, the full moon on July 3 leads the way. It falls in Capricorn, your solar twelfth house, and illuminates something that is hidden. Pluto forms a close conjunction with this full moon, suggesting power issues may surface. But if they do, you're in the driver's seat.

The new moon in Cancer on July 19 occurs in your solar sixth house of daily work. This moon should bring new opportunities—a new job, new responsibilities, a promotion—

the possibilities are wide open. Saturn forms a challenging angle to this new moon, though, so there could be some hoops to jump through before the opportunities appear.

FINANCES, OTHER STUFF

On July 3, Mars finally leaves Virgo and enters fellow air sign Libra. This transit, which lasts until August 23, should benefit you in several ways. It bolsters your already lively mentality, infuses you with more physical energy, makes you more sociable, and also may prompt you to take an unexpected trip overseas. Mars now forms a beneficial angle to Jupiter in Gemini, so it energizes Jupiter's tendency to expand whatever it touches.

The second Mercury retro of the year extends from July 14 to August 8, and you should know the drill by now. Just to refresh your memory, though, read about it in the Big Picture section for your sign. This retro occurs in your partnership area, so be sure to communicate clearly with both business and romantic partners.

CAREER

During the Mercury retro period cited above, stick to your current projects and revitalize projects/ideas from the past. Don't start something new. Fortunately, Venus and Jupiter are traveling together through Gemini and your daily work area, bringing luck and expansion as well as an artistic bent to your perceptions. If you use these qualities during the retro period, it will help to mitigate Mercury's shenanigans.

ROMANCE

With Venus and Jupiter traveling together through Gemini until August 7, an office flirtation may heat up. If a romance develops—and the signs suggest it's a possibility—be careful that you don't mix business with pleasure. It is easy to be misunderstood during any Mercury retrograde. You've also got Mars and Saturn forming beneficial angles to your natal sun sign and to both Venus and Jupiter. It's a bonus that prompts you to be more outgoing, heightens your sexuality, and strengthens your connection with your partner.

BEST DAYS, CHALLENGING DAYS
Big ouch day: July 14, when Mercury turns retrograde in Leo, your opposite sign.

August—Aquarius

LUNAR HIGHLIGHTS
With three lunations this month, August may drive you a little nuts, but there's plenty to celebrate, too. The action begins with the August 1 full moon in your sign, Aquarius. This one should illuminate something in your personal life and, thanks to an exact and harmonious angle from Jupiter, the news looks excellent.

August 17 features a new moon in Leo, your opposite sign. This one ushers in a new partnership—business or romantic—and may bring an opportunity for you to strut your stuff. Whether you're pinpointing upcoming trends for a client or reading the future for your boss, people are now aware of your considerable talents.

On August 31 a full moon in Pisces illuminates a financial issue or concern. Neptune forms a wide conjunction with this full moon, indicating a possibility that you don't get the full scoop. Be sure to dig for the facts before making a decision. Your intuition could prove helpful.

FINANCES, OTHER STUFF
Mercury turns direct on August 8. Wait a day or two, then get to work on whatever you have postponed during the retro period. Whether it's applying for a mortgage or dealing with insurance and tax issues, you can now rest assured that you are in a much stronger bargaining position.

The day before Mercury turns direct, Venus enters water sign Cancer, where it will be until September 6. Read about the repercussions of this transit under the Career and Romance sections.

CAREER

With Venus in your daily work area during the dates cited above, everything you do in your daily work routine will impact the larger picture of your career. This is always true, of course, but with Venus now forming a beneficial angle to your professional area, the flow goes your way. Others find your ideas appealing, you gather the support you may need to launch a project, and you could get a raise. Jupiter remains in Gemini during this period, making sure that whatever you do is fun and pleasurable and expands your venues in some way. Once Mars enters Scorpio and your career area on August 23, you're a veritable powerhouse of energy. That transit lasts until October 6.

ROMANCE

Venus in Cancer is an intuitive placement for this planet, so be sure to listen to your hunches and intuitive guidance, particularly in your romantic relationships. An office flirtation or romance could heat up, particularly after August 23, when Mars enters passionate Scorpio. Be careful that you don't break any hearts, Aquarius. If the relationship goes south, you still have to work with this person.

BEST DAYS, CHALLENGING DAYS

August 8: Mercury turns direct.

September—Aquarius

LUNAR HIGHLIGHTS

It should be a calmer month, compared to August, at any rate. But then again, you never know for sure! So let's take a closer look at this month's lunations. The new moon on September 15 is in Virgo, that area of your chart that governs other people's resources. This could mean that your partner, spouse, or someone else with whom you share resources could get a significant raise. It's also possible that you get a break in insurance or taxes or have a chance to attend (or conduct?) a seminar on an esoteric topic. This new moon can also bring about psychic experiences.

On September 29, the full moon in Aries illuminates your conscious mind. Expect news related to siblings, communication, your immediate neighborhood, travel. Uranus is closely conjunct to this full moon, so buckle up, Aquarius! It's going to be a wild, unpredictable ride.

FINANCES, OTHER STUFF

The new moon brings financial opportunities. That's a major part of the financial stuff this month. Also, until September 16, Mercury is in Virgo, in that same area of your chart as the new moon. This transit suggests discussions and focus on joint finances. In other areas to watch, Mercury transits Libra, a fellow air sign, between September 16 and October 5. You're going to be thinking a lot about foreign travel, your educational goals, that unpublished manuscript you've stashed in a bottom drawer. You'll be talking about these things with anyone who will listen.

CAREER

Between September 6 and October 3, Venus transits Leo, your opposite sign, suggesting your heart's focus is on partnerships, both romantic and professional. Let's look at the latter. It's possible that you and your business partner agree on the broad strokes, but not on the finer details. Or vice versa. Whichever it is, do some research, get your facts together, trust your instincts. When Mercury transits Libra between September 16 and October 3, you may be in a better position to make a decision that is fair to all parties.

ROMANCE

You should be feeling pretty good about things during Venus's transit. You and your partner will feel passionate about each other, even if you disagree on some of your individual ideas about things. You've got Mercury in an air sign (dates above) during part of this transit, which should bolster your confidence in whatever you're feeling and thinking. In addition, Jupiter is in air sign Gemini, which means the odds are stacked in your favor, Aquarius. Hey, just kick back and enjoy whatever comes your way in the romance and creativity department.

BEST DAYS, CHALLENGING DAYS
September 6. A definite shift in emotional energies. Venus enters Leo and your partnership area that day.

October—Aquarius

LUNAR HIGHLIGHTS
It's a gentler month, with lunations in signs that are compatible with your sun sign. Plus, there's a shift in a major planet. Let's take a closer look. On October 15, a new moon in Libra should be very much to your liking. It brings new opportunities for foreign travel and business dealings abroad, education and publishing, and the development of your spirituality. Jupiter forms a strong, beneficial angle to this new moon, suggesting that the new opportunities expand your life in some way.

October 29 features a full moon in Taurus that lights up your domestic environment and home life. Neptune forms a wide but beneficial angle to this full moon, suggesting ideals and idealism are part of the news you hear related to your family.

FINANCES, OTHER STUFF
Between October 3 and 28, Venus transits Virgo and that area of your chart that symbolizes shared resources. This transit could bring a significant raise to your partner or a break in taxes and/or insurance. Read the fine print in any contract that you sign during this period. Details are vital.

October 5 brings two transits: Mercury enters Scorpio and transits it until October 29, and Saturn enters Scorpio and transits that sign for the next two and a half years. Read about Saturn's transit under the Big Picture section for your sign. The Mercury transit brings deeper intuition and a kind of relentless need to get to the bottom of something.

CAREER
Once Saturn enters Scorpio and your career area, there can any number of repercussions. One thing is for sure, however. Saturn demands that you meet your responsibilities and obligations. It brings structure to your career, and even though there may be delays in some professional matters, this transit should ultimately benefit your career.

ROMANCE
The transit to anticipate is when Venus moves through Libra between October 28 and November 21. This one should bring romance while you're traveling or with someone you meet through a course or workshop you take, through publishing or perhaps a spiritual group to which you belong. Mars transits Sagittarius between October 6 and November 16, energizing your contacts with friends and groups and triggering lots of activity in your social life. So it's possible that you meet a romantic interest through friends.

BEST DAYS, CHALLENGING DAYS
October 28 looks very nice. Venus enters fellow air sign Libra that day.

November—Aquarius

LUNAR HIGHLIGHTS
Okay, two eclipses this month: you ready for a wild ride? The first eclipse, solar, occurs on November 13 in Scorpio, your career area. This eclipse should be positive for you and bring in new professional opportunities. A promotion might be in the offing or a raise or even a new career path. Whatever unfolds, you're going to be in very good shape.

On November 28, the lunar eclipse in Gemini really suits

you. Jupiter forms a close conjunction with the eclipse degree, so any news you hear or emotions you feel about a romantic relationship should be positive. This eclipse could also impact your creativity and your kids, all in positive, uplifting ways.

FINANCES, OTHER STUFF
Between November 16 and December 25, Mars transits earth sign Capricorn and your solar twelfth house. This transit should bring issues you've buried over the years, power you've disowned. It might be a good time to start meditating, take up yoga, or see a therapist. This transit also favors goal-setting and forms a strong, supportive angle to your career area.

CAREER
Most of the action this month is in the career arena. The solar eclipse brings opportunities. The Mars transit in Capricorn is your professional booster rocket. Between November 21 and December 15, Venus transits Scorpio and your career area, bolstering the effects of the solar eclipse. In short, even with the Thanksgiving holidays this month, you should be able to push forward with your ideas and projects, gain the support you may need, and make significant professional strides.

ROMANCE
Venus remains in Libra until November 21, and during this period you're in the mood to be romanced and loved, seduced and loved. If your partner is on your wavelength, then expect flowers, jewelry, books, chocolates, whatever it is that you most enjoy. When Venus transits Scorpio between November 21 and December 15, your emotions are more intense and powerful. You're extremely focused on your career and professional obligations. That said, an office flirtation could develop into a full-blown romance.

BEST DAYS, CHALLENGING DAYS
Challenge and a mercury retro alert: November 6 to 26, Mercury is retrograde in Sagittarius, your solar eleventh

house. This is the last Merc retro of the year, that's the good news. The not so good news is that it impacts your friendships, travel, finances, every area of your life. Reread the section in Big Picture on Mercury retrogrades.

December—Aquarius

LUNAR HIGHLIGHTS
December 13 boasts a new moon in Sagittarius, which should steer new opportunities your way in friendships and group associations and with education, publishing, and foreign travel. Not too bad for the last new moon of 2012, right? On a larger scale, this new moon could trigger more rhetoric about the end of the Mayan calendar on December 21, 2012. Read on for more on that.

The full moon on December 28 falls in Cancer and should illuminate and bring news about your daily work routine and the daily maintenance of your health. Uranus forms a challenging angle to this full moon, though, so the news could be troubling. Don't let it upset your New Year's Eve plans, though. Just go with the flow, Aquarius. Offer no resistance.

FINANCES, OTHER STUFF
Mercury transits Sagittarius between December 10 and 31, and then it enters Capricorn, which takes you into 2013. The first transit puts you in the holiday mood—gift shopping, partying with friends, getting together with family. You become quite the social creature. The second Mercury transit puts you in a goal-setting frame of mind, perfect for setting your new year agenda. So get busy, Aquarius. What are your resolutions and desires for 2013?

CAREER
Now that Saturn is in Scorpio, transiting your career area, you could be encountering delays, but you also could be reaping the benefits of your hard work and efficiency. It all depends on what you've been doing in your professional

life for the last several years. On December 25, Mars enters your sign, a wonderful bonus not only for your career, but for you personally. Your physical energy is stronger, your drive is remarkable, you are eager and willing to get things done. This transit takes you into early February 2013.

ROMANCE
Venus, again. Sigh. If it weren't for Venus, where would any of us be? On December 15, it enters Sagittarius. If you aren't involved right now, keep your social calendar open. You may meet a special someone through friends, a group to which you belong, or even while traveling. If you are involved, then you and your partner may be spending a lot of time with friends. You may be brainstorming, partying, or simply enjoying the company of like-minded individuals.

BEST DAYS, CHALLENGING DAYS
If you're listening to all the hype about the end of days, then the entire month of December is likely to be challenging for you. Your best course is to ignore all of it and just live your life. The world won't be ending on December 21. Really.

Happy New Year!

13

Pisces

The Big Picture in 2012

Welcome to 2012, Pisces! It's a year of personal power and prosperity and one in which your spirituality, ideals, and imagination will influence all that you do.

Your ruler, Neptune, enters your sign on February 3 and will be there for the next fourteen years. This transit heightens all the qualities for which you're known. Your imagination will be tinged with the unusual, with a focus on the mysterious, the unknown, the psychic. Your creative talents should blossom. Your ideals reach new heights, and you try to figure out how to integrate them more readily into your life.

Saturn occupies two signs this year—Libra and Scorpio, which it enters on October 5. The first transit, through Libra, has been going on since late October 2009, so you should be accustomed to its energy by now. It forms an angle to your sun that requires an attitude adjustment on your part. Your spouse or partner may not get the raise or promotion that he/she hoped for, and there could be some delays concerning mortgages and loans. Once Saturn enters fellow water sign Scorpio on October 5, things ease up considerably for the next two and a half years. Saturn will be forming a beneficial angle to your sun then, and your life generally will move along at a more measured and stable pace.

Neptune entered Pisces on April 4, 2011. But by early

August 2011, it had slipped back into Aquarius. Neptune symbolizes our higher ideals, escapism, fiction, spirituality, and our blind spots. It seeks to dissolve boundaries between us and others. One possible repercussion of this transit is prolonged religious wars, which proliferated during Uranus's transit in Pisces from early 2003. February 3, 2012, it enters Pisces again and won't move on until January 2026. The important thing to remember with this transit is that Neptune can create confusion, but can also lead you to create something truly inspired.

Pluto starts off the year in compatible earth sign Capricorn and your solar eleventh house, where it has been since November 2008. You're accustomed to its energy now. Its transit, which lasts until 2024, is bringing profound and permanent change globally, evident in the economic challenges that now face the U.S. Most institutions are in the throes of great change—the health-care industry, the petroleum and insurance industries, mortgages/lending, housing, aviation, even the Internet. You name it, and Pluto's fingerprint can be found.

On a personal level, this planet's transit through Capricorn enables you to achieve your dreams and goals. You'll be able to lay out a strategy and garner the support of helpful people. Any groups you join are likely to support your interests and passions. Your approach to friendships and what you hope for in those relationships will change. Pluto's changes are rarely sudden, but they usually work at deep levels and make us aware of just how special life is.

Jupiter's transit through Taurus from January 1 to June 11 is in a compatible earth sign and expands your conscious mind. You might obtain additional schooling to learn new skills, may write a book, start a blog, build a Web site, take workshops in topics that intrigue you. Your daily life is expanded in a significant way too, with new people and experiences that broaden your awareness.

Between June 11 and June 25, 2013, Jupiter transits air sign Gemini and your solar fourth house. This transit expands your domestic environment in some way—a birth, someone moves in, you add onto your existing home, find a larger home . . . you get the idea. Jupiter expands whatever it touches.

Uranus entered Aries in March 2011. This transit is in your solar second house of finances, so there will be sudden and unpredictable changes in what you earn and what you think about the way you make your living.

They say that timing is everything, so with that in mind let's look at some specific areas in your life in 2012.

Romance/Creativity

The most romantic and creative time for you all year falls between August 7 and September 6, when Venus transits Cancer and the love/romance area of your chart. Not only do others find you more appealing, seductive, and radiant, but you feel that way about yourself too. You attract who and what you need when you need it. If you're single and looking, then be sure that during this period you do a lot of what you enjoy.

If you're in a committed relationship, then you and your partner rediscover each other. Plan a trip out of town, to some secluded, romantic spot. Spend time together doing whatever you both enjoy.

Another good time frame: November 21 to December 15, when Venus transits fellow water sign Scorpio and your solar ninth house. During this transit you're more social, which increases your chances of meeting someone special.

A deepening commitment in an existing relationship is possible from October 3 to 28, when Venus transits Virgo and the partnership area of your chart. You and your partner may decide to move in together, get engaged, or get married.

CAREER
One of the most important periods falls between December 15 and January 9, 2013, when Venus transits Sagittarius and the career area of your chart. You should see things start to happen two days earlier, on the thirteenth, when

the new moon in Sadge ushers in new professional opportunities. Another super period for your career and just about everything else in your life occurs on or around February 21, with a new moon in your sign.

BEST TIMES FOR

Buying or selling a home: May 24 to June 7, when Mercury transits Gemini and your solar fourth house.

Family reunions: The above dates or when Venus is moving direct in Gemini between April 3 and May 15 and June 27 and August 7.

Financial matters: February 8 to March 5, when Venus transits Aries and the financial area of your chart.

Signing contracts: When Mercury is moving direct!

MERCURY RETROGRADES

Every year Mercury—the planet of communication and travel—turns retrograde three times. During this period it's wise not to sign contracts (unless you don't mind renegotiating when Mercury is moving direct), to check and recheck travel plans or, better yet, don't travel, and to communicate as succinctly as possible. Refrain from buying any large-ticket items or electronics during this time too. Often computers and appliances go on the fritz, cars act up, data is lost . . . you get the idea. Be sure to back up all files before the dates below:

March 12–April 4: Mercury retrograde in Aries, your solar second house of finances.

July 14–August 8: Mercury retrograde in Leo, your solar sixth house of daily work.

November 6–26: Mercury retrograde in Sagittarius and your solar tenth house of career.

ECLIPSES

Solar eclipses tend to trigger external events that bring about change according to the sign and house in which they fall. Lunar eclipses trigger inner, emotional events according to the sign and house in which they fall. Any eclipse marks both beginnings and endings. The solar and lunar eclipse in a pair falls in opposite signs. If you're interested in detailed information on eclipses, take a look at Celeste Teal's excellent and definitive book, *Eclipses: Predicting World Events & Personal Transformation.*

If you were born under or around the time of an eclipse, it's to your advantage to take a look at your birth chart to find out exactly where the eclipses will impact you.

Most years feature four eclipses—two solar, two lunar, with the set separated by about two weeks. In November and December 2011, there were solar and lunar eclipses, so this year the first eclipses fall during May and June.

May 20: Solar eclipse at 0 degrees Gemini. This one should bring new opportunities to your domestic situation.

June 4: Lunar eclipse in Sagittarius, your solar tenth house. Positive career news.

November 13: Solar eclipse in Scorpio, your solar ninth house. New opportunities in education, publishing, adventure.

November 28: Lunar eclipse, Gemini, your solar fourth house. Jupiter forms a five-degree conjunction to the eclipse degree, suggesting that news you receive around this time will be cause for celebration! It relates to your home life.

LUCKIEST DAY OF THE YEAR
Every year there's one day when Jupiter and the sun meet up, and luck, serendipity, and expansion are the hallmarks. This year that day falls on May 13, with a conjunction in Taurus.

January—Pisces

LUNAR HIGHLIGHTS
The year gets off to a running start with a full moon in fellow water sign Cancer on January 9. This one should illuminate a romantic relationship, a creative project, or something about your children. News about any of these areas is likely. Since the moon is in Cancer, it's also possible you hear news about your family and/or parents.

Mars forms a beneficial angle to this full moon, suggesting heightened activity.

On January 23, the new moon in Aquarius occurs in your solar twelfth house. This new moon brings opportunities to delve into your own unconscious. You might go into therapy or take up meditation, yoga, or some other mind/body discipline. Uranus forms a beneficial angle to this new moon, so the opportunities could surface rapidly and unexpectedly.

FINANCES, OTHER STUFF

Between January 14 and February 28, Venus transits your sign, Pisces, which facilitates many areas of your personal life. Things flow your way—even money! With Mercury in Capricorn between January 8 and 27, your communication skills are strong, and friends prove helpful. The contacts you make during this period could be excellent for your career and daily work.

CAREER

Mars begins the year in Virgo, where it remains until July 3. It will be retrograde between January 24 and April 4. But while it's moving direct, a potential business partner could surface. Or if you already have a business partner, then the two of you iron out the finer details of your agreement. During the retro period just take care of current business rather than implementing new procedures or techniques.

ROMANCE

While Venus is in your sign between January 14 and February 8, you enjoy one of the most romantic and creative periods all year. If you aren't involved when this transit starts, you will certainly be looking. Keep your social calendar wide open during this time. Listen closely to your intuition. Use your wonderful imagination to attract the partner you want.

Jupiter is in Taurus until June 11. This transit benefits

you. Taurus is an earth sign compatible with your water-sign sun, and it expands everything it touches. As it transits your solar third house, romance may be as close as your own neighborhood!

BEST DAYS, CHALLENGING DAYS
January 24 could be challenging—Mars turns retrograde in Virgo, your partnership area.

February—Pisces

LUNAR HIGHLIGHTS
The full moon on February 7 is in Leo, your solar sixth house. This one should bring news or insights about your daily work routine and the daily maintenance of your health. You should expect a bit of general craziness around this time, with people in your environment vying for your attention and approval.

The new moon on February 21 is in your sign, Pisces. This new moon occurs just once a year and it's worth preparing for. Create a wish board with images of what you would like to experience or achieve or have this year. Post the wish board where you'll see it often. Back each desire with emotion, but don't worry about how these wishes will come true. Just know that they will.

FINANCES, OTHER STUFF
Jupiter continues to bring expansion and luck into various areas of your life and urges you to practice gratitude. As you find things in your experience for which you're grateful, the likelier it is that you'll experience even more people and situations and events for which you're grateful. Like attracts like. That's part of Jupiter's message. Since it corules your sign, its message is doubly important for you.

Venus transits Aries and your financial area between February 8 and March 5, a period that favors your earnings, investments, and attitude toward money. Financially, then, things go your way. A raise? Possibly. Also possible: royalty check, insurance payment, a tax break.

CAREER
Between January 27 and February 13, Mercury transits Aquarius. It's a good period to pitch ideas, move your own professional agenda forward, and brainstorm with coworkers. Then, between February 13 and March 2, it's in your sign, Pisces, and your conscious mind becomes a psychic sponge, absorbing information from the ether! You're able to navigate professional matters on a purely intuitive basis.

ROMANCE
While Venus transits fire sign Aries between February 8 and March 5, your passions are up front and center. You may be feeling more possessive about your partner and could experience jealousy, but you may also be more loving. During part of this transit Mercury will be in your sign, so there should be a deep telepathic connection between you and the one you love. If you aren't involved, you could be actively seeking companionship and romance.

BEST DAYS, CHALLENGING DAYS
One of the best days? February 13, when Mercury enters your sign.

March—Pisces

LUNAR HIGHLIGHTS
The full moon in Virgo, your opposite sign, on March 8 lights up your partnership area. Mars is widely conjunct this full moon, bringing a whirlwind of activity and news about a business or romantic partnership. Pluto forms a wide, beneficial angle to this moon, so there may be power issues and transformative emotions surfacing.

March 22 brings a new moon in Aries, your second house. This one should usher in new financial opportunities for you, Pisces. Possibilities? A raise for either you or your partner, an insurance payment, royalty check, tax break, or even an inheritance.

FINANCES, OTHER STUFF

The new moon in Aries and your financial area is the big money news in March. But there are some other things going on too that you should know about. Between March 2 and May 9, Mercury transits Aries and your financial area. Mercury is retrograde between March 12 and April 4. While it's moving in direct motion, lots of financial discussions ensue. You might be negotiating a contract, moving your accounts to a different bank, or talking about loans or a mortgage. Anything and everything to do with money could be a topic of discussion. During the retro period follow the suggestions in the Big Picture section for your sign under Mercury retrogrades.

CAREER

Between March 5 and April 3, Venus transits Taurus and travels with expansive Jupiter. This duo should bring a broad depth to your communications, make your ideas appealing to others, and bring attention to you, your professional skills, and your goals. You may be more stubborn than usual about some professional or personal matter. Taurus is an earth sign compatible with your water-sign sun, so this is a friendly transit for you.

ROMANCE

The Venus transit through Taurus should be quite positive for your love life. You and your partner are close and communicate well, and you're pretty contented with things generally. With Mercury in Aries during part of this transit, your mind is on fire with ideas, and you're eager to share them. If you aren't involved right now, then romance may find you in your own neighborhood!

BEST DAYS, CHALLENGING DAYS
March 12. Mercury turns retrograde.

April—Pisces

LUNAR HIGHLIGHTS
A full moon in Libra occurs on April 6 in your solar eighth house—one of the financial houses. This one should illuminate resources you share with others—typically a spouse or partner—so there could be news for your partner about his or her earnings. This full moon could also bring news about a relationship, friendship, or artistic project—that's the Libra part of it.

The new moon in Taurus on April 21 looks good for you. Taurus, an earth sign, is compatible with your water-sign sun, and this new moon should trigger new opportunities in your daily life. You may find a new neighborhood that you like, and this could prompt you to begin considering a move. You might have an opportunity to take a class or workshop in a topic that interests you.

FINANCES, OTHER STUFF
Mercury turns direct on April 4, good news always for your finances—and for every other area of your life. After that date, it's fine to sign contracts, apply for a mortgage, pitch ideas, submit projects, move your agenda ahead. Saturn continues its journey through Libra and your solar eighth house until October 5, when it will enter Scorpio, a fellow water sign. While it's in Libra, your partner could experience delays in finances, and you may experience delays related to insurance and taxes, mortgages and loans. Once Saturn enters Scorpio it will form a strong angle to your sun, and you'll benefit from the transit.

CAREER
From April 3 to August 1, Venus transits Gemini and your fourth house and is opposed to your career area. This tran-

sit suggests that you may figure out a way to work from your home, and because this transit is long for Venus, you'll have plenty of time to do it. Venus is retrograde between May 15 and June 27, so the periods on either side of these dates work best.

Mars turns direct on April 14 in Virgo, your opposite sign, and remains there until July 3. During this transit your focus could be on finding the right business partner.

ROMANCE
Back to the Venus transit. This one should benefit your love life and your home life. You and your partner may engage in more conversation than you do normally or could become involved in some sort of creative project together. Once Mercury turns direct on the fourth, you and your partner lift yourselves out of any misunderstandings.

BEST DAYS, CHALLENGING DAYS
April 4: celebrate. Mercury turns direct!

May—Pisces

LUNAR HIGHLIGHTS
The full moon on May 5 falls in Scorpio, a fellow water sign. This one highlights a trip abroad—one you're on or planning to take—and there could be news about it. Pluto forms a wide but beneficial angle to this full moon, so it appears that the news is transformative, powerful. With Neptune, your ruler, now in your sign, your idealism is important to you, and the news you hear could be connected somehow to integrating this idealism more readily into your life.

The new moon in Gemini on May 20 is also a solar eclipse and should bring new opportunities to your domestic environment. Your family and even your parents could be involved. Uranus forms a wide, beneficial angle to the eclipse degree, so opportunities may come out of nowhere. Just be ready to seize them!

FINANCES, OTHER STUFF
Venus turns retrograde in Gemini on May 15, so have your financial affairs in order by then. It turns direct again on June 27. On either side of these two dates, apply for mortgages and loans and get your insurance and tax matters taken care of. If you're in the market for any large-ticket items, try to buy them when Venus is moving direct.

CAREER
Mercury transits Taurus from May 9 to 24, a transit that should benefit you. You're able to communicate clearly, and your ideas are grounded. In fact, your wonderful Piscean imagination should be more practical during this transit. Oh, you can still trip the light fantastic, but now you'll realize how you can communicate your feelings and perceptions to others.

ROMANCE
Ok, so your love life could be a tad rough when Venus retrogrades during the dates mentioned under finances. But it won't be *that* rough. It simply prompts you to think before you speak, to frame your feelings in a way your partner will better understand. Besides, you've still got Jupiter in Taurus, the earthiest of the earth signs, seeking to expand your venues on all fronts.

BEST DAYS, CHALLENGING DAYS
May 15—Venus turns retrograde. Not horrendously challenging, but not stellar either. It's what you make of it that counts.

June—Pisces

LUNAR HIGHLIGHTS
June 4 features a lunar eclipse in Sagittarius, your career area. This one brings news and stirs emotions about professional matters and relationships. The eclipse should be positive for you, Pisces, and with Uranus forming a wide, beneficial angle to the eclipse degree the news comes out of the blue.

June 19: the second new moon in Gemini. This one ushers in new opportunities in your domestic environment, much as last month's solar eclipse did. But you don't have to relinquish anything as you may have had to do under the solar eclipse. Sit back and enjoy the opportunities that surface! Possibilities? A birth in the family, a move, someone moves in or out, you launch a home-based business.

FINANCES, OTHER STUFF
Until June 7, Mercury is in Gemini. Think of this transit as the gift of gab that enables you to make friends with anyone, anywhere. Between June 7 and 25, Mercury moves through fellow water sign Cancer, and your intuition deepens. Use it to make decisions about your finances, romance, your creativity, your career and ... well, just about everything!

Venus turns direct in Gemini on June 27, so after that date buy your large-ticket items without worrying about whether you may have to return them.

CAREER
It seems that much of the month's emphasis is on Gemini. Jupiter enters that sign on June 11 and remains there until June 25, 2013. It is opposite your career area during this transit, which may mean increased responsibility for you in your work. It could also mean that you may be looking for a new job or career path, that your current position isn't answering all your needs, or that you take a course to hone your skills.

ROMANCE

Between June 27 and August 7, Venus travels with Jupiter in Gemini, a wonderful combination that should bring joy and happiness to your home life—and love life. You and your partner may move in together, get engaged, perhaps set a wedding date. You may also move or add on to your existing home, or someone may move in. Expansion and luck are key.

BEST DAYS, CHALLENGING DAYS

June 11 and June 27 should be among the best days this month. The first date is when Jupiter enters Gemini, and the second date is when Venus turns direct. Also notable this month? On June 25, Saturn turns direct in Libra, your career area. Now you can move full steam ahead on everything in your professional life.

July—Pisces

LUNAR HIGHLIGHTS

Now that the eclipses are over, July looks calmer! On July 3, the full moon in compatible earth sign Capricorn illuminates a friendship or goals that you have. Pluto forms a close conjunction with this full moon, strengthening your resolve to do things your way. Uranus forms an exact and challenging angle to Pluto during this moon, so be prepared for the unexpected.

On July 19, the new moon in Cancer occurs in that region of your chart that rules romance and love, creativity, enjoyment, children. New opportunities could surface in any of these areas. A birth is possible, a new relationship, a new creative project.

FINANCES, OTHER STUFF

Okay, Mars finally moves into another sign on July 3. It joins Saturn in Libra, your solar eighth house. This transit, which lasts until August 23, energizes resources you share with others—notably a partner or spouse. It may prompt you to apply for a mortgage or loan, to refinance your home, or to ask for a raise.

Between July 14 and August 8, Mercury is retrograde in Leo. It's the second retro this year, and by now you know what you should and shouldn't do. Reread the section on Mercury retros in the Big Picture for your sign.

CAREER
On either side of those Mercury retro dates, Mercury works to bolster your professional stuff. It strengthens your flair for expressing yourself in bold, dramatic terms, so it's excellent for pushing your concerns, projects, and agenda forward. Uranus in Aries does the same thing, but more erratically. It is retrograde between July 13 and December 13.

ROMANCE
Now that Venus is moving direct in Gemini, your love life should be smoother, more to your liking. You're working up to the transit in August, when Venus will enter fellow water sign Cancer and your romance area, marking one of the most romantic and creative times for you all year. So until then be mindful of your desires and be kind and loving toward your partner. If you aren't involved, keep your social calendar open. Embrace the unknown.

BEST DAYS, CHALLENGING DAYS
July 14: difficult. Mercury turns retrograde.

August—Pisces

LUNAR HIGHLIGHTS
There are two full moons and a new moon this month. It spells chaos, excitement, frenetic activity. But let's take a closer look. The action begins on August 1, with a full moon in air sign Aquarius, your solar twelfth house. This moon illuminates whatever is hidden in your life and brings it to

the surface where you must deal with it. Uranus forms a beneficial angle to this moon, indicative of surprise and a suddenness to events and news.

On August 17, the new moon in fire sign Leo should bring new opportunities in your daily work routine that enable you to exhibit your vast talents. Saturn forms an exact, beneficial angle to this new moon, so any opportunity that comes your way is a serious one and should be given careful consideration.

On August 31, the full moon in your sign highlights a personal issue or concern. You hear news or gain insights about this issue. Neptune forms a wide conjunction with this full moon, which could mean you don't have all the scoop on what's going on or that your ideals are somehow involved.

FINANCES, OTHER STUFF

Big news first: Mercury turns direct on August 8. By now you should know what this means. Between August 7 and September 6, Venus moves through fellow water sign Cancer, and between August 23 and October 6, Mars transits fellow water sign Scorpio. At the same time Neptune is in your sign, and Pluto is in compatible earth sign Capricorn. The positions of these planets place a lot of emphasis on water-sign attributes—imagination, intuition, emotions, your inner world. Pluto in Capricorn helps to ground all of it, to make it tangible, real, and ultimately transformative.

CAREER

Uranus in Aries continues to form a beneficial angle to your career area. Unfortunately, it's retrograde until December 13, but even when retrograde we feel its impact. Your best ideas, for instance, may be happening while you sleep and dream, during relaxed moments when you daydream, even during meditations. It seems counterintuitive to the action sign that Aries usually is, but all its fierce energy is turned inward while the planet is retrograde. So be sure you've got tools on your nightstand—pen, notepad, night light—for recording any morsels you recall from your dreams. Keep your iPhone, Blackberry, cell phone handy for snapping photos of things that move your passions. You know the saying: do what you love, and the money follows.

ROMANCE
As Venus transits Cancer, you enjoy one of the most creative and romantic periods all year. You and your partner are seeing eye to eye on most issues, enjoying each other's company, and bringing new ideas and goals to the table. You could be collaborating on a creative project too.

If you're not involved, who cares? Not you. You're enjoying yourself too much to be pining away for something or someone you don't have yet. And *yet* is the operative word. Focus and attention are key. If you want to meet a special someone, then make a list of traits that you would like to have in a partner. Be specific, but don't obsess about it.

BEST DAYS, CHALLENGING DAYS
Best? August 8, when Mercury turns direct.

September—Pisces

LUNAR HIGHLIGHTS
The new moon on September 15 is in Virgo, your opposite sign. Mercury is closely conjunct, and Mars forms a wide but beneficial angle to it. This one should bring new opportunities in partnerships—business and romantic. Events happen quickly, so be sure you're ready to seize the opportunities as they surface.

The full moon in Aries on September 29 brings news about finances. You may have an unexpected expense or could receive an unexpected royalty check, loan repayment, insurance check. Things are apt to be somewhat chaotic around the time of this full moon, thanks in part to a close conjunction from Uranus. But you deal with it all in your usual way, by going with the flow.

FINANCES, OTHER STUFF
The major financial aspects this month are mentioned above, under the full moon in Aries. Between September 16 and October 5, Mercury will be in Libra, your solar eighth house, so you may be discussing topics like mortgages and insurance. When you aren't discussing these topics, you're thinking about them. Saturn and Mercury are traveling together during this period, which can create a sense that things are more serious or dire than they actually are.

CAREER
Next month, Saturn enters fellow water sign Scorpio, where it will be for the next two and a half years. In the Big Picture for your sign, reread the section on this important transit. There are several ways to prepare for it now so you can make the most of it. Take an honest look at your career path and your daily job, and ask yourself if you're happy. If you are, then strive to bring more of this happiness into your life by doing more of what you enjoy. If you're not happy in your career, then do the grunt work, Pisces. Research the qualifications you need to have another kind of career.

ROMANCE
Between September 6 and October 3, Venus transits fire sign Leo. Your passions are running high and furiously. A flirtation at work or with someone you meet through a coworker could become a romantic relationship quickly. Just be careful that things don't burn out just as quickly. Try to pace yourself. Mars is in Scorpio until October 6, heightening your sexuality.

BEST DAYS, CHALLENGING DAYS
Pluto turns direct on September 17, so you may feel the energy as a release.

October—Pisces

LUNAR HIGHLIGHTS
On October 15, the new moon in Libra occurs in your solar eighth house. This one should bring new financial opportunities in investments and stocks, insurance and taxes, and for your partner's earnings. You also have the benefit of Saturn now in Scorpio (as of October 5), forming a beneficial angle to your sun. Saturn strengthens these opportunities.

October 29 features a full moon in Taurus, an earth sign compatible with your water-sign sun. This one illuminates an issue or concern in your daily life or neighborhood or with a sibling or communication. Neptune in your sign forms a beneficial angle to this full moon, suggesting that any news you receive or insights you gain may be related to your ideals.

FINANCES, OTHER STUFF
October 5 is a big date. Saturn enters Scorpio, and for the next two and a half years you benefit from this planet's energy. Structures in your life will be strengthened, your ability to dig deeply for answers will be more powerful and directed, and your intuition should deepen. If you travel abroad, it won't just be for fun. You might be on some sort of quest. Read about this transit in the Big Picture section for your sign.

CAREER
In addition to Saturn's transit into Scorpio on October 5, Mercury also enters that sign the same day. The two travel together until October 29, so your conscious mind will be more disciplined, intuitive, structured. It's a good time to flesh out new ideas, push your own professional agenda forward, and even to look for a new job or career path if you're dissatisfied with your current ones.

ROMANCE
Between October 3 and 28, Venus transits Virgo, your opposite sign. This period favors deepening a commitment to the one you love. You and your partner may decide to move in together, buy a home, get engaged or marry, start a family. If you're not involved when this transit begins, your energy may turn toward business partnerships, and it could be you find the love of your life in that way!

BEST DAYS, CHALLENGING DAYS
Once Venus transits Libra between October 28 and November 21, Jupiter in Gemini forms a strong, supportive angle to it. This duo, then, should strengthen the area of joint finances. Also, be aware that Mars transits Sadge from October 6 to November 16, and this transit acts as a booster rocket for your career. You may be traveling more internationally during this period or could attend a workshop to hone your professional skills.

November—Pisces

LUNAR HIGHLIGHTS
Two eclipses are in the lineup this month. The first, on November 13, is a solar eclipse in fellow water sign Scorpio, your solar ninth house. This one looks positive for you, Pisces. It brings new opportunities in foreign travel, research and investigation, education, publishing, and expanding your business interests abroad.

Two weeks later, on November 28, the lunar eclipse in Gemini occurs in your solar fourth house, within five degrees of Jupiter. This eclipse brings news and insights concerning home, family, your domestic situation, your parents. The news and insights somehow expand your venue and knowledge, and you may be able to use what you learn in a creative project.

FINANCES, OTHER STUFF

The 2012 hype is probably blasting through the media 24/7. The best way to navigate it is to ignore it. Stay abreast of the news, certainly, but whenever you hear the hype, turn your attention elsewhere. This should be fairly easy to do because you're going to be busy this month. Mars transits Capricorn between November 16 and December 25, so your social calendar heats up, and you're on everyone's party list. Distractions. Good.

Mercury is retrograde in Sadge between November 6 and 26, the last retro of the year for this planet. You know what to do and not do!

CAREER

With Mars in Capricorn during the dates mentioned above, your goals and professional desires are as pressing as your social life. You get an additional boost, though, when Venus joins Saturn in Scorpio between November 21 and December 15. Venus facilitates professional matters through your focus, desire, and attention to what you're doing in your career. With Mercury retrograde for much of the month, though, your best bet is to stick to current projects and clear out anything that is backlogged.

ROMANCE

Once Venus enters Scorpio on November 21, your passions deepen and your intuition is remarkable. Listen to that inner voice in all matters concerning relationships, love, and romance. You'll need to rely on your intuition a lot while Mercury is retrograde too. Try not to say anything that will hurt your partner and that you can't retract. Times may be stressful now, but that's no excuse.

BEST DAYS, CHALLENGING DAYS

Best day? November 26, when Mercury turns direct again!

December—Pisces

LUNAR HIGHLIGHTS
The new moon on December 13, the last of 2012, occurs in Sagittarius and probably will really dial up the media hype about the end of the world on December 21. On a personal level, though, it should be interesting, particularly for your career. New opportunities surface—a new career path, a new job, a raise or promotion, more foreign travel. If you're changing jobs/careers, then you may take some courses to sharpen your skills. You may even dust off an old manuscript, rework it, and start submitting it.

On December 28, the full moon in Cancer brings new insights into a romantic relationship or creative project or about one of your children. One of your parents could be involved in this equation too. You may be sticking close to home around this time, perhaps choosing to celebrate New Year's Eve with family and close friends.

FINANCES, OTHER STUFF
With Mercury now moving in direct motion, you're a much happier camper. So is everyone around you. Between December 10 and 31, it transits Sadge, the same sign as the new moon on the thirteenth. It forms a beneficial angle to your financial area, suggesting that you can sell just about anything to anyone—an idea, product, lifestyle, manuscript, home—take your pick.

CAREER
With Mercury in Sadge during the above dates, you're in a prime position to take advantage of the general goodwill that prevails around the holidays. But unique gifts for coworkers and bosses won't bust the bank! Throw a party for the people with whom you work. Be as generous to others as others are to you. Get the idea here, Pisces? It's the giving season. Once Venus begins to transit Sadge on December 15, this goodwill takes you into the new year. Things definitely flow your way. You land the promotion, the raise, or the job you desire.

ROMANCE
Whether you're involved or not, Venus's transit through Sadge is accompanied by passionate feelings, a need for movement and excitement, an itch to travel. If you have a partner, then the two of you may get away for a few days to some far-flung port. If you're not involved, your capacity for enjoyment is such so that you have fun with friends and family and even when traveling solo.

BEST DAYS, CHALLENGING DAYS
December 31, when Mercury enters Capricorn. This earth sign suits you and enables you to reach for the highest goals and resolutions for 2013.

Happy New Year!

PART TWO

Another Viewpoint

Navigating the Waves of Change
by Nancy McMoneagle

Anxiety reigns about the ending of the Maya calendar on December 21, 2012. The first question to ask might be: is it real? I'm reminded of the angst and fear surrounding Y2K, when, in spite of that would-be disaster, there were no apocalyptic scenarios as some had imagined happening at the turn of the century.

So it is with the would-be Maya calendar "end of times." We have already experienced waves of change, numerous endings and new beginnings. We don't have to wait for December 21, 2012, for the end of times as we've known them! Since 2010 there have been a number of intense planetary transits (the positions and interactions among the planets and their effects on us and earthly matters) reminiscent of economic events of the 1930s, which included the Great Depression, and the social, revolutionary changes of the 1960s.

Yes, 2012 is likely going to be another year of intense change, and we're already seeing and feeling the winds of these changes—both personally and collectively—as the planets energetically dance with and battle against each other. How can we best direct and use these energies instead of being paralyzed by fear of the future? In which areas of life are we being asked to make major changes? What outworn systems, beliefs, relationships, and just plain stuff that no longer serve our greater good do we need to release?

Let's take a look at what's going on with the more challenging planets and the astrological weather fronts for 2012. Let's explore how you can best navigate and put them to good use, given your sun sign's innate qualities and how your solar chart is being activated. I hope that after you read this, you'll be more excited than anxious about the times ahead and aware of the potential the planets bring. I hope you come away with ideas on making optimum choices for yourself.

The Major Planetary Players

SATURN, Capricorn's ruler, is known as the Teacher, the "Cosmic Cop," Stern Taskmaster, and the Wise Old Man, among other colorful titles. Saturn represents limitations, structures, fear, responsibility, lessons, and the urge for safety and security. It has been in Libra, the sign of balance, harmony and relationships, since July 21, 2010. As of October 5, 2012, it will be in intense, passionate, and transformative Scorpio and remain there for about two and a half years.

Saturn asks us to downsize and simplify, to prune from our lives what's no longer working. When in Libra, it urges us to be responsible and equitable in all things, most especially in our relationships. When it moves into Scorpio in October of 2012, its focus will shift to dealing with lessons in letting go, surrendering to change, understanding more about our money matters and sexuality and how we use both. Saturn in Scorpio will also activate power and control issues, how we approach birth and death, and ask that we probe the depths of almost everything—from our own shadow sides to what's buried in the depths of the oceans and underground.

When dealing with Saturnian energy, if you're anxious about loss, refocus on what you *do* want in your life, define what your intentions are, and how you want to feel. Saturn wants us to be clear and responsible, to take a stand for what we want. Given Libra's propensity to take long considerations for all the possibilities before making a decision, you may want to keep the following quote by Bryce Courtney in mind: "If you sit in the middle of the road, you will get hit by traffic from both directions!" From now until October 5, decide to "go for gold"!

Saturn's location in your astrological chart (both at birth and where it transits) and the area of the chart it rules indicate which areas of life are most affected and where you need to focus. This is where your important life lessons will be coming from.

URANUS rules Aquarius and is known as the Awakener—rather like Prometheus, who broke the Olympian rules and gave fire to humanity. Uranus is about the urge to be free and represents inventions, originality, sudden change, revolution, and revelation. For the first time in eighty-four years, Uranus is now in fiery, pioneering Aries for about the next seven years, where we'll see major technological breakthroughs and a greater emphasis on individual rights. The last time this happened was from 1927 to 1935, when the following events occurred:

FDR created the New Deal, curbing corporate power in the wake of the 1929 Wall Street crash and the ensuing Great Depression.

Gandhi's civil disobedience

Adolf Hitler came into power, and the first concentration camps were formed by the Nazis.

Dr. Alexis Carrel developed the artificial heart, and penicillin was discovered.

Remarkable things can and have happened with Uranus in Aries. How can we use this forceful energy this time around? Uranus's location in your chart shows where you want to do things your way and where you want to be free. Its transits will let you know where you need to free yourself up and get out of a rut!

PLUTO, "Lord of the Underworld," is the ruler of Scorpio and represents death and rebirth, destruction and transformation. It rules atomic power, crime, waste, recycling, dictatorships, and things hidden, like Earth's buried riches and our dark sides, our phobias and obsessions. Pluto takes about 248 years to travel through the zodiac, and from 2008 to January 20, 2024, it's in the structure-loving, authoritative sign of Capricorn. The last time Pluto was in Capricorn was from 1762 to 1778, and coincided with: the Boston Tea Party in 1773, the American Revolution (1775–1783), and the Declaration of Independence.

While in Capricorn, Pluto locates and eliminates decay in structures and systems, as we've seen happening within a number of corporations since the unsustainable real estate speculation and banking crisis that began in 2008. After exposing corruption in these institutions and the greed and dishonesty of authorities who abuse their power, Pluto then helps to regenerate these systems. For example, where corporations are dying, we're seeing the birth of new systems—the creation of new co-ops and bankrupt companies being run as worker-owned cooperatives.

Pluto's location in your chart illustrates where you will undergo some major transformation and regeneration. It also provides insight as to the role you may be destined to play and where you need to plumb the depths in order to access and use your personal power.

The Major Challenge

The most challenging transit in 2012, which lasts until March 2019, is Uranus's. It demands that we become more aware of the impact our personal lifestyles have had on others—humans, animals, all existing life. We need to make necessary changes to free ourselves from behaviors that are destructive, such as mindless consumption of Earth's resources. Pluto and Uranus are two powerhouse planets, and when they're in the initiating and power-driven signs of Aries and Capricorn, they show us how we must change . . . or die. This dynamic duo will motivate us through shocking (Uranus) events to revolutionize and transform (Pluto) our actions.

In the mid-1960s, Uranus and Pluto were together (conjunct) in Virgo opposite Saturn in Pisces. Values changed then, just as they will now, a result of the current square between these two cosmic heavyweights. In the 1960s, we saw the computer and space age unfold, the struggle for equality for blacks and women, and a counterculture revolution with the youth of America demanding freedom from what they perceived as oppression by the "Establishment." New patterns of relating ("free love") came into being even as women were demanding equality between the sexes, symbolized by burning bras and advent of the birth control pill. It was a time of major new beginnings as well as clashes between generations and opposing ideologies.

By consciously and productively using the dynamic energy created by the square-dance of Uranus and Pluto during 2012 and beyond, we could see innovative technology emerge. Possibilities: how to rid ourselves from dependence on oil (Zero Point energy?), ventures deeper into space, our first walk on Mars, and massive changes to our entire approach to daily life due to a sudden event that shocks us into more creative and fruitful action. One thing is certain, we will not be numbing out in shopping malls or on video games. Uranus says, "I bring you fire, use it wisely," and Pluto says, "Change or die!" Heads up, everyone!

How You Can Best Navigate the Waves

Wherever Saturn, Uranus, and Pluto fall in your chart and the houses they rule will determine in which areas of life you'll be surrendering old structures, beliefs, relationships—*anything* that no longer serves you (Saturn's influence); where you'll be freeing yourself up and making changes, some of which may be sudden and unexpected (Uranus); and where your life is being transformed at a very profound level (Pluto).

A thumbnail sketch follows on what's happening with each sun sign. In addition to your sun sign, if you know your rising sign (ascendant) and what sign the moon was in at your birth, the information for those signs will apply to you as well.

ARIES
Independent and pioneering, you have had Saturn testing your relationship arena for the past couple of years, helping you realize the importance of connections with others. Starting in October, 2012, Saturn will be asking you to focus on the three major things we often joke about: death, sex, and taxes! Seriously, make sure you pay attention to getting rid of any debt you've incurred. Examine any joint financial ventures you're involved in and make sure they (along with your taxes and insurance) are in good order.

Also take a good look at how you use your sexual energy. Is it a way to feel at one with someone? Do you use it for power or as a control mechanism? Is it just for fun or procreation, or is sex something entirely different for you? If you find yourself thinking more about death and what happens when we leave this life, it might be a good time to read on the subject or talk with a spiritual advisor. Consider participating in a self-development program that will help you experience and understand other states of consciousness.

Uranus and Pluto will be challenging you over the next few years to free yourself from old ways of being into new forms of expression. The vehicle could be a new career or taking on a more powerful position in your current occupation.

TAURUS
Dependable, sensual Taurus will stretch your philosophical boundaries over the next few years as Pluto transits your solar ninth house. You may decide to travel overseas or return to school or church as you seek additional knowledge and a deeper understanding of universal truths.

At the forefront of your mind could be questions like: *Why am I here? What's my purpose? What's it all about?* Uranus could activate your dreams, giving you sudden, unexpected ideas, information, and answers to these questions. This material rises from the depths of your unconscious, so it would be wise to keep a dream journal.

Your work and health arena has had Saturn bearing down on it since 2010. Hopefully you've used Saturn's discipline to your advantage by establishing a good health regimen, relinquishing bad habits, and being patient with coworkers who may have been a drag. In October 2012, Saturn will enter your area of relationships for a couple of years. This transit will change the focus from work and health to primary relationships. Relationships that have outlived their purpose may well end after Saturn's testing, but after going through the rigors of Saturn's trials, your solid relationships will become even stronger.

GEMINI
With Saturn in Libra until early October, it's a time for curious and adaptable Gemini to get serious about expressing your creative sides. Once Saturn enters Scorpio, you'll find yourself concentrating on having a good health program and a more functional daily routine over the next couple of years. Your fun-loving nature may feel buried with responsibility, but it's important that you honor Saturn's energy, as it's helping you prepare for a time of more visibility, possibly receiving a form of recognition for your efforts.

Don't be surprised if some long-standing goals unexpectedly change due to significant realizations you're having about yourself, insights about the nature of life and death, and what you want to do and be before you leave the planet. Your friends, too, may suddenly change, bringing very different kinds of people into your social circles who will also share your interest in transformational and metaphysical topics. As ever, Gemini, stay flexible and open to the possibilities. This is a time for discovering answers to age-old mysteries.

CANCER
As a home-loving individual, you've had Saturn pressing additional responsibilities on you on the home front since

2010. You may have taken on the challenge of making renovations or repairs to your house, or some of you may have been responsible for the care of a parent or relative. Saturn's stay here has also asked you to delve into the root of some old, familial patterns that you no longer need and can now release. This release will strengthen you and your life at the very foundation of your being.

In October, Saturn will move into your area of creativity, children, and romance. It's time to get serious about expressing your creative side, come out of your shell, and allow yourself some fun, even if you feel whatever "fun" activity you engage in must have a purpose! This is not the best time to gamble. Be careful of risky speculations. Uranus and Pluto are in your areas of career and relationship, so make sure you're flexible and ready for change in the career arena. Pay attention to how you and your significant other are interacting. Are you empowering each other or engaging in power struggles? You can use these next few years to free yourself from nonproductive games of manipulation and control, and instead focus your energy on optimal development in your major relationship.

LEO

As you vibrant Leos know, it's vital that you have a way to shine and express yourselves creatively. With Saturn in your solar third house of communications until October 2012, this is a time to hunker down and write your book or screenplay, teach a course, create a new Web site, or communicate what you want to share through art or music. When Saturn moves into Scorpio in October, you'll be focusing more on home and family matters, perhaps scrutinizing some past family dynamics that you can now release. You may also focus that Saturnian energy on finding new ways to feel secure.

Keep in mind that Saturn will assist you in strengthening your foundations wherever needed—from your house to your inner being. You're being motivated by Uranus and Pluto to revise your belief systems, including your religious and/or spiritual beliefs. Watch for unexpected insights, possibly from a trip to a foreign country or a class you take. As a result, there may be major changes in your daily life or at work. With Pluto in your sixth house of work and health, adopt a healthy daily regimen for your body and mind, and give due consideration to other perspectives presented to you in the workplace and elsewhere. Pluto is helping you totally transform your daily life.

VIRGO
As an industrious, exacting individual, you're being asked to use your discriminating abilities in your financial affairs and to give careful thought to what you truly value in life. How is your self-esteem doing these days? Saturn is helping you prune away old values (like the need for perfection!) that may have been holding back a healthy sense of self-worth.

When Saturn goes into Scorpio in October, it will highlight your need to change ways of thinking. It will help you identify and release any habits that aren't serving you well. Saturn's gift of discipline will help you communicate more clearly, use your already well-developed analytical skills, and possibly motivate you to write that book you've had on your mind for years.

Uranus will also be helping you let go of the old, outworn ways of thinking and being, possibly with some sudden, unexpected events that illuminate hidden subconscious patterns. You may even feel like parts of you are dying and being reborn at lightning speed. Between its energy and that of Pluto activating your creativity, don't be surprised if your creative self-expression takes new forms that you never before considered possible!

LIBRA
Until October of 2012, you peace-loving Libras may feel Saturn has weighed you down with more responsibility than usual. You have to decide in which direction you'll go. Think back to about fourteen years ago, and you'll get a sense of whether you should continue or stop whatever you began back then. Saturn brings the discipline and clar-

ity to do what YOU need to do and be—not what others expect of you or what you think you ought to do to please others. Libra, this is about redefining yourself!

When Saturn moves into Scorpio in early October, you'll be paying more attention to what you truly value in life, including everything from self-confidence to income. With the transformative effects of Scorpio, you may change a number of values to reflect the true you, instead of the person who has put self second and lived for others' approval.

Meanwhile, Uranus and Pluto are also helping you make changes, particularly in the areas of home and relationships. If you're not in a relationship, you may well meet someone to whom you're suddenly attracted. If you're already in a relationship, be ready to put some sparkle back into it as you free yourself from the same old stuff!

SCORPIO

You passionate souls are already looking for the buried riches in your daily life. You take nothing for granted in your communications. You probe the depths of meaning in everything that's written or said, no matter how mundane the topic. Pluto is relentless in making even the most prosaic events significant.

Until early October, Pluto is demanding major changes to help you release ways that don't serve you well—like giving up obsessive thoughts and actions or feeling the need to be in control all the time. This powerful planet will help you see what's underneath these urges and use all that energy for being a commanding presence.

Along with that ongoing dynamic, Uranus is giving you the opportunity to free yourself from the boring aspects of work. You might change jobs or alter the way you've gone about fulfilling your daily duties. Since 2010, Saturn has been helping you complete old business, deal with your fears, and recognize your buried strengths.

As of October 5, 2012, when Saturn goes into your sign, it will be your turn over the next couple of years to "shed your old skin" and allow your transformed self to emerge. Saturn asks that you take on additional responsibilities.

You bring some projects from either seven or fourteen years ago to a close and prepare for new beginnings. Since Saturn holds back the ebullience of the sun to a certain degree, you may feel less energized than usual. So take good care of your health, and make time for rest and relaxation!

SAGITTARIUS

Since 2010, with Saturn in your area of friendship, social consciousness, and goals, you may have been spending a lot of time with friends or involved with some group activities. All the while, you have been figuring out what your next adventure will be and what you want to accomplish.

When Saturn goes into probing Scorpio in October 2012, you'll be prompted to focus on projects that need completion. You'll be spending some quiet time reflecting on where your life has taken you and determining where you want to go from here. Uranus in Aries urges you to take innovative approaches to your creative enterprises, romance, and child-rearing. For those with kids, don't be surprised if they rebel or act in unexpected ways, even display some genius. Uranus activates this area of your solar chart.

If you get involved in a sudden love affair, have a good time, but don't necessarily expect it to last. Uranus sweeps in like a tornado, changes everything around, fills you with a sense of life, then moves out as quickly as it arrived. Meanwhile, Pluto in Capricorn is transiting your financial area, transforming your bank account and values. It's a good time to be careful about your financial outflow (this is not the best time to buy that boat!) and focus on your inner values and realize how they support you far more consistently than money ever could.

CAPRICORN

You're the hard worker and responsible one. Now you have the "gift" of Pluto, Mr. Transformation, in your sign, tearing down your outworn ways of being and rejuvenating you with a whole new sense of self. Pluto's way is to ferret out and remove the old, useless beliefs, relationships, and behaviors, then slowly rebuild what has been ripped out or torn down into a wonderful new form that will serve you far better than what you had before. The process, however, isn't fun.

Like the butterfly's struggle to emerge from the cocoon, the transformation isn't easy but the end result is breathtaking. Meanwhile, Uranus is in your area of home and family, also demanding that you make major changes in your life. You may be thinking of moving or want to make some inventive changes to your home—rewire the house or add some cool new technology, like that 80-inch HD 3-D television you've been eyeing!

If you've gotten a promotion at work or otherwise have heavy responsibilities weighing you down professionally, it's due to Saturn's transit through Libra since 2010. Saturn has been testing who and what you are choosing to be in the "outside world." In October 2012, it moves to your area of goals, friends, and desires, so the next few years are about defining your intentions and using your incredible building and executive skills to manifest them—possibly with a friend.

AQUARIUS

Your views about life are being tested. You've been trying to understand yourself and your place in the universe. In October 2012, Saturn moves into an area of your chart that corresponds with career, reputation, and achievements in the outer world. Over the next couple of years you may find your career either reaching a peak of success or discover that you're ready to take on something new and different. Though you may find you have a lot of extra responsibilities, this could also be one of the most rewarding times in your life.

Uranus in your area of communications is birthing new and different ways of thinking about your daily activities, perhaps even prodding you to delve into new interests that could involve science or cutting edge technology or even studying astrology! Pluto, meanwhile, is helping you uncover the hidden part of your nature, prompting you to delve ever deeper into discovering aspects of yourself that have been buried and now need to come to light. Let it help you take out the "psychic garbage" and free you up for the new you that will be emerging a few years from now!

PISCES

For the past year or more, you probably have been thinking a lot about death and transformation on a number of levels—physical, emotional, psychological, spiritual. It's been a heavy time. Maybe you've had to deal with the loss of someone close. As Saturn moves into your area of higher knowledge and belief systems starting in October, you may be considering what such transformation means for your life purpose, connection to God, and other such philosophical and spiritual questions.

As a result of your discoveries, your hopes and intentions for the future are going through great change. At the same time, your values and economic situation are also changing. If possible, put money aside. Uranus, the planet of surprises and sudden change, is transiting your house of income and values. Sometimes people decide to change how they earn their income or free themselves from unnecessary stuff. Now would be a good time to unload things that no longer bring you joy or serve a good purpose—material items as well as old principles that no longer serve you well.

FOR EVERYONE!

Pluto demands transformation, Saturn wants viable structures, and Uranus wants big changes to occur NOW. So instead of fearing what is to come in 2012, make this a time of new beginnings. Have fun by productively using these planets' energies for creatively transforming your life—wherever you most want and need to do so. This is the time to eliminate the old outmoded structures in your lives while allowing for and creating new possibilities ... things you never considered before!

Nancy McMoneagle offers astrological consultations out of the Astrological Services Division of Intuitive Intelligence Applications (www.mceagle.com), a consulting company she co-owns and operates with her husband, Joseph McMoneagle. Nancy and Joe live in the foothills of the Blue Ridge Mountains in central Virginia with their two dogs and six feline fur children.

PART THREE

The Emergence of a Thirteenth Zodiac Sign

On January 10, 2011, the *Minneapolis Star Tribune* carried an article about the emergence of a possible thirteenth zodiac sign. The story apparently zipped around cyberspace at the speed of light and was picked up by CNN, ABC, and NBC. Network coverage on this topic struck me as weird: since when do they cover astrology?

It was covered because an astronomer—not an astrologer—made the announcement about the thirteenth sign and presented a new set of dates for all the signs, shifting the zodiac. Paul Kunkle, who teaches astronomy at a junior college in Minneapolis, pointed out that the zodiac periods were set up by the Babylonians millennia ago. Since then, the moon's gravitational pull has made the earth wobble on its axis, which has created a month difference in the stars' alignment over time. "When astrologers say the sun is in Pisces, it's really not in Pisces," said Kunkle. "Most horoscope readers who consider themselves Pisces are actually Aquarians."

Here is how the dates line up under Kunkle's theory:

Aries: April 18–May 13
Taurus: May 13–June 21
Gemini: June 21–July 20
Cancer: July 20–August 10
Leo: August 10–September 16
Virgo: September 16–October 30
Libra: October 30–November 23

Scorpio: November 23–November 29
Ophiuchus: November 29–December 17
Sagittarius: December 17–January 20
Capricorn: January 20–February 16
Aquarius: February 16–March 11
Pisces: March 11–April 18

Notice the new sign for November 29 to December 17? That's Ophiuchus (*OFF-ee-YOO-kuss*), the serpent bearer, which in Kunkle's view now belongs in the mainstream zodiac.

However, Kunkle's dates are irrelevant for Western astrology; he's actually referring to sidereal astrology, which is oriented to the constellations. Tropical astrology, the most common form in the Western world, is based on the seasons. It's geocentric—related to life on Earth. In tropical astrology, if you were born between February 19 and March 20, you're still a Pisces!

The irony is that the ancient Babylonians knew about Ophiuchus, but because they didn't want a zodiac with thirteen signs, they tossed it out. They supposedly thought that thirteen wasn't as tidy as twelve. It was one of the forty-eight constellations listed by the second-century astronomer Ptolemy and one of the eighty-eight modern constellations. As you can see, though Ophiuchus maybe be new to us, it has been around for centuries.

But what should we make of its recent reappearance in the astrological conversation? Perhaps, in a larger context, its rediscovery signals the emergence of a new planetary archetype, and its importance can be found in what it might be telling us about humanity and ourselves at this juncture in time. That's where synchronicity enters the picture.

Planets are archetypes—Mars, for instance, is the mythological god of war; Venus is the mythological goddess of love. A planet's discovery often coincides with a shift in mass consciousness that comes about as certain world events and situations unfold. For example, in 1930, a new planet was discovered as a result of aberrations in the orbit of Uranus. The planet was named Pluto, after the god of the underworld. In mythology, Pluto is associated with Hades—hell—and with immense power and destruction. In Latin literature, Pluto also rules the dead. In astrology, this planet came to be associated with profound and irrevocable change, transformation, strange taboos, dictators, decadence, disasters, atomic power, gangsters (Mafia), sexuality, the sexual act, sexual power, death, dying, rebirth, explosions, power struggles—you get the idea.

The world events surrounding its discovery included two world wars; the emergence of atomic weapons; and the rise of Nazis, Hitler, concentration camps, and the annihilation of six million Jews and minority groups. It also saw the birth of psychoanalysis, notably the work of Sigmund Freud, which focuses on sexuality, and Carl Jung, whose work deals with mythology, dreams, archetypes, and synchronicity. So what kind of archetype might be emerging with the *rediscovery* of Ophiuchus?

Well, it's the only astrological sign based on a real person: Asclepius. By the ancient Greeks in 27 B.C., he was regarded as a healer, and in the Roman pantheon, he is a son of Apollo. He supposedly learned the secrets of preventing death when he observed one serpent bringing healing herbs to another. He raised the dead using this herb. In order to prevent the entire human race from becoming immortal under his care, Zeus supposedly killed him with a bolt of lightning, then later suffered a pang of conscience and placed his image in the heavens to honor his good works.

Ophiuchus is usually depicted as grasping a snake—thus his name as the serpent bearer—and has one foot resting firmly against Scorpius (the scorpion). In honor of Asclepius, snakes were often used in healing rituals, and nonvenomous snakes were allowed to crawl on the floor in dormitories where the sick and injured slept. Cults grew up around Asclepius in Greece and Rome, and pilgrims supposedly flocked to his healing temples from 300 B.C. onward. Ritual purification would be followed by offerings or sacrifices to the god, and by spending the night in the holiest part of the sanctuary so that dreams would occur. Any dreams or visions were reported to a priest, who would prescribe the appropriate therapy by interpreting what the dreams meant.

Just from the mythology, we can glimpse some of the components of the archetype: healer, alternative medicine, the power of groups (pilgrims flocking to the temples), magic (raising the dead), dream interpretation, cult mentality, violence and violent deaths, sudden unexpected events (thunderbolts), resisting and questioning authority, pushing against the status quo, a greater independence from authoritarian rule (sounds like what has been going on in Egypt, and the Middle East and North Africa in general) and greater dependence on the self and the local community.

Other components of this archetype include what author and physician Dean Radin calls "the global mind, the collective consciousness of everyone on the planet." This phrase grew out of Radin's involvement in the Global Consciousness Project. In 1998, Princeton's Dr. Roger Nelson, in conjunction with the Institute of Noetic Sciences, began an Internet-based experiment aimed at monitoring this global mind. Through dozens of random number generators situated worldwide, the idea is that, according to Dean Radin, "as mind moves, so does matter." The findings, so far, are intriguing.

Networks of random number generators are present at sixty-five sites worldwide. Once a minute, the generated numbers are downloaded and analyzed for consistency. The process is explained in detail on the project's Web site, which can be found at www.gcpdot.com. The purpose of the project, according to the Web site, is "to examine subtle correlations that may reflect the presence and activity of consciousness in the world. We predict structure in what should be random data, associated with major world events."

So, during events that are of global interest, the focused attention and emotional outpouring worldwide brings about a notable difference in the results. The Web site maintains a GCP dot that registers these fluctuations in the global mind in real time, covered 24/7 by the media. Hours before the first plane hit the World Trade Center, these random number generators went a bit nuts, and the button turned red. If you read what it says about colors on the Global Consciousness Project Web site, you'll see that red indicates a variance in the statistical analysis of these generators—an event that mass consciousness registers, sometimes before the event occurs, it seems. The same thing happened during the original O.J. Simpson trial. And shortly before the Tucson shootings involving Representative Gabrielle Gifford earlier this year. In other words, these generators registered the fluctuations in consciousness.

Magnetic fluctuation impacts human beings, and it may be creating a sensitivity in certain types of individuals, which is part of this emerging paradigm. Planetary empaths are individuals who seem to be so intimately connected to fluctuations in the earth that they experience physical symptoms for days and sometimes weeks before a natural disaster occurs. Their "symptoms" are astonishingly similar and often coincide with the change in colors in the GCP dot. One woman in California, for instance, knows that when her left ear starts ringing and throbbing painfully, an earthquake is imminent. Another woman is seized by vertigo before a quake.

There's no question a paradigm shift of some sort is underway. This shift in mass consciousness may be what the rediscovery of Ophiuchus presages.

That said, there are troubling facts emerging that suggest this paradigm shift may occur *as a result of* global warming, an increase in natural disasters, a widening disparity between rich and poor, and increased political and religious strife worldwide. We've covered some of the facts in other posts—about the massive deaths of birds and other wildlife, for instance. Here are some additional facts:

- In 2010, natural disasters killed more than a quarter million people and displaced millions. According to Swiss Re, the largest reinsurer in the world, the finan-

cial losses from these natural disasters exceeded two hundred twenty-two billion dollars.
- Greenland's ice sheet melted at a record rate in 2010.
- 2005 and 2010 are tied for the warmest years on record.
- The last pole shift occurred nearly eight hundred thousand years ago. Some scientists believe we're long overdue. Others believe a pole shift is already under way.

So this rediscovery of Ophiuchus may be a warning, or it may be prompting us to really examine our collective beliefs and desires. What do we *want* not only for ourselves and our loved ones, but for the planet?

SYDNEY OMARR

Born on August 5, 1926, in Philadelphia, Pennsylvania, **Sydney Omarr** was the only person ever given full-time duty in the U.S. Army as an astologer. He is regarded as the most erudite astrologer of our time and the best known, through his syndicated column and his radio and television programs (he was Merv Griffin's "resident astrologer"). Omarr has been called the most "knowledgeable astrologer since Evangeline Adams." His forecasts of Nixon's downfall, the end of World War II in mid-August of 1945, the assassination of John F. Kennedy, Roosevelt's election to a fourth term and his death in office ... these and many others are on the record and quoted enough to be considered "legendary."

◉ SIGNET

Also Available

SYDNEY OMARR'S® DAY-BY-DAY ASTROLOGICAL GUIDES FOR THE YEAR 2012

These expert forecasts for 2012 offer valuable insights about the past and extraordinary predictions about the future:

- What to expect from relationships and family partners
- New career opportunities for success in the future
- Lucky days for every month of the year

...and much more! Don't face the future blindly—let the Zodiac be your guide.

AVAILABLE FOR ALL TWELVE ASTROLOGICAL SIGNS

Available wherever books are sold or at penguin.com

Penguin Group (USA) Online

What will you be reading tomorrow?

Tom Clancy, Patricia Cornwell, W.E.B. Griffin,
Nora Roberts, William Gibson, Robin Cook,
Brian Jacques, Catherine Coulter, Stephen King,
Dean Koontz, Ken Follett, Clive Cussler,
Eric Jerome Dickey, John Sandford,
Terry McMillan, Sue Monk Kidd, Amy Tan,
J. R. Ward, Laurell K. Hamilton,
Charlaine Harris, Christine Feehan...

You'll find them all at
penguin.com

*Read excerpts and newsletters,
find tour schedules and reading group guides,
and enter contests.*

Subscribe to Penguin Group (USA) newsletters
and get an exclusive inside look
at exciting new titles and the authors you love
long before everyone else does.

PENGUIN GROUP (USA)
us.penguingroup.com